Motivating Students

EDITED BY
SALLY BROWN
STEVE ARMSTRONG
GAIL THOMPSON

D1645296

RoutledgeFalmer
Taylor & Francis Group

LONDON AND NEW YORK

First published in 1998 by Kogan Page Limited

Reprinted in 2002

Apart from any fair dealing for the purposes of research or private study, or criticism or review, as permitted under the Copyright, Designs and Patents Act 1988, this publication may only be reproduced, stored or transmitted, in any form or by any means, with the prior permission in writing of the publishers, or in the case of reprographic reproduction in accordance with the terms and licences issued by the CLA. Enquiries concerning reproduction outside those terms should be sent to the publishers at the undermentioned address:

Transferred to Digital Printing 2004
by RoutledgeFalmer
11 New Fetter Lane,
London EC4P 4EE

RoutledgeFalmer is an imprint of the Taylor & Francis Group

© Sally Brown, Steve Armstrong and Gail Thompson 1998

British Library Cataloguing in Publication Data

A CIP record for this book is available from the British Library.

ISBN 0 7494 2494 X

Typeset by JS Typesetting, Wellingborough, Northants.
Printed in England by Selwood Printing Ltd. West Sussex

Contents

Notes on Contributors

Steve Armstrong is Senior Lecturer and Teaching Fellow with the Business School at the University of Sunderland. His research interests lie in the field of cognitive style, particularly its effects on inter-personal relationships in a work environment.

Anne Baldwin was previously a research assistant in Educational Development Services at the University of Plymouth and is now travelling in Australia.

Philip Barker is Professor of Applied Computing within the School of Computing and Mathematics at the University of Teesside. He is an author, researcher and consultant of international acclaim who specialises in the application of human–computer interaction to the problems of using computers for the support of teaching and learning. Further details on his research group's activities can be found at the following Web sites: http://www.telesys.com/pbarker and http://www.scm-tees.ac.uk/groups/isrg

Liz Beaty is Head of Learning Development at Coventry University and co-Chair elect for SEDA. Liz researches in the area of student learning and accreditation of teachers in Higher Education.

Selena Bolingbroke is Education Researcher at Middlesex University Students' Union. She worked previously on the QHE Project at the University of Central England, and has published in the areas of student funding, quality assurance and professional bodies.

David Botterill is Head of the School of Hospitality, Leisure and Tourism in the Faculty of Business, Leisure and Food at University of Wales Institute, Cardiff. His current research interests focus on destination image and marketing and government policy formation in relation to education and training for the hospitality, leisure and tourism sectors. David plays a role in several national forums including the National Liaison Group for Tourism Education.

Sally Brown is Head of Quality Enhancement at the University of Northumbria at Newcastle. She is Vice-Chair of SEDA and is the Association's Publications Coordinator. She publishes widely and runs workshops in Britain and abroad on issues of teaching, learning and particularly assessment.

Alan Bleakley is a Senior Lecturer at Cornwall College, where he runs undergraduate and postgraduate courses in Education and Counselling for the Universities of Plymouth and Exeter. He is widely published and a regular contributor to conferences.

Noel Entwistle is Bell Professor of Education and Director of the Centre for Research on Learning and Instruction at the University of Edinburgh. He currently edits the journal, *Higher Education.*

Della Fazey is the Sub Dean of the Faculty of Arts and Social Sciences and the Director of Undergraduate Study in the School of Sport, Health and Physical Education Sciences (SSHAPES). In 1996 she completed a two-year, Department for Education and Employment-funded secondment as Director of the Bangor Guidance and Learner Autonomy Project. She teaches and researches learning in lifetime development.

John Fazey is the Director of the University of Wales Bangor Centre for Learning Development and Training which supports staff and educational development activity at UWBangor and provides training services in the wider community. Current research projects in post-compulsory education include testing frameworks for evaluating training and the role of feedback in learning and about learning. He teaches and researches student learning, skill development and understanding.

Linda France is Research Projects Assistant in the Centre for Learning and Teaching at the University of Brighton. Her interests are in student learning and she has undertaken a number of action research projects within the University.

Hazel Fullerton is Head of Educational Development Services at the University of Plymouth. She publishes widely on Higher Education issues increasingly concerned with how students and HEIs will move into the next century.

Colin Gray is Director of External Affairs in the Open University Business School. His current research interests focus on drivers of management development in small and large companies, information learning and management needs of small firms and the impact of motivational factors (both economic and non-economic) on SME development, economic growth and SME and large firm linkages.

Kay Greasley is currently undertaking an MPhil studying the relationship between gender and approaches to learning in Higher Education, funded by Sheffield Hallam University. She also teaches Organizational Behaviour at the University of Derby.

Ron Iphofen is a medical sociologist with a background in adult education based in the Faculty of Health Studies, University of Wales, Bangor. He teaches on a wide range of health professional courses and acts as a consultant on research to Health Authorities and Trusts. His research interests include motives in health and in learning.

Kim Issroff is a lecturer in the Higher Education Research and Development Unit at University College London. Her research interests include computer-supported collaborative learning, technology in teaching and learning in Higher Education and affective aspects of learning technologies.

Eleri Jones is Dean of Resources and Special Projects in the Faculty of Business, Leisure and Food at University of Wales Institute, Cardiff. Her current research interests focus on the development of a coherent framework for the support of lifelong learning and issues of work-based and open and distance learning, especially the use of multimedia techniques to support lifelong learning, management and organizational development. She has recently established the Centre for the Support of Lifelong Learning at UWIC. She is the co-author of a range of papers on management development and multimedia authoring.

Debbie Keeling is Lecturer in the Faculty of Business, Leisure and Food and Researcher in the Centre for the Support of Lifelong Learning, both at University of Wales Institute, Cardiff. Her current research interests focus on the role of motivation in promoting lifelong learning. She is particularly interested in Work-Based Learning and the impact of organizational systems on the uptake and success of learning opportunities.

Linda Leach is a member of the Academic and Staff Development department of Wellington Polytechnic, New Zealand. She is involved in jointly running Bachelor and Masters Programmes in Education.

Martin Luck is Lecturer in Animal Physiology at the University of Nottingham's School of Biology. His scientific specialism is reproductive biology. He also works part-time as an Advisor for the University's Teaching Enhancement Office with a brief to promote good practice in teaching and learning. He takes a special interest in skill development and in the relationship between research and teaching in Higher Education.

Rhona Magee is a senior lecturer in Educational Development Services at the University of Plymouth.

Julie Mortimer is currently working as an Educational Consultant in the Centre for Advances in Higher Education in the University of Northumbria. She is involved in teaching lecturers who are studying educational theory and practice. Her research interests focus upon assessment.

Guyon Neutze is a member of the Academic and Staff Development department of Wellington Polytechnic, New Zealand. He is involved in jointly running Bachelor and Masters Programmes in Education.

Stephen Newstead is a Professor of Psychology at the University of Plymouth and was from 1995 to 1996 president of the British Psychological Society (BPS). His on-going concern with the teaching of the discipline has involved him in chairing the special group for Teaching Psychology and he edits the refereed journal Psychology Teaching Review on their behalf.

Phil Race is Emeritus Professor of Educational Development at the University of Glamorgan. Following early retirement he is now an independent consultant on teaching, learning and assessment and is Programme Director for the Durham University Certificate in Higher Education.

Teresa del Soldato works at the Institute of Educational Technology, at the Open University, UK. Her research focus on affective aspects of learning and the use of new technologies in teaching environments. She has also been involved in European projects developing a multimedia database for learning material.

Ian Solomonides is First Year Tutor in the Department of Mechanical and Manufacturing Engineering at Nottingham Trent University and a coordinator for the university's 'Sharing Excellence' project. His research has concentrated on the quality of student learning and the student learning experience.

Gail Thompson is Senior Lecturer with the University of Sunderland Business School. She is currently carrying out research into various aspects of the student experience of Higher Education, with particular emphasis on stress and its effect on learning.

Paul Wellington is Senior Lecturer in Mechanical Engineering at Monash University, and was chairman of the initial organizing committee which established this multidisciplinary programme.

Gillian Winfield is a Research Fellow at CEDAR (the Centre for Educational Development, Appraisal and Research) at the University of Warwick, having held the post of Student Activities Manager in their Students' Union when the research published here was carried out.

Nick Zepke is a member of the Academic and Staff Development department of Wellington Polytechnic, New Zealand. He is involved in jointly running Bachelor and Masters Programmes in Education. He is also editor of *Connections*, a journal on Higher Education issues.

1

The Art of Motivating Students in Higher Education?

Sally Brown, Steve Armstrong and Gail Thompson

Well-motivated students have always succeeded in Higher Education and will continue to do so: the challenge has always been to stimulate, engender and enhance the motivation of those students whose enthusiasm for learning cannot be taken for granted. In mass systems, where large amorphous groups are taught by over-stretched staff in resource-poor environments, ways in which to encourage all students to give their best to their studies are eagerly sought by those whose business it is to teach them. This book aims to explore ways of doing so, balancing theoretical approaches with practical ideas and case studies. The chapters are organised into four sections:

- The impact of teaching on student motivation

- Motivating diverse students

- The impact of university practices on motivation

- The impact of assessment on motivation.

SECTION ONE: THE IMPACT OF TEACHING ON STUDENT MOTIVATION

The five chapters in this section examine the ways in which lecturers affect the extent to which students are motivated to learn. Chapter 2 discusses some of the issues involved in using Computer-Based Learning (CBL) approaches to promote student motivation by making learning more interactive. Phil Barker argues by reference to a case study that CBL, by offering greater flexibility in curriculum delivery methods can generate student enthusiasm, as long as it is well-designed, although he feels there is much further development work needed.

In the next chapter, Noel Entwistle suggests that effective curriculum delivery relies not just on effective teaching methods to engage students in learning, but also on clearly developed conceptions of the teaching and learning processes

1

which build on lecturers' understanding of the factors that affect student motivation. He describes some of the preliminary findings of his team who have designed a questionnaire ASSIST (Approaches and Study Skills Inventory for Students) based on the earlier Approaches to Study Inventory (Entwistle and Ramsden, 1983) to provide a fuller picture of how students are studying.

Chapter 4 looks at causal links between what teachers and students themselves do to bring about effective learning. Ian Solomonides' studies also makes use of the ASSIST questionnaire, and he concludes that interventions to promote student motivation are doomed unless a systemic approach is adopted to improving learning.

Ron Iphofen, in Chapter 5 argues that taking responsibility for learning depends on teachers' and students' mutual recognition of and respect for each other's motives. He suggests that learner responsibility is a joint accomplishment of learners, their teachers and the institutions in which learning takes place and that a balance must be achieved if the process is to be a positive one.

The final chapter in Section one is by Phil Race. He discusses the changing student profile of universities in the 1990s and provides a practical overview of how different classroom teaching practices can be used to promote effective student learning in a variety of contexts.

SECTION TWO: MOTIVATING DIVERSE STUDENTS

The second section looks at the diversity of students currently in Higher Education and explores some of the characteristics of students that affect motivation. Chapter 7 by Della Fazey and John Fazey explores some theoretical perspectives on enhancing the motivation of students for learning and describes three elements that are particularly relevant: the extent to which students feel they have personal control and responsibility over their learning, the presence of a climate that encourages adaptive motivational orientations, and the existence of a value system to promote high student expectations and to sustain lifelong high level learning.

Kim Isroff and Teresa del Soldato argue in the next chapter for a rethinking of the ways in which teaching is undertaken in conventional institutions. This follows studies using questionnaires and interviews on student motivation undertaken by the authors in a conventional university and in the Open University, the UK's best established provider of distance learning. They discuss a range of factors including age, gender, study approaches and the extent to which students feel themselves to be autonomous learners.

Chapter 9 develops these themes further. Rhona Magee, Ann Baldwin, Stephen Newstead and Hazel Fullerton report on a large-scale study during induction of more than 600 students from a range of disciplines, using the revised Study Processes Questionnaire (Biggs, 1987). They conclude that each of these factors does impact on student motivation, but that there are no significant interactions between them.

Chapter 10 by Gillian Winfield and Selena Bolingbroke explores students' motivation beyond the curriculum, looking at a particular group of students who might be expected to have greater motivation than most students. With fieldwork undertaken at two very diverse HE institutions, Middlesex University and the University of Warwick, they discuss factors affecting why students became student representatives.

In Chapter 11, Kay Greasley asks whether gender affects approaches to learning. She concludes that it does in matters such as fear of failure, the depth of approach adopted and preferences for intrinsic or extrinsic motivation. Her conclusions indicate that this is something university teachers need to take into account when planning and delivering the curriculum.

Linda France and Liz Beaty suggest in Chapter 12 that encouraging student motivation is more complex than the relationship between the individual lecturer and their students. They explore a range of study orientations based on the first year experience at the University of Brighton using case studies and discuss a new orientation they have defined which they have termed 'independence orientation', associated with students' desires to make the experience of studying part of personal growth towards autonomy.

SECTION THREE: THE IMPACT OF UNIVERSITY PRACTICES ON MOTIVATION

In Chapter 13, Gail Thompson describes her studies at the University of Sunderland investigating how stress prevents students from doing their best, particularly considering those elements which involve personal control and the person–environment fit. Staff–student relationships still have tremendous impact on the effectiveness of student learning, she suggests, and universities do well to keep this in mind if students are to achieve their potential.

In Chapter 14 Martin Luck writes about undergraduate research projects. He asks whether we are properly motivating our students to recognize the full value of their research projects, and concludes that there is still plenty to be done in this field. He suggests that students need to be encouraged to recognize the extrinsic as well as the intrinsic value of project work, particularly as a vehicle for the development of transferable skills.

Paul Wellington provides an Australian perspective on project work in Chapter 15. He describes how teams of students worked in multidisciplinary teams on peer-assessed projects offered by local manufacturing companies. He found significant motivational development in students undertaking the work in terms of increased confidence, better group working skills, the ability to apply knowledge to practical contexts, developing their own expertise and in being challenged by competition.

Motivational perspectives and work-based learning are the subject of the next chapter by Debbie Keeling, Eleri Jones, David Botterill and Colin Gray. Their exploratory study used focus groups in the financial industries sector in Cardiff to identify factors that influence individual participation in Work-Based Learning (WBL). Their conclusions indicate that if WBL is to succeed, organizations need to take seriously students' needs for support in learning development and for effective communication of all kinds within the organization.

In the final chapter of this section, Alan Bleakley takes a very different stance and asks university teachers to re-examine their practices and to concentrate on making learning a powerful experience in which the love of wisdom as a form of beauty is foregrounded. He passionately defends the notion that if we are to move away from the intellectual stagnation that beleaguers much of Higher Education today, we must reject the ugly and the dull in favour of the aesthetic practice of learning.

SECTION FOUR: THE IMPACT OF ASSESSMENT ON MOTIVATION

In Chapter 18 Julie Mortimer writes about the way in which she has used portfolios as an effective learning tool to enable students to develop their abilities to reflect on their practice. An important feature of the work is the use of self- and peer assessment to involve students fully in their own learning, processes she regards as highly motivating for the students involved.

Stephen Newstead writes next about individual differences in student motivation, looking particularly at the factors that affect whether or not a student is likely to be motivated to cheat. He suggests that certain kinds of assessment instruments are more likely than others to prompt a surface approach to learning and that cheating is often associated with these kinds of approach. Gender and age both seem to be factors in play here, with male students reported as more likely than females to cheat and younger students inclined to break the rules rather than mature ones, who are likely to have stronger intrinsic motivation.

A study from New Zealand is the basis of the last chapter of the book. Linda Leach, Guyon Neutze and Nick Zepke argue that the adult learners they teach tend to be more motivated when assessment is integral to learning, when they have an element of control over their learning, where there is a balance between maintenance and transformative learning and assessment and when there are opportunities for them to engage deeply with the subject matter they are learning. Learners need to be consulted about the processes and practices of learning, they suggest, if they are to maximize their potential.

The aim of this book is to increase awareness of the factors that influence student motivation, with the explicit purpose of using this understanding to bring about improvements in curriculum design, delivery and assessment in our practices in Higher Education. Under-motivated students are hard to teach, gain little benefit from their studies and drain the resources of the institutions in which they study, contributing to poor completion rates and stretching the capacities and the patience of their tutors. We will never be able to rouse every student into a state of enthusiastic participation for their own learning, but there is much that can be done, when the factors that influence student motivation inform the ways in which we work. It is to be hoped that this book will contribute in some way to a greater awareness of these issues, with the result that we can put it into practice in our own working contexts.

REFERENCES

Biggs, J B (1987) *Student Approaches to Learning and Studying*, Australian Council for Educational Research, Melbourne.

Entwistle, N J and Ramsden, P (1983) *Understanding Student Learning*, Croom Helm, London.

SECTION ONE:
The Impact of Teaching on Student Motivation

2

Interactivity as an Extrinsic Motivating Force in Learning

Philip Barker

INTRODUCTION

With growing student numbers and the more widespread availability of computer-based resources, conventional approaches to teaching and learning have often been criticized for their lack of 'interactivity'. It is well known that computers, if used correctly, can have a highly motivating effect on student learning. It seems reasonable therefore that this technology should be used to support conventional teaching and learning activities and, at the same time, be used to develop new approaches. This chapter discusses some of the issues involved in realizing these goals.

Learning is often regarded as either a temporary or a permanent change in behaviour and knowledge that arises as a consequence of some internal or external stimulus. It involves the internal development and reorganization of relevant physico-cognitive structures and processes (Card *et al.*, 1983). The external stimuli involved usually take the form of organized pedagogic and experiential activities that are often designed so that learning is optimized (Barker, 1995a). Learning, of course, is rarely, if ever, a linear process; it often involves trial and error approaches, hit and miss strategies and can sometimes result in mal-learning (Barker, 1994). Invariably, the success of a learning process

7

is often critically dependent upon the frequency, level, quality and type of *feedback* that is given to learners during the 'critical phases' of a learning task. This feedback might be made available in an explicit way or it might form an implicit part of the learning process itself. Feedback is important because it can significantly influence *motivation* – that is, an individual's desire to succeed in some task or activity.

Invariably, the effectiveness and efficiency of learning depend, among other things, upon both *intrinsic* (from within) and *extrinsic* (from without) motivation. For example, although there are exceptions, it is often the case that good teachers motivate students whereas bad ones can have a de-motivating effect (extrinsic factor). Similarly, enthusiastic and enquiring students often achieve very much more (pedagogically) than those who lack these basic intrinsic qualities. Obviously, students show a wide range of learning motivations. Therefore, when designing learning resources that are to be used to facilitate the implementation of new courses, it is imperative that we consider how to create materials that can cater for a user population that exhibits a wide range of intrinsic motivation.

One of the major attractions of computer-based learning (CBL) techniques is the potential that they offer to cater for the particular needs of specific individuals. Implicit in this are the possibilities that these approaches offer in supporting the learning activities of large populations of learners in which there is a diverse range of cognitive and physical capabilities, motivational drive and pre-course skills and knowledge. Although the basic technology to support CBL is now very powerful, the problems of developing highly adaptable software systems that achieve high levels of student motivation are still quite difficult ones to solve.

Bearing in mind what has been said above, it is my belief that, from a pedagogic perspective, *interactivity* is one of the most important characteristics of computer-based teaching and learning systems. Because of its importance within the context of courseware design and electronic course delivery (ECD), this chapter discusses the basic nature of interactivity in terms of cognitive state changes and message passing – with a view to (a) identifying sought-after knowledge states, and (b) designing messages that facilitate progressive transitions between these states (Barker, 1994). It then discusses how interactivity can be used to prevent the onset of mal-learning and how this paradigm can also be used to provide a powerful extrinsic motivational force to stimulate student learning. A case study that illustrates our approach to the development of resources to support electronic course delivery is then briefly described and discussed.

INTERACTIVITY, MOTIVATION AND COURSE DEVELOPMENT

The world in which we exist can be interpreted in terms of two basic types of entity: objects and processes. Processes are important because they provide the mechanisms by which objects are able to change their form and behaviour. Such changes usually take place as a result of various 'perturbational forces' that can influence a system's state space. The term 'interactivity' refers to the ability of one process to influence the progress of another in a controlled way (Barker, 1994). Within the context of an educational setting, these processes are essentially learning and skill development processes that result in the creation of many different kinds of knowledge state. The message-passing activity that takes place as a result of the interaction between students and learning resources constitutes a *communicative dialogue* that is intended to promote the development and enhancement of knowledge states (Barker, 1989).

The importance of message passing (and the dialogues that they involve) is that they facilitate the process of mental model-building. The development of cognitive models is a fundamental aspect of learning activity. People develop models as a result of their experiences and use them to store information and knowledge. Of course, they can also be used to guide any further necessary learning and study that is needed – through the identification of 'gaps' or 'holes' in our understanding. The richness of a person's mental model-set for a particular subject domain determines how well that person understands the concepts and topics involved and can solve problems in this area. Experts have very rich mental models relating to their area of expertise, whereas novices have relatively poor models of the domain in question.

For a variety of reasons, during any model-building process it is possible for someone to build an incorrect model and thereby use this to derive incorrect answers to questions relating to it. The onset of incorrect model building is often referred to as *mal-learning*. The importance of interactivity and feedback is that, if they are used correctly, mal-learning processes can be detected at an early stage; they can then be rectified in appropriate ways. Through the use of suitably designed monitoring processes, the influence of mal-learning can thus, in principle, be minimized, thereby leading to the successful creation of reliable mental models and confidence that these models will be sufficient to cope with all the situations in which they are likely to be needed. It is my belief that mental models play a fundamental role in all human activities, particularly those relating to learning. It is therefore important that, when designing new courses, we consider the fundamental purpose of these models and the effects that interactivity and feedback can have on their development.

With this in mind, it is obviously imperative that as course designers we should consider any guidelines or evidence that might usefully be applied to the future development of any new courses in which we are involved. This is particularly so in cases where such evidence enables us to incorporate (into the creation of learning and teaching materials) mechanisms that will lead to substantial increases in performance and student motivation (Barker, 1995b; Vosniadou *et al.*, 1994).

In our view, two very important factors that must be considered are (a) the way in which a course is delivered (for example, through books, lectures, electronic course delivery, the Internet, and so on), and (b) the 'agent' with whom the primary motivational responsibility for learning resides, namely, the instructor (using a teacher-centred approach) or the learner (in situations where student-centred strategies are employed). For a variety of reasons, giving students responsibility for managing their own learning is becoming an increasingly popular trend within higher education. If we accept that this is a reasonable approach to adopt, the question then arises as to how new courses should be designed in order to accommodate this requirement, while at the same time achieving high levels of student motivation. As has been suggested earlier in this chapter, we believe that this can be accomplished through the appropriate use of interactive, computer-based technologies. Not only can these can be employed to supplement conventional approaches to teaching and learning but, they can also be used to produce totally electronic learning environments (Barker, 1997a).

One approach to the realization of this requirement is through the use of 'electronic lectures' (Barker, 1997b). An electronic lecture is one in which a lecturer uses a computer-based presentation package to deliver his or her material within the confines of a traditional lecture theatre that is fitted out with appropriate screen projection facilities. From the point of view of learning perspectives, there are four main advantages to adopting this approach to lecturing (compared with the use of conventional OHP-based presentations) (Barker *et al.*, 1995a). First, electronic lectures can be made interactive. Second, they can easily be distributed to students: on floppy disk, on CD-ROM or via an in-house intranet facility. Third, the basic lectures can be augmented in various ways (to cater for the individual needs of different students). Finally, it is possible to build in to the lectures various types of self-assessment exercise for students to use in order to gauge their progress and assess their understanding. Using approaches such as this, it becomes much easier for students and teachers to detect the onset of the mal-learning processes.

A natural extension to the approach described above is to move towards putting the whole of a course into electronic form. This strategy is often referred to by the term 'Electronic Course Delivery'. Some of the many advantages of the ECD approach are discussed in detail in Barker (1997a). These include: much wider access to course materials; greater flexibility with respect to how learning materials are accessed by students and the ability to provide toolsets and environments that facilitate more effective and efficient learning activities. In addition, the use of computer-based materials can lead to enhanced levels of student motivation – both in the context of individual and group learning activities.

In my view, the use of ECD can be regarded as just a stepping stone in the transition towards student-centred, intranet-based courses (Forsythe, 1996). Naturally, if this approach is to become the norm in the future, then it is important that we undertake research in order to identify best practice and express this in terms of an appropriately documented collection of guidelines and procedures. With this as a long-term objective, my own work in this area has focused on attempting to identify some of the major issues involved in reorganizing courses to fit into this new paradigm. The approach that we have adopted is briefly discussed in the case study that is presented in the following section.

CASE STUDY

Earlier in this chapter, motivation was loosely defined as being an individual's desire to succeed with respect to the various activities in which he or she becomes involved. It is my belief, therefore, that we can encourage student motivation by providing learning environments and support infrastructures that are conducive to successful learning activities. Our design methodology for learning resource development therefore involves identifying the inhibiting factors which prevent learning and then designing systems that overcome these problems.

In the case of lecture-based courses, one of the main problems that we identified was giving students access to 'on demand' information and materials relating to courses as and when they needed them. The two approaches that we adopted to overcome this problem were based on: (a) the creation of an Electronic Open Access Student Information Service (Barker *et al.*, 1995b; Barker, 1997c), and (b) making a conscious movement towards the implementation of the student-centred learning paradigm discussed in the previous section. This case study deals with the second of these two initiatives.

In order to assess the feasibility of converting a conventionally taught (lecture-based) course into one which is accessible through the Internet (using an 'information on demand' paradigm), we restructured one of our current courses (G56036: Human–Computer Interaction) so as to involve a substantial element of student-centred learning. Because of our uncertainty of success (in terms of student motivation to use these resources and the overall effectiveness of the ensuing course), we were not prepared to just 'throw away the old and wheel in the new'. We therefore decided that one-third of the original course should be made accessible electronically through a departmental intranet facility (using student-centred learning strategies) while the other two-thirds should still be delivered using conventional (teacher-centred) lecturing techniques (possibly involving the use of electronic lectures similar to those described in the previous section).

Rather than just being a lecture-driven course, the modified course would now consist of two parallel strands of learning activity. The main issue that the course redesign process therefore had to resolve was identifying which parts of the course would best be implemented using student self-study techniques and which should remain as lecture-based material. Of course, the two streams of learning activity were not to be regarded as totally independent, unrelated processes; wherever possible, we thought the two strands should support each other and be synchronized in time and content. That is, activities being undertaken in one learning strand should be reinforced by those taking place in the other – although this is not always easy to do. In addition, it was also necessary to identify those characteristics and attributes of the 'new medium' that we could usefully exploit to the advantage of the students following the course.

Naturally, it was anticipated that students would use computer workstations for the realization of the self-study strand of the course. These might be campus-based (and attached directly to our campus-wide local area network) or they might be portable computers that are used off-campus – in the home or in

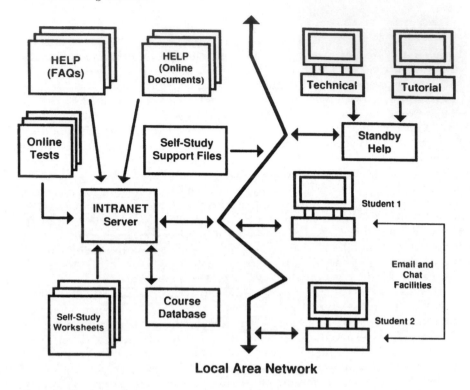

Local Area Network

Figure 2.1   *Towards a student self-study environment*

student hostels through the use of a modem. The basic logical organization of the self-study strand of the course is illustrated schematically in Figure 2.1.

The main development activity involved in implementing the student-centred learning modules was the creation of a hyperlinked set of electronic documents. Together, these defined: (a) the nature of the material to be studied (in terms of a set of 20 worksheets) and supporting files, and (b) the learning and assessment processes involved. Online help facilities were made available in the form of electronic texts (manuals and sets of 'Frequently Asked Questions', FAQs), email and interactive 'chat' facilities.

The electronic documents that formed the basic building blocks of the system were created on a personal computer (PC) using Microsoft's Word for Windows (Version 6) word-processing package. Completed Word documents were then imported into a PC-based HTML (HyperText Markup Language) editing system (HotMetal PRO from the SoftQuad Corporation) ready for mounting on a UNIX-based intranet server as HTML files. The hyperlinks between the different files were added using the HTML editing system. All the HTML files mounted on the intranet could subsequently be accessed using both a Netscape (graphical) or a Lynx (text-based) browser. The implementation of the online testing facilities required the creation of appropriate 'Common Gateway Interface'

(CGI) software to be mounted on the server. This software was written in the Perl programming language. An electronic comment facility was also made available to students so that they could send us feedback about this part of the course.

Although we have not yet conducted a formal evaluation of the self-study strand of the course, the feedback facility has enabled us to gauge some of the students' attitudes to the course. In general, the tone of the feedback that we have received from the students has been positively supportive. The most common student comments have related to: the usefulness of the online self-assessment tests as both an indicator of progress and as a motivational resource; the advantages of being able to access materials on a 24-hour a day basis; and the attractiveness of being able to develop flexible working patterns as a result of not having to go to formally scheduled classes.

From the course manager's perspective, one of the most attractive features of the system is its ability to keep a close eye on what students are doing. This involves keeping automated records of student activity on the system, keeping 'mark books' that reflect performance in the online tests and, if necessary, sending out various cautionary messages to students and staff relating to specific difficulties that particular students may be encountering.

CONCLUSION

The advent of new teaching and learning technologies has meant that radical changes are now necessary within higher and further education, if our institutions of learning are to remain competitive (Armstrong *et al.*, 1997). Bearing this in mind, for one reason or another, many academic organizations are now therefore exploring the possibilities of using these new technologies to support student-managed, self-study activities in a more extensive way than they have in the past. In our view, students welcome these initiatives with mixed feelings. Some students enthusiastically accept the types of change that are involved whereas others are much more reticent and sceptical about them, particularly, in situations where computer-based systems are involved. Despite this, it is apparent from our research that computers can be used as an effective motivational resource within a learning context provided that appropriately designed software and support infrastructures are made available. Indeed, many students feel that the strength of computer-based systems lies primarily in two main areas. First, the ability of the computer to make learning materials and environments more widely accessible in an 'anywhere, anytime, as and when needed' fashion; second, their significant potential for the close monitoring (of what students are doing) and delivery of appropriate comments and feedback (to aid and reinforce their learning activities).

Of course, even though computer-based systems have tremendous potential for the support of teaching and learning activities, it is my belief that considerable thought will have to be given to how best to achieve the goals identified above, especially if motivating learning experiences are to be the net result of the time and effort that are invested.

REFERENCES

Armstrong, S, Thompson, G and Brown, S (1997) *Facing up to Radical Changes in Universities and Colleges*, Kogan Page, London.

Barker, P G (1989) *Basic Principles of Human–Computer Interface Design*, Hutchinson Computer Studies Series, Century Hutchinson, London.

Barker, P G (1994) 'Designing interactive learning', in de Jong, T and Sarti, L (eds), *Design and Production of Multimedia and Simulation-based Learning Material*, Kluwer Academic Publishers, Dordrecht. 1–30.

Barker, P G (1995a) 'Interface design for learning', in Chapman, G M (ed.), *Computer-Based Learning in Science*, Proceedings of the International Conference CBLIS '95, 30th June–4th July, Opava, Czech Republic, Open Education & Sciences, Opava, Czech Republic, 3–18.

Barker, P G (1995b) 'Emerging principles of performance support', in Raitt, D I and Jeapes, B (eds), *Online Information '95, Proceedings of the 19th Online Information Meeting, Olympia, London*, 5–7 December, Learned Information (Europe) Ltd, Oxford.

Barker, P G (1997a) 'Electronic Course Delivery', Special Edition of *Innovations in Education and Training Technology International*, 34, 1, 1–69.

Barker, P G (1997b) 'Assessing attitudes to electronic lectures', in Armstrong, S, Thompson, G and Brown, S (eds), *Facing up to Radical Changes in Universities and Colleges*, Kogan Page, London.

Barker, P G (1997c) 'Flexible access to learning resources through electronic course delivery', in Hudson, R, Maslin-Prothero, SE and Oates, L (eds), *Flexible Learning in Action – Case Studies in Higher Education*, Kogan Page, London.

Barker, P G, Banerji, A K, Richards, S and Tan, C M, (1995a) 'A global performance support system for students and staff', *Innovations in Education and Training International*, 32, 1, 35–44.

Barker, P G, Beacham, N, Hudson, S R G and Tan, C M, (1995b) 'Document handling in an electronic OASIS', *The New Review of Document and Text Management*, 1, 1–17.

Card, S K, Moran, T P and Newell, A (1983) *The Psychology of Human-Computer Interaction*, Lawrence Erlbaum Associates, Hillside, NJ.

Forsythe, I (1996) *Teaching and Learning Materials and the Internet*, Kogan Page, London.

Vosniadou, S, De Corte, E and Mandl, H (1994) 'Technology-based learning environments: psychological and educational foundations', *NATO ASI Series F*, 137, Springer-Verlag, Berlin.

3

Motivation and Approaches to Learning: Motivating and Conceptions of Teaching

Noel Entwistle

INTRODUCTION

This chapter contrasts a conventional psychological view of motivation as a stable individual trait with one which recognizes the role of teaching in motivating students. Even where the relative stability of motivation is stressed, it is still necessary to recognize its complexity. The chapter starts from the way motivation is still used by some academic staff in discussing students, and tries to establish a more differentiated conception of motivation. From that view of motivation, it is possible to see how contrasting conceptions of teaching in Higher Education influence attempts at motivating students towards higher quality learning.

Interviews with academic staff often suggest that two variables alone can predict levels of success in studying, namely, ability level and motivation (Marton *et al.*, 1997, p.6):

> There are two kinds of [weak students] really: the downright indolent [or those who put efforts into other than academic work] and . . . some who don't understand . . . [Again there is the student who] is not very well motivated; he takes the courses largely because he likes other courses even less. He may be doing his degree on that basis . . . only attending university because there's nothing else more intelligent occurred to him to do.

In this comment, the blame for poor performance is laid squarely at the student's door, and other comments made it clear that these lecturers did not believe it was their responsibility to motivate students. 'If they are not motivated, they shouldn't be here', was a typical comment. Not only does this attitude lead to explanations of inadequate learning in terms of the student's lack of ability or application, it also suggests that motivation is a unitary characteristic of which students themselves may have a lot or a little. Certain people are motivated, others are not. Also, the direction of causality is clear. Strong motivation leads to success, while a lack of it results in failure.

In psychological terms, the concept of motivation has been used as a way of describing certain kinds of behaviour and to try to explain the different amounts, and kinds, of effort which are put into a particular activity. That effort has an amount and a direction. But the idea that there are different kinds of effort as well immediately begins to suggest that simple links between motivation and achievement will need to be reconsidered. The next section explores the conception of motivation as it is now viewed in research on student learning, and tries to indicate how a more complex view of its links with student learning can help academic staff to think more critically, and imaginatively, about their teaching.

CHANGING CONCEPTIONS OF MOTIVATION

For many years now, research findings have shown a fairly strong relationship between academic motivation and levels of performance in Higher Education (see, for example, Entwistle and Wilson, 1977). But even in the early studies it was recognized that causality operated in both directions. High motivation leads to success, certainly, but good results also increase motivation. It was also clear from earlier research that motivation is not a unitary concept, but instead is multifaceted, in the ways suggested by Pintrich (1988). He has described three kinds of goal-oriented motivation – *mastery* (understanding the course material for oneself), *extrinsic* (concentrating on obtaining the qualification), and *relative ability* (competitive striving to do better than others). The form, as well as the amount, of motivation affect the outcomes. The forms of motivation in relation to learning and studying can be summarized as follows.

Extrinsic motivation

- is instrumental in form;
- focuses on satisfactory completion of the course;
- is strongly influenced by external rewards and pressures;
- leads to a surface approach to learning and fear of failure;
- produces learning outcomes which are inflexible and not readily transferable to other contexts.

Intrinsic motivation

- reflects a personal goal;
- derives from interest in the subject area;
- depends on personal engagement with tasks chosen;
- depends on feelings of competence and confidence;

- leads to a deep approach and conceptual understanding;
- produces learning outcomes which are flexible and transferable.

Achievement motivation

- is competitive, but can become egotistical and selfish;
- focuses on personal levels of achievement;
- depends on time-management and organised studying;
- treats tasks as personal challenges;
- leads to a strategic, but also versatile, approach to studying;
- produces learning outcomes which include sensitivity to context, but often not sensitivity to persons.

Briefly summarizing some of the main conclusions of research on motivation and learning in Higher Education, we can say that motivation in Higher Education:

- describes the amount of effort put into an activity and its goal;
- has some consistency, but can also change;
- affects, but is also affected by, the level of performance;
- is influenced by perceptions of teaching and learning tasks;
- comes in contrasting forms; and
- its current form and level are a reaction to circumstances, but are also dependent on the past personal history, and habits of thought and studying of that person.

There is, by now, clear evidence that the form of motivation shown is closely related to the approach to learning adopted by students (see, for example, Biggs, 1987; Entwistle, 1988a). The three distinct forms of motivation – extrinsic, intrinsic and achievement – map closely on to those described by Pintrich as extrinsic, mastery and relative ability.

In the earlier research, motivation was still seen as a stable personality trait, and interpreting the motives as 'filtering' the students' perceptions of the learning environment. That is still part of the perspective presented in current models of student learning (Meyer, 1991; Entwistle, 1998), but now we shall also look at the relationship working in the opposite direction, with motivation being affected by teaching and assessment, as we shall see later.

MEASURING MOTIVATION AND APPROACHES TO STUDYING

While the trait-like characteristics of motivation were overstated in the past, the degree of consistency of motivation, and the general habits of studying associated with them, allow self-report inventories to be used to describe students' current ways of studying. In our own studies, we have used the Approaches to Studying Inventory (ASI) (Entwistle and Ramsden, 1983) and subsequent variants of it to measure the relative strengths of different forms of motivation and approaches to learning and studying (Entwistle and Tait, 1990).

Currently, we are developing a questionnaire – ASSIST (Approaches and Study Skills Inventory for Students) – which incorporates a developed version of the ASI, but also includes additional scales to provide a fuller picture of the ways students are studying. Using ASSIST with a sample of 1231 first-year students from six universities, Hilary Tait and I have been able to show, using maximum likelihood factor analysis, not only how approaches to studying were related to preparation for higher education, conceptions of learning (Marton and Saljo, 1997), and learning orientations (Beaty *et al.*, 1997), but also how differing approaches are associated with equivalent preferences for different kinds of teaching (see Table 3.1).

In the analysis, Factor I linked the deep approach with an intrinsic orientation (interest in the course content itself) and a conception of learning as transforming the information presented, but it was also related to preferences for 'deep' teaching – clear explanations combined with intellectual challenge. Factor IV presented the opposite picture of students with an academic extrinsic orientation (drifting into Higher Education on the 'conveyor belt' of educational progression), who saw learning as reproducing, were syllabus-bound, and preferred lectures and books which focused directly and narrowly on assessment requirements without demanding much personal engagement with the course content. Factor III described students who lacked confidence in their prior knowledge and adopted an instrumental approach associated with a fear of failure. The remaining factor (II) describes the strategic approach shown by students who have a strong, competitive form of achievement motivation and well-organized study methods.

Table 3.1 presents a paradox in considering how to improve student motivation and learning. Students with an intrinsic orientation, who saw learning as transforming, preferred teaching that supported that approach, but students with an academic extrinsic orientation who saw learning as reproducing preferred quite a different kind of teaching. Is it possible to cater for students with such different kinds and levels of motivation? And should we?

MOTIVATING STUDENTS BY TEACHING

As we suggested earlier, some colleagues feel that it is none of their business to motivate students. Remember the comment from lecturers used at the beginning of this chapter? Poor performance was attributable to a combination of low ability and laziness. The fault thus lay entirely with the student. However, one of the lecturers saw a certain paradox in offering this explanation (Marton *et al.*, 1997, p. 13):

Table 3.1 *Factor loadings on approaches and preferences for teaching*

	Factor			
	I	*II*	*III*	*IV*
Preparation for higher education				
Independent studying		.37		
Prior knowledge			−.41	
Study skills		.42		
Organizing own work		.41		
Learning orientations				
Intrinsic orientation	.62			
Personal extrinsic			.30	
Academic extrinsic				.35
No clear goal		−.33		
Conceptions of learning				
Learning as reproducing				.35
Learning as transforming	.50			
Approaches to studying				
Deep approach				
Seeking meaning	.68			
Relating ideas	.73			
Use of evidence	.69			
Interest in ideas	.70			
Strategic approach				
Organized studying		.77		
Time management		.94		
Monitoring effectiveness	.41	.45		
Achievement motivation		.75		
Instrumental approach				
Lack of understanding			.65	
Lack of purpose			.38	
Syllabus boundness				.34
Fear of failure			.69	
Preferences for teaching				
Lectures deep	.52			
Books deep	.57			
Exams deep	.42			
Course deep	.44			
Lectures surface				.42
Books surface				.39
Exams surface				.51
Course surface			.43	

Note: N = 1231, 44.0% variance.

The main trouble is unwillingness to get down to work, but having said this, there is no doubt a paradox . . . in that at some time in the past, in order for a person to have got here, presumably he had been willing, and something is going on which diminishes this willingness.

Students, however, resolved that particular paradox without any difficulty at all. One said:

So often are students bored by uninspired teaching or disenchanted by badly taught material. While university lecturers are undoubtedly knowledgeable, they are totally untrained and unexamined in the art of communication . . . The completely incorrect assumption is that anyone with a good degree will automatically be able to impart this knowledge to others.

Whether or not staff believe it is their job to motivate students, research findings make it very clear that their ways of teaching and designing assessment will, nevertheless, have strong influences on student motivation. And these ways of teaching and assessing reflect lecturers' beliefs about the nature of teaching and learning.

CONCEPTIONS OF TEACHING

Although the recent emphasis on quality in teaching is likely to have improved the experiences of students, there remains enormous variability in the quality of teaching among individual lecturers, and also in the culture of teaching found in different departments and universities. Recent research into the experiences of teachers in Higher Education has been paralleling the earlier work on the experiences on students (see, for example, Prosser *et al.*, 1994) to identify equivalent concepts describing teaching. And different conceptions of teaching also seem to affect the extent to which lecturers see one of their functions as motivating students.

The research on student learning has shown how students' conceptions of learning lead to equivalent approaches to learning and studying. It is reasonable, therefore, to anticipate that lecturers will also show coherence between their conceptions of learning, their conceptions of teaching, and their approaches to teaching. Edited extracts from two interviews with science lecturers can be used to illustrate these expected connections (Prosser, personal communication).

Lecturer A: Teaching as encouraging understanding

- *Conception of learning:* The kind of learning we want to have in education is a process of invention, rather than a process of ingestion of information. If you're really going to learn something, then you have to invent it for yourself. It doesn't matter that someone three or four hundred years ago was the first person to invent this, the fact that you're engaged in the same sort of inquiry as they were, doesn't take away from you the act of invention on your part.

- *Conception of teaching:* I like to make a distinction between having something as a presence and something somewhat removed from that, as a concept. Lectures provide a presence that a book doesn't, and you can utilize that in the lecture by a directly engaging question. The lecturer can actually engage (the student) in that question, in a much more interactive mode. Teaching also has a theatrical element to it. I suppose I'm saying that the function of the lecture is to bring inquiry to life, the inquiry that learning is.

- *Approach to teaching:* Students learn, over the years, to get into *lecture mode* very readily. What they'll do is walk into a lecture theatre, and it's automatic – most of the brain shuts down, and all that's left active is this very narrow channel which connects the eye to the hand. The whole basis for my style of lecturing is to defeat that lecture mode, to give another dimension an opportunity to operate. I'm constantly challenging the students in the lecture to think something through for themselves. I think that generates a certain sense of – I think intrigue is a good word, but wonderment is another one, appreciation is another one, and understanding is related to that. (And) in my preparation I actually have to create this (situation) every time, rather than just remember (the content). (The lecture) is a conversation in which there's active listening involved.

Lecturer B: Teaching as transmitting information

- *Conception of learning:* It is my duty and responsibility to help students develop the specific knowledge and skills which are needed to pass the examinations, although I'm fully aware that this might narrow the kind of education I am giving to the students. Still, I think the theory of learning is pretty clear on this, like the old saying goes, 'Practice makes perfect'. Students have to put effort into learning the lecture material and to develop problem-solving skills. If they learn them, then they will be able to cope with the exams.

- *Conception of teaching:* I put great emphasis on behavioural objectives and making sure that I cover the syllabus thoroughly. I also think it is important that the students take away a good set of notes. It gives them confidence if they have those notes to study from. They also give them a clear idea of what they have to know in order to pass the exam, and I'll help them by essentially writing the notes for them.

- *Approach to teaching:* In preparing a lecture, I decide what it is that I want the students to be able to do as a result of the lecture. I also plan the lectures so that I know exactly what notes I want the students to get. Students don't have to decide when to take notes: I dictate them. In my teaching, I also try to make the students realize the importance of being accurate, for example, in the way they write up lab reports . . . (and) I also give a lot of (tests) to make sure they know their stuff.

Running through the first extract is the lecturer's conviction that learning, and teaching involve the active construction of meaning, and that conviction is then expressed through the teaching methods adopted. These connections may seem to be logically inevitable: they certainly emerge as empirical relationships in recent analyses (Prosser *et al.*, 1994; Trigwell and Prosser, 1996). The second extract also reflects this coherence, but with very different beliefs about learning and students. While the first lecturer quoted above is seeking to motivate through intellectual challenge and appeals to experience, the other one is limiting the content and directing the students towards rote learning activities. The forms of motivation being evoked are thus very different, and may be expected to lead to qualitatively different outcomes of learning.

Murray and Macdonald (1997), in their review of several other studies, find similar differences in conceptions of teaching, but their own survey findings indicate that there are also marked disparities between the conceptions lecturers *espouse* and the teaching approaches they actually *adopt*, particularly where conditions make their preferred approach difficult to implement. And in another recent study, van Driel and his colleagues (1997) report that lecturers who are intent on transmitting information also blame students for poor performance and low levels of motivation. This can be seen as a shifting of blame by lecturers who have a very restricted view of the ways in which teaching affects learning.

Lecturers who encourage understanding generally either have had extensive prior training in teaching, or have independently reflected on the underlying purposes of teaching and its effects on learning. It seems that the more developed conception of learning has some of the characteristics of the *versatile* style of learning described by Pask (1988), but, in their case, integrating different teaching strategies. They are able to transmit information as well as other lecturers, but also to engage those students who are prepared to become interested in the fundamental questions of the discipline. Such staff are thus likely to be providing the bare bones of the syllabus as well, for those students who are not prepared to engage with the course.

Perhaps the main conclusion to draw from the research on contrasting conceptions of teaching is the need to help academic staff to develop a more sophisticated conception of the teaching–learning process which will enable them to break out of traditional views about university teaching. Then, they will be able to reflect imaginatively on the teaching of their own subject area in ways which will point to effective ways of organizing courses and approaching teaching. Providing a set of 'tips' to improve technique is a good way of introducing colleagues to alternative methods of teaching, but an adequate conceptual framework is essential if that teaching is to engage students with the intellectual excitement of academic disciplines, and so move it from competence to excellence. In so doing, such teachers will be motivating students towards the underlying ideals of a university education, not just to the routine passing of examinations.

REFERENCES

Beaty, E, Gibbs, G and Morgan, A (1997) 'Learning orientations and study contracts', in Marton, F, Hounsell, D J and Entwistle, N J (eds), *The Experience of Learning*, 2nd edition, Scottish Academic Press, Edinburgh.

Biggs, J B (1987). *Student Approaches to Learning and Studying*, Australian Council for Educational Research, Melbourne.

Entwistle, N J (1988a) 'Motivational factors in students' approaches to learning', in Schmeck, R R (ed.), *Learning Strategies and Learning Styles*, Plenum, New York.

Entwistle, N J (1988b) *Styles of Learning and Teaching*, David Fulton, London.

Entwistle, N J (1998) 'Improving teaching through research on student learning', in Forest, J J F (ed.), *University Teaching: International Perspectives*, Garland, New York (in press).

Entwistle, N J and Ramsden, P (1983) *Understanding Student Learning*, Croom Helm, London.

Entwistle, N J and Tait, H (1990) 'Approaches to learning, evaluations of teaching, and preferences for contrasting academic environments', *Higher Education*, 19, 169–94.

Entwistle, N J and Wilson, J D (1977) *Degrees of Excellence: The Academic Achievement Game*, Hodder & Stoughton, London.

Marton, F, Hounsell, D J and Entwistle, N J (1997) (eds), *The Experience of Learning*, 2nd edition, Scottish Academic Press, Edinburgh.

Marton, F, and Saljo, R (1997) 'Approaches to learning', in Marton, F, Hounsell, D J and Entwistle, N J (eds), *The Experience of Learning*, 2nd edition, Scottish Academic Press, Edinburgh.

Meyer, J H F (1991) 'Study orchestration: the manifestation, interpretation and consequences of contextualised approaches to learning', *Higher Education*, 22, 297–316.

Murray, K and Macdonald, R (1997) 'The disjunction between lecturers' conceptions of teaching and their claimed educational practice', *Higher Education*, 33, 331–49.

Pask, G (1988) 'Learning strategies, teaching strategies and conceptual or learning style', in Schmeck, R R (ed), *Learning Strategies and Learning Styles*, Plenum Press, New York.

Pintrich, P R (1988) 'A process-oriented view of student motivation and cognition', in Sark, J S and Mets, L (eds), *Improving Teaching and Learning through Research*, New Directions for Institutional Research, vol. 57, pp. 55–70), Jossey-Bass, San Francisco.

Prosser, M, Trigwell, K and Taylor, P (1994) 'A phenomenographic study of academics' conceptions of science learning and teaching', *Learning and Instruction*, 4, 217–32.

Trigwell, K and Prosser, M (1996) 'Changing approaches to teaching: a relational perspective', *Studies in Higher Education*, 21, 275–84.

Van Driel, J H, Verloop, N, Van Werven, H I and Dekkers, H (1997) 'Teachers' craft knowledge and curriculum innovation in higher engineering education', *Higher Education*, 34, 105–22.

4

Intervention and Motivation: What Affects What?

Ian Solomonides

INTRODUCTION

Have you seen this list of criteria before?

- Teaching, Learning and Assessment
- Student Progression and Achievement
- Student Support and Guidance
- Learning Resources
- Quality Assurance and Enhancement
- Curriculum Design, Content and Organization.

If like us you have been all too familiar with the list above and the implications of it to your department, school, or university, then you may have gone through the process of quality assessment. Our experience (satisfactory) as a department of Mechanical Engineering within the Nottingham Trent University is one thing, but now we are a department of mechanical and manufacturing engineering following a merger in September 1996. In our preparations for any future quality assessment or audit we have asked some quite fundamental questions about the quality of teaching and learning that we encourage. Perhaps for the first time 'education' was and is firmly on the department's agenda. Quite a powerful statement, but justified by activities such as a whole departmental workshop (all 50 academics and 40 research and support staff) where staff identified departmental strengths and weaknesses. A major issue to be raised during this day was that of poor student motivation and measures for its improvement.

This chapter is about how to integrate staff interest and concern about student motivation into their everyday activities. It is about research and how a series of previously unprecedented activities in the department have led to applied engineering research being associated with fundamental educational research, as well as staff and student development. It is quite an eclectic chapter, discussing pockets of activity that, although initially unrelated, have come to effect more broadly on the system of teaching and learning in the department than had been perceived. This chapter extends the work previously reported to SEDA (Solomonides and Swannell, 1996) and encourages devolved staff development activities so that action for improvement or change has been owned and managed locally. We start with the research carried out by the author and where this is now being integrated into further departmental work.

RESEARCH INTO STUDENT APPROACHES TO STUDY: BACKGROUND

The author's research is concerned with interventions into students' approaches to study. This is fully reported elsewhere (Solomonides, 1996), but briefly, this involved first-year undergraduates in a series of workshops aimed at developing their approaches to study. The workshops were based on Gibbs' (1981) activities. Approaches to study were quantified using the 60-item Revised Approach to Study Inventory (RASI) (Entwistle and Tait, 1993) which was also subjected to a validity and reliability study using local data (see Table 4.1). Quantitative outcomes were supplemented using a qualitative analysis of essays written by students during the 'learning to learn' workshops. General findings about the context emerged as well as utility problems for the RASI.

The literature on student approaches to study has given us the now familiar terms of deep, surface, strategic and apathetic approaches to study, along with descriptions of the consequences of adopting these approaches. The RASI incorporates a section of 60 items comprised of statements about learning. Each respondent is invited to indicate their level of agreement with each statement on a five-point Likert scale. Variable scores are aggregated into scales and sub-scales as shown below. It should be noted that each of the three main scales (deep, strategic and surface) each have an overriding motivational element or intention (as shown thus * in Figure 4.1).

It was concluded that the author's intervention did not promote the preferential deep approach and did not affect motivations. It was also established that subsequent years of the local degree courses were associated with progressively deteriorating approaches. Even students who were exposed to the intervention followed a similar pattern of deteriorating motivations and approaches, suggesting that the local course context and its demands had a greater influence on the approach of students than did the intervention. It was also found that assessment outcomes were unrelated to the extent to which students took a deep approach. There appeared therefore to be a mis-match between the approach students adopted to pass examinations and those that are required for high quality learning outcomes. It is suggested more co-ordinated, coherent and diverse actions for changing local course demands are needed before an improvement in student approaches and, most importantly, their motivations will be observed.

Table 4.1   *Oblimin analysis matrix for the 60-item RASI*

	F1	F2	F3	F4	Alpha
Deep Approach					.83
Intention to Understand	–	–	–	79	.47
Active Learning	–	–	–	67	.60
Relating Ideas	–	–	–	81	.55
Use of Evidence	–	–	–	70	.63
Surface Approach					.78
Intention to Reproduce	–	–	69	–	.38
Passive Learning	–	–	62	–	.45
Unrelated Memorizing	–	–	74	–	.58
Fear of Failure	–	–	70	–	.74
Strategic Approach					.80
Intention to Excel	–	–	–	43	.42
Alert to Assessment Demands	–	55	–	–	.65
Study Organization	–	75	–	–	.56
Time Management	–	75	–	–	.75
Apathetic Approach					.81
Lack of Direction	–	–52	51	–	.62
Lack of Interest	–	–42	52	–	.76
Academic Self Confidence	–	–	–97	–	.70

Factor Correlations		F1	F2	F3
	F2	–	–	–
	F3	.4	.5	–
	F4	–.3	.2	–.3

Note: Maximum Likelihood Oblimin Factors explained 60 per cent of the variance. Loadings below 0.3 are omitted. Decimal points generally removed. Alpha refers to Cronbach's Alpha for each of the scales and sub-scales, n = 567 (representing all full-time and part-time students).

Deep (16 Items, 4 for each of:)
Intention to Understand*
Active Learning
Relating Ideas
Use of Evidence

Surface (16 Items, 4 for each of:)
Intention to Reproduce*
Passive Learning
Unrelated Memorizing
Fear of Failure

Strategic (16 Items, 4 for each of:)
Intention to Excel*
Alertness to Demands
Study Organization
Time Management

Apathetic (8 Items, 4 for each of:)
Lack of Direction
Lack of Interest

Academic Self Confidence (4 Items)

Figure 4.1   *RASI main scales and sub-scales*

These conclusions are broadly supported elsewhere (cf Ramsden *et al.*, 1986; Meyer *et al.*, 1994; Norton and Crowley, 1995) and by the results from the qualitative analysis which indicated similar dominating effects of course context over approach. Some individual students did gain from the intervention in that they reported being in a better position to evaluate their relationships with the course following the workshops. It appeared that some students could be described as being in tension between the desire to take a deep approach and the adoption of less desirable approaches as promoted and encouraged by the course context. It is suggested that questions regarding the integrity of the intervention are thereby left unresolved even though the immediate group level effects of it are quite clear.

This paradox between success of the intervention at the individual level and failure of the intervention at a group level has again been reported elsewhere (cf Meyer *et al.*, 1994). Reported successes in changing students' learning behaviour are generally based on work at the individual, or at most a very small cohort level. The problems of intervening on a scale that copes with large numbers of students are legion. There is therefore an in-built inadequacy in terms of dealing with all students' behaviours and motivations in the same way. This of course is also in tension with the economies of scale that Higher Education is now rebuilding itself around. There may therefore be some merit in pursuing a method of identifying and supporting those students most at risk of failing. Gibbs (1981) alluded to this conclusion but there has been very little research since then into how group level interventions might help identify students at risk who can then be engaged at the individual level.

RESEARCH INTO STUDENT APPROACHES TO STUDY: CURRENT ISSUES

Since the author's research was published, the RASI has undergone further modifications to produce a version known as ASSIST (Approaches and Study Skills Inventory for Students) (Tait, 1996). Trialed at Edinburgh, Nottingham Trent and elsewhere, this inventory recognizes the sometimes shaky relationship between approaches and their (previously) defining motivations. Indeed, the scoring key for ASSIST confirms that:

> empirical relationships between items and between sub scales are, in part, a function of the specific discipline and the particular learning environment experienced by the student and so are liable to vary somewhat . . . the fourth sub scale (the motivational element) is more likely to vary . . . *In research there would generally be an advantage in treating motives as separate variables.* (my emphasis)

In this respect, and if using Factor Analysis on variables like these, the assumptions made about how scale items cluster together may not be equally valid for different student populations. This supports the need to analyse data relative to the context in which they were obtained, and to develop a 'map' or model of the local context within which action can develop.

The identification of students with 'potential weaknesses', especially within a cross-sectional or snap-shot study like the author's, cannot reliably be judged against external criteria. The analysis needs to be introspective so that the students' motivations and performance can be judged against internal, local conditions. Whether the prevailing conditions are supportive or not of learning for understanding, and whether or not the local students take 'appropriate' approaches are a wider issue that the author has questioned and then found largely disappointing answers. These have revealed a spiralling deterioration of approach over time within the local system.

Research suggested students passing the course would seem to utilize more appropriately the skill elements of the strategic approach when dealing with assessment than those that fail. Those failing tend towards an apathetic approach. The other approaches do not seem to be as instrumental in assessment outcome loadings, suggesting that:

- some aspects of the strategic approach are influential in determining student success or failure;

- even more concerning is that the assessment system is not being seen by students to be rewarding the preferable deep approach to study (but that is another issue for future development and discussion).

These findings may also indicate a future need for inventories of student approaches to study to be constructed so as to be subject-specific or context-specific. In this respect, the constructs of approaches to study may be significantly altered by the nature of the context to which they are meant to relate. In an attempt to consider these alterations in a way that factor analysis fails to appreciate, we have embarked on a new trail of research using neural net algorithms.

The author is concerned with far more than the statistical vagaries of inventory analysis, and has come to recognize the importance of discipline tutors researching their own practice and the effects that this indirectly may have on student motivation. Further, the pressures of external audit and quality assessment, along with the drive for internal cost effectiveness have changed the way in which many colleagues look at the students they are responsible for. This has placed a greater emphasis on trying to understand what motivates students appropriately and discover the methods by which students can be fully integrated into the engineering education culture. From a developmental point of view, the author's department is now engaged in a series of innovations, for example:

- participation in the HEFCE's Fund for the Development of Teaching and Learning project, with the author co-ordinating the department's efforts in 'sharing excellence' and the peer observation and support of colleagues;

- staff workshops of the kind reported at the beginning of this chapter;

- development of new and higher impacting methods of student to staff feedback, for example, several course tutors have followed the author's example of interviewing all students each semester;

- the development of a neural net and interface which will serve to do several things:

  - identify students at risk of failing so that intervention at an individual level can be designed and implemented by a pastoral tutor (the author);

  - include engineering research in fundamental educational research so that colleagues can have access to a technology and application they recognize as being their own, while being exposed to issues and problems of research in education.

The benefits of this last point cannot be over-emphasized. There is a tradition involved in discipline teaching in Higher Education which may need to be reassessed before improvements in student motivation are observed. As Eysenck and Piper (1987) suggest, there may be an epistemology of each discipline that enables many lecturers to dismiss findings of educational research as being unsound:

> The way in which the student has to learn about, say, physics or engineering, it is claimed, is peculiar to the subject, because the criteria by which good evidence is distinguished from bad and truth from falsehood is the very basis of the discipline. It is accepted that such is the case for all subjects. All, that is, except the one which refuses to stay in its discrete territory. When education brings its methods of analysis and applies its criteria of rigour to investigating how physics or engineering is taught, then it is asked to justify itself, not against its own paradigms of veracity, but rather against those of the subject matter taught.

With respect to this, it is likely that there is some reticence or inertia within the Higher Education system as a whole to adopt sound and well-grounded principles which have been formulated with the aim of improving motivation and the quality of student learning. The author's research was conducted from within an engineering context in the hope that any findings would be recognized and accepted by the department they were intended to inform. It seems reasonably clear that the demands as they stood locally were not encouraging high quality learning outcomes. The central problem for further research may not solely be in verifying this suggestion but also in getting such suggestions recognized by the culture from which they have emerged. It can and should be argued that mechanisms for bringing educational research closer to the culture are required. In the local context, this is where the neural net is useful.

NEURAL NETWORKS AND THE IDENTIFICATION OF STUDENTS AT RISK OF FAILING

Neural nets involve the modelling and prediction of systematic events. Previous attempts at this kind of modelling are typically associated with developing computer based applications. Entwistle, Tait and Speth (1994) and Tait and Entwistle (1996) devised and produced a computer-based diagnostic system that identifies students at risk of failing. The package is known as PASS (Personalized Advice on Study Skills), made up of three Hyper-Card shells. One of these shells, 'Student View', relies on the RASI, and its subsequent analysis, as the basis for a diagnosis and 'treatment' being prescribed. The author is not at this stage concerned with the validity of advice that PASS gives to students, but is more concerned with the way in which the RASI is analysed within such computer-based systems. Conventional systems have one major flaw – they are inflexible in statistical interpretation of the RASI scores against differing contexts and as such will tend to consider all students in all disciplines as fundamentally similar. Given the comments already made in this chapter, what is needed is a much more flexible system, one which recognizes which student learning constructs and motives are most suited to a particular discipline and the context in which it is learned. These loci could then be used as datum against which students could be profiled. In this manner a series of criteria for passing students might be established, and those students significantly differing from the criteria would then be flagged as at risk of failing. This type of system would have to be more flexible and context sensitive than that produced by Entwistle *et al.* (1994).

Programmes using statistical algorithms to solve linear numerical problems are limited in their interpretative capabilities. In an attempt to examine the possibility of developing a more flexible system, the author consulted colleagues with respect to the computer applications known as neural networks. These significantly extend the previous work on expert systems by enabling the neural network, the computer program, to 'learn' from its environment, that is, the data supplied to it. In brief, a neural network is a multi-variate analytical program which can train itself to recognize relationships within data sets. It is trained by being repeatedly shown one set of data in random order. The program effectively 'learns' to evaluate inherent patterns within the data against external criteria and to draw inference from these patterns. Ultimately, the net will be capable of accepting new, unseen data, and then indicating probable outcomes based on the previous training runs.

Theoretically, then, it is possible to program such a network to accept data from the RASI or some other profile and to 'look for' links between these data, context data and academic or other outcomes, on a retrospective basis. Tied into the local student tracking system, and over a period of time, the network would therefore 'learn' to distinguish and generalize profiles of students most likely to succeed or to fail. Thereafter, the system could be used to identify students who would benefit from specified forms and content of learning intervention, and retrospectively to evaluate courses and the approaches and motivations they promote (cf Prosser and Trigwell, 1990). Clearly, there is

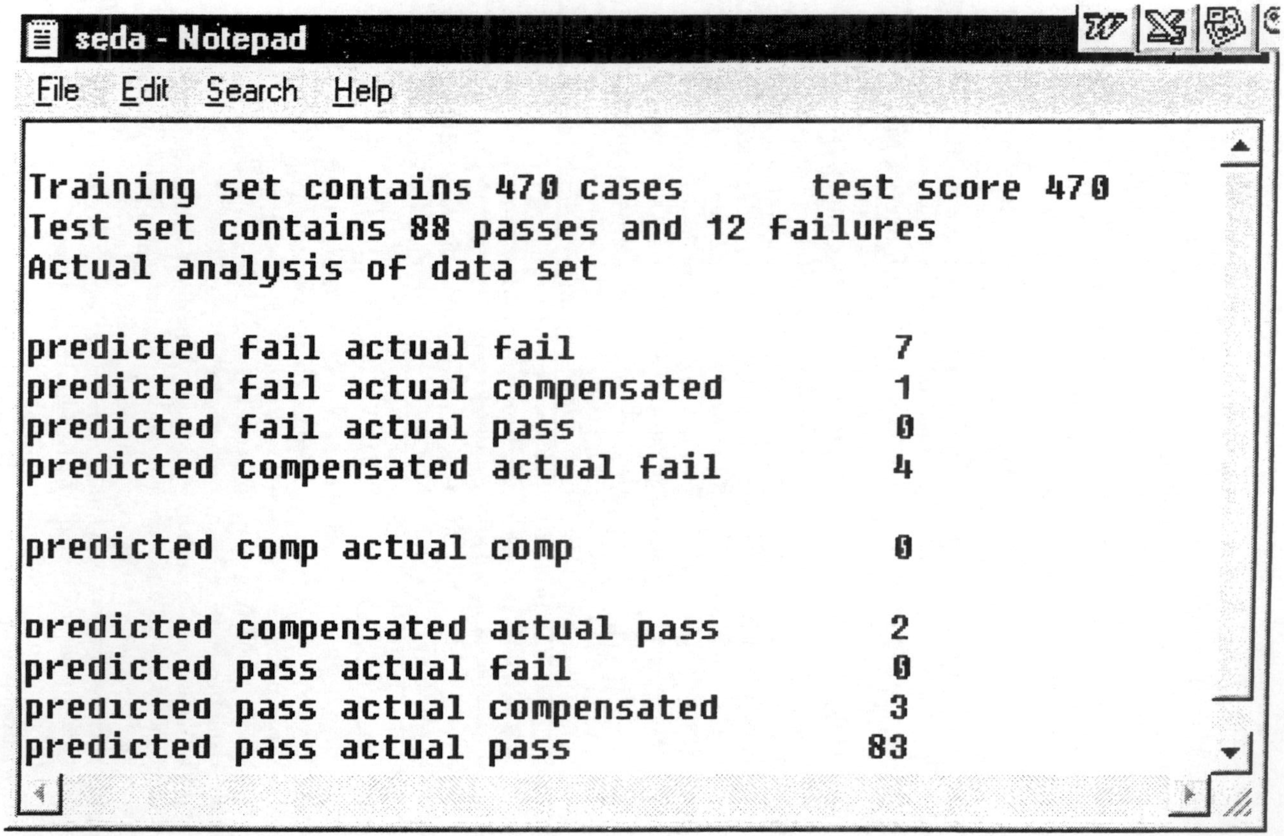

```
seda - Notepad
File  Edit  Search  Help

Training set contains 470 cases      test score 470
Test set contains 88 passes and 12 failures
Actual analysis of data set

predicted fail actual fail                      7
predicted fail actual compensated               1
predicted fail actual pass                      0
predicted compensated actual fail               4

predicted comp actual comp                      0

predicted compensated actual pass               2
predicted pass actual fail                      0
predicted pass actual compensated               3
predicted pass actual pass                     83
```

Figure 4.2 *Neural net output window*

a series of technical, psychological and ethical issues to be researched in the development of such a system. The work reported here is in the early stages but is showing promise. Figure 4.2 is an example of a typical test output for the neural net we are developing.

What can be seen from the window is that the neural net has been shown 470 randomly selected RASI profiles and the associated academic performance scores so that it may ascertain the 'fingerprint' of students who failed compared to students who passed as a prelude to examining a further 100 unseen RASI profiles.

Within the unseen data there were 88 RASI profiles from passing students and 12 from failing students. The neural net successfully predicted seven failures and 83 passes. In other words, once the net has been trained using locally based data, when it is then shown a new set of data the net is capable of identifying at least seven of the students who did in fact fail. The consequences of this should be clear to anyone trying to identify students at risk of failing. There are problems at the time of writing with getting a 100 per cent hit rate (which should be possible considering the academic outcomes of the students who supplied the data is known), but it is probable that this is a consequence of the utility problems of the RASI discussed above. Data acquired using the latest ASSIST will hopefully produce a highly reliable and context sensitive package . . . watch this space.

CONCLUSIONS

This work has further confirmed the author's belief that in his department, the motivation of students and the quality of learning that takes place within it are system dependent (Biggs, 1993; Solomonides, 1996). The natural outcome of this is that interventions into student motivation are doomed to failure unless they take the system into account. Broadly, the research to date suggests that any intervention should be consonant with the system it intends to impact on, as students could be identified who, despite seeing the benefits of the author's original intervention, were unwilling to take the chance of change. More specifically, the author's findings have made a small contribution to the understanding of what a strategic approach to study is at the local level. In this respect, the strategic approach has been shown to be less concerned with intention or motivation and more concerned with skill.

The research supports previous findings regarding the difficulties of forcing changes in students' motivations and intentions by group level intervention. While the nature and the content of the author's intervention were broadly well received, the results from the RASI data suggest that it had no effect on the approach to study, motivation, or academic outcome of the participating students. This is not the same as saying that students were unchanged regarding their ability to evaluate their motivations towards, and their relationships with, the learning environment following the intervention. Some students did report an increased awareness in this respect. The integrity of the intervention is undecided because the system where the intervention is found may militate against such an intervention having any effect at all at the group level.

Likewise, the methods of analysis applied are unable to offer substantial conclusive evidence regarding effects at the individual level. It is suggested that on a quantitative basis, the development of the neural net analysis may offer a more insightful and context-related method of exploring the relationship between an individual student's attitudes and his or her success or failure.

These conclusions lead to a wider corollary regarding the nature of improving the quality of student learning. As students enter into Higher Education they become part of, contribute to, and have a relationship with a system of teaching and learning. Intervention into only one part of the system (for example, just the students) erroneously presumes that the intervention will have a sufficiently disruptive effect so as to alter other (often more powerful) system elements. Predictably it seems now, such a disruptive effect was not identified or triggered by this research. So what are the benefits for departments engaging in educational research and development at the local level? The practical benefits in conducting the research are:

- in determining where and how interventions in a broader sense might be targeted;

- in identifying how students might be encouraged to reflect on their experience of learning in support of a developed approach to study and related motivation;

- in the inclusion of previously sceptical or otherwise reticent colleagues in the research of their own practice, especially at a qualitative level;

- in the establishment of educational research as being a necessary and legitimate part of discipline provision;

- in providing some insights and evidence which will be of great benefit in future quality audit;

- in simply finding out things that were previously just assumed or even misconceived.

ACKNOWLEDGEMENTS

This chapter is dedicated to the memory of Mike O'Neil, a local colleague and researcher who was always interested in my work. I hope I can carry on the tradition of promoting research and enquiry at The Nottingham Trent University which he had done so much to establish.

I am also grateful to Noel Entwistle and Hilary Tait for providing often unpublished information regarding the inventories and for discussing various concepts and ideas with me.

REFERENCES

Biggs, J B (1993) 'From theory to practice: a cognitive systems based approach', *Higher Education Research and Development*, 12, 1, 73-85.

Entwistle, N and Tait, H (1993) 'Identifying students at risk through ineffective study strategies', *European Association for Research on Learning and Instruction (EARLI): 1993 Symposium on Student Learning*, Aix en Provence, France.

Entwistle, N, Tait, H and Speth, C (1994) *Identifying and Advising Students At Risk from Deficient Study Skills: A Computer Based Package for Departments*, Centre for Research on Learning and Instruction, Edinburgh University, Edinburgh.

Eysenck, M W and Piper, D W (1987) 'A word is worth a thousand pictures', in Richardson J T E, Eysenck M W and Piper D W (eds) *Student Learning: Research in Education and Cognitive Psychology*, SRHE, Guildford, pp.208-2.

Gibbs, G (1981) *Teaching Students to Learn*, OU Press, Buckingham, pp.61-71.

Meyer, J H F, Cliffe, A F and Dunne, T T (1994) 'Impressions of disadvantage: II – monitoring and assisting the student at risk', *Higher Education*, 27, 95-117.

Norton, L and Crowley, M (1995) 'Can students be helped to learn how to learn? An evaluation of an approaches to learning programme for first year degree students', *Higher Education*, 29, 307-28.

Prosser, M and Trigwell, K (1990) 'Student evaluations of teaching and courses: student study strategies as a criterion of validity', *Higher Education*, 20, 135-42.

Ramsden, P, Bestwick, D G and Bowden, J A (1986) 'Effects of learning skills interventions on first year university students' learning', *Human Learning*, 5, 151-64.

Solomonides, I P (1996) *Learning Intervention and the Approach to Study of Engineering Undergraduates*, PhD Thesis, The Nottingham Trent University.

Solomonides, I P and Swannell, M J (1996) 'Encouraging students: making the passive active at The Nottingham Trent University', in Wisker, G and Brown, S (eds), *Enabling Student Learning*, Kogan Page and SEDA, London, pp.102-15.

Tait, H (1996) Personal communication with the author.

Tait, H and Entwistle, N (1996) 'Identifying students at risk through ineffective study strategies', *Higher Education*, 31, 97-116.

5

Understanding Motives in Learning: Mature Students and Learner Responsibility

Ron Iphofen

INTRODUCTION: THEORETICAL BACKGROUND

Theorizing about motivation in learning has progressed from basic stimulus-response ideas towards an interest in more authentic motivational accounts produced in learning dialogues. This chapter argues that taking responsibility for learning depends upon educators' and learners' mutual recognition of and respect for their motives.

The bases for a sociopsychological understanding of motivation lie within the sociology of accounts (summarized in Buttny, 1993) and attribution theory (outlined by Weiner, 1991). Both approaches stress that interpersonal communication processes act as determinants of motive attributions. Motives are 'not subjective springs of action in the individual' (Wright Mills, 1940, p.905) but should be seen as the linguistic or paralinguistic modes of communication used by humans to interpret and manipulate phenomena in their world. Any complete motivational account produces a rationale in which an actor, an act and a scene are linked by some mechanism; and the rationale will be coloured by an evaluation of the audience for the statement (Burke 1962). Thus, accounts of the pursuit of a particular educational course must appear 'legitimate' by linking intentions to outcomes and must incorporate an allocation of responsibility for actions.

As accounts for action, motives cannot be assumed to be permanent, to dominate behaviour, nor to be set in a fixed priority list. Success motives, for example, can be achieved in many ways. Motives change according to time and place. They can become 'stabilized' in an institutionalized set of attributions when there is acceptance across a community of the reasons for particular actions. The psychological stability of individuals need not rest on the degree to which they 'internalize' the typical attribution profiles for their society. Their stability may just as much depend upon the individual correctly interpreting a situation as calling for the offering of a particular motive (Bhatia, 1993). For example, a student may be reluctant to reveal their 'real reasons' for attending a course if they believe those reasons to be institutionally unacceptable. The interesting question is how students come to identify and attribute certain needs and wants as relevant to themselves and their future goals and to feel that they will be accepted as legitimate.

If this is the case for individuals, it is likely to be more complicated for a group. Students in a class hold a variety of educational motives. The group's motivational profile changes as the group matures and as shared incidents impinge upon the group's history. Consequently, a range of motivational profiles and priorities emerges in any setting. Effective educational systems meet the requirements of such a variety of motives.

METHODOLOGICAL PROBLEMS

Research into adult students' motives has employed variants of factor and cluster analysis using in-depth interview, 'reason-seeking' questionnaires and psycho-metric measures (Boshier, 1976). Such an approach leads to a failure to separate aspiration from other factors linked to participation (Jarvis, 1983, pp.65–8; McGivney, 1990, pp.23 ff.). It adopts the reductionist view that motives are an internal psychodynamic 'charge' called forth through stimulus or response mechanisms or revealed with skilled probing. This is partly why some participants appear inadequately motivated. Factor analyses artificially fragment motivational accounts and do not look in detail at the emergent process of accounting for entering and pursuing courses of education.

Similarly, tests for reliability and validity cannot separate measures of the research instrument from measures of the strength of attributions which have become institutionalized. Their snapshot nature cannot test the stability and consistency of particular motive accounts.

Questionnaires and projective devices unnaturally force a focusing. A factor analysis of frequently given reasons only elicits a count of responses deemed apt in the context of that discourse event: the response to a questionnaire. The authentic production of attributions in human discourse is the essential site for motive investigation. Motives should emerge according to criteria established by the mutually interested parties, not those of the visiting behavioural scientist.

OBSERVING LEARNER MOTIVES

The notion that motives are plural, complex, dynamic and observable only in terms of their use in a specific context implies a certain relativism. But most people know that only certain things can be said or admitted in certain situations. When individuals are assumed to be 'not motivated' because they do not participate in Higher Education, we are making a value judgement. When students are regarded as 'un-motivated' when they participate for the 'wrong reasons', we are effectively prioritizing motives or applying a hierarchy of credibility (Becker, 1967). In the same way, an intrinsic/extrinsic motive categorization ignores the complexity of dynamic accounts. If I enthuse about something (my intrinsic motive) to students who then learn due to my enthusing, have they caught my intrinsic energy or are they extrinsically driven by motives outside themselves?

The failure to realize inherent value judgements produces the assumption that intrinsic is better than extrinsic motivation. When we make the judgement that there are right and wrong reasons for action, we need to set the context to that judgement. As contexts change, so does the rhetorical power of a motive. To suggest that some rewards are more legitimate than others is to hierarchize the motives to which such rewards apply.

Rarely are students 'de-motivated' by the Higher Education experience. This suggests that the experience extracted all inspiration to act. Instead, students' motives change and we, as educators, participate in that change and in the students' disenchantment. We must be prepared to ask: what do we or the institution or society do to cause this change? If students are motivated only by assessment, that says something about the way students perceive the rewards of Higher Education, and the society within which those rewards become measures of an individual's potential, and the way we structure the curriculum to comply with those demands.

ADULT EDUCATIONAL MOTIVES

Fostering a corporate educational spirit is impossible if institutional mission statements fail to match practice. The broad aims of institutions and the specific motives of individuals come together in the accomplishment of particular educational goals. My research into the motives of adult residential college students aimed to discover how far their motives were influenced by biographical factors or by their progress through the educational institution (Iphofen, 1996).

Their strongest motivational orientation was 'instrumental' in the sense of aspiration towards Higher Education and valued occupations. It is too simple to portray this as extrinsic motivation. Students use institutions and their motives remain stable while they gain confidence in their ability to achieve their goals. Confidence boosting is one advantage of all preparatory courses for mature students. By enhancing familiarity with a Higher Educational environment, students are reassured that they are in the right place. Despite disadvantages, the value of a residential 'therapeutic community' lies in offering mutual support and understanding while students develop their new learner identities.

Ongoing research with mature nursing students suggests their initial willingness to take responsibility as autonomous learners, but they soon meet institutional constraints which adjust their expectations downward (Lavelle *et al.*,1997). This may be a feature of curriculum, organization or staff. As part of an action-oriented project the students were confronted with this knowledge and challenged to do something about it. As Harri-Augstein and Thomas (1991) recommend, a dialogue about learning was established. Previously dissatisfied students discovered something which directly affected their ability to learn effectively, which appeared to be outside their control and which they resented.

There is a problem making profound changes to the institutional infrastructure in which this process occurs. We cannot experiment by changing the staff nor can we do much about centralized funding and course validation arrangements which constrain both class size and course content. This is a particular problem of certain professional health care training courses and the control applied by NHS managers on human resource demands. The connection between employers and Higher Education is not so clear-cut in non-vocational courses, but none the less remains an influence on central authorities who allow the economy to condition the educational infrastructure.

ENCOURAGING MOTIVATION BY 'USING MOTIVES TO LEARN'

The DfEE studies on individual commitment to learn used the category of 'non-motivated' (Tremlett *et al.*, 1995, p.21). This included non-learners who preferred 'to relax' after work, to 'spend time with the family', were 'too busy' to learn or 'did not need to learn new things'. Other so-called non-motivated learners had, in fact, learned transferable skills for specific purposes. They had achieved short-term learning goals. Such people are motivated, to do different things.

The assumption that non-participants are non-learners implies that learning only takes place in institutions. People also learn from television, the tabloid press, and conversation. Their motives include getting a job, caring for the family and enjoying life. Non-participants feel they have accomplished many of these things to standards which they have set themselves. They may have learned some 'wrong' things in my judgement, but they have still learned. This is one reason why adult learning awareness-raising in popular culture is emphasized (Uden, 1994, p.28).

Participants in my valued learning setting may seem less well motivated when they focus on relevance and what is essential for the forthcoming exam. Yet they too are motivated towards clear, short-term goals. In a similar way, drop-out statistics are employed as a measure of commitment, although the factors behind student wastage can vary widely. Again, some researchers regard this as evidence of 'de-motivation' (Purdey and Gale, 1988, pp.45–52).

What is really happening is a change in the institutionalized attribution complex among Higher Education students and a persistence in the attributions of non-participants which devalues education. Educators consider legitimate motives to include valuing the university learning experience and an abiding interest in the topic or discipline. In many respects, these are the ideals. We complain when students do not offer similar motives but such ideals have not always been universally dominant. Lecturers are not uniformly dedicated either to their subject or to the experience of learning. We must decide how to relate our perception of student needs with their views about what they want. This means taking the entire complex of their motive attributions seriously and placing that in the context of the available distribution of learning resources.

Creating a conducive learning environment requires making the best use of the available opportunities and removing obstacles to learning. Students must be adequately informed about the educational opportunities that exist and guidance must indicate variations in quality and be specific to individual requirements. Advice given by providers is not impartial. Guides exist to advertise institutions. If students find themselves in the wrong institution or course, then some of the blame may lie with the corporate image-makers.

Staff must show that they care about the goals and ideals of the learning institution. Cynicism, self-seeking and pessimism more easily cascade down an organization than up it. No successful modern business enterprise lacks a mission statement; nor the means to implement goals and evaluate achievements. Alternative funding systems have been proposed both by the government and the Dearing Report.

But ability is also a vital resource and errors are made by admitting students to maintain targets without unlocking their potential to learn. Sampling the Higher Education experience, improving access based on realistic chances to succeed, and increasing incentives for adult learning are ways in which the opportunity may be made realistic.

When individuals conduct their own personal opportunity-cost analysis, they must calculate that the pursuit of Higher Education is worth effort. One in five respondents in the DfEE survey did not have a choice; employers required them to attend courses. Such motives do not deliver students with a commitment to learn, only a calculated incentive to pass the course. If continuing professional development progresses in a similar way, much of the joy of learning will be threatened.

Commitment by both learners and educators is a function of making realistic choices. This is only possible if real alternatives exist. Thus, the increasing uniformity of Higher Education may be disempowering and, therefore, prevents learners and educators alike from taking responsibility for learning. Learners must have a sense of value for money and value for the time which they have invested. They will not be reassured by TQA visits and HEQC reports. They make their own judgements of worth based on delivery methods, class sizes, organized and clear curricula, flexibility and variety to cater for individual differences. (See Watts, 1990, pp.74–5; Tremlett and Park, 1995, pp.15–20; Uden, 1994, pp.28–35 for fuller discussions of each of these issues.)

Institutionalized provision is used by students for their own purposes, whatever we hold to be the 'real reasons' or even the 'best reasons' for doing it. Ideally, we seek congruence between the motives of the student and those of the institutional provider.

CULTIVATING MOTIVATIONAL CONGRUENCE

Given the constraints on Higher Education, students and lecturers must share the responsibility for learning. Lecturers could deride motives which come low on their own priority list or they could use those motives along with their own in a dialogue about the learning experience. Cultivating such a responsive environment cannot merely mean the imposition of an integrative curriculum or an andragogical pedagogy. Teaching Quality Assessment refers to 'enhancing the quality of the learning experience' and we can do this by engaging in discourse with students which includes consideration of the following topics:

- *clarifying reward structures:* gains from the successful completion of courses must be clarified. Any devaluation of degree qualifications must be openly discussed. Other motives for engaging a course might then be seen as important.

- *sharing success tricks:* learners can be encouraged by discovering practices successfully adopted by those they emulate. Ideas for achieving exam success may sound instrumental, but they can enhance the learning experience.

- *addressing practical needs:* learners' needs are frequently practical: how to write a good assignment, conduct effective information retrieval, or use equipment. Modelling, over-the-shoulder work and systematic instruction can be employed in a concerted manner to suit learners' needs. Teachers identify such good practices but may not employ them believing that, at the Higher Education level, there are few practical solutions to these problems.

- *practical andragogy:* principles of relevance, student orientation, experiential learning and problem-centredness are valued. But it is contrary to andragogy to impose autonomy upon learners who are not ready for it. With some topics and with some learners, autonomy and responsibility for learning may take time to cultivate. Didactic teaching can be given if students desire it, even if it counters valued educational principles. They must judge when the time is right for autonomy.

- *matching rhetoric:* Educators need persuasive rationales for action. Learners need to be convinced of the 'good reasons' for learning particular things. It is not enough to employ student subcultural vocabularies, they date and the educator becomes anachronized.

- *variations in learning styles:* learning can be turned into leisure by judicious time management. Successful learners use simple self-rewards and gain satisfaction by personal control of a 'best time to work'.

- *disclosure – sharing vulnerabilities:* we should be prepared to discuss exams we have failed or lecturers we didn't like. The conditions of failure must be confronted.

- *display – pride in competencies:* at the same time we should encourage apt immodesty as a means of boosting confidence. If we are prepared to reveal our competencies, students will see this as acceptable pride. It also enhances co-operative learning: students can share in each other's collective expertise.

- *success and failure biographies:* exclaiming 'I can do that too!' models successful careers. The observation that someone worse off than oneself succeeded also acts as a model. Mature students are particularly encouraged by examples of late learning successes. Their aspirations are encouraged and are seen as achievable.

● *pedagogical content:* commitment can be encouraged by using proven means of successful teaching. This assumes that content alone does not stimulate interest, but if delivered in an imaginative way, learners' attitudes towards content changes. Innovative curricula and assessment produce students who are excited into sharing our vocabularies of motive, our reasons for learning and our ideals about how intellects should be developed.

All the above are motivational narratives which offer practical means for achieving success. They suggest ways in which responsibility can be taken for learning and commitment can be enhanced (Uden, 1994, p.13). They reduce anxiety and boost confidence. Apart from the constraints of politics and economy, such discourse creates the conducive environment we need.

CONCLUSION

The Secretary of State's guidance for the DfEE's research into individual commitment to learning was: 'Individuals must be persuaded that training pays and that they should take responsibility for their own development' (Tremlett and Park, 1995, p.35). But some individuals have no evidence that training pays. Can and should individuals be persuaded of something that contradicts their experience? How can individuals take responsibility for their own development, if they cannot control those institutions which are assumed to hold the necessary learning resources? Individuals are concerned about their own development. They may simply hold different views from ours.

Government funding and centralized management dictate the dominant rationales for Higher Education. The main participants – students and staff – have had to subordinate their idealized motives to those of the institutional provider. Personal growth and intellectual discipline are acceptable motives if secondary to the achievement of qualifications and professional credentials. If individuals remain unconvinced that credentialism is a primary motive for participation, then they will not participate. However, if the rhetoric of credentialism is accepted, educators must accept that content remains secondary to the achievement of qualifications. Higher Education has succumbed to government and employer rhetoric which is why it has problems motivating students. This is the institutionalized attribution complex which we need to change.

We all know that the ideals of Higher Education are fine in an ideal world. But realities of finance, politics and administration force students and staff to forego the luxury of ideals. The learning dialogue between educators and learners is the vehicle through which the compromises between the ideal and the real are conducted. As educators, we are being dishonest if we pretend that the university ideal can be maintained in the face of political and economic constraints. Further, we are unfair to students in expecting them to hold the highest ideals in the face of the practical need to adopt the most effective learning methods for higher education success. When students cheat or manipulate the system it is not they who have failed, but us, since we did not resist the encroachment of short-term, credentialist views of learning.

The Secretary of State's statement could be re-cast as: 'Individuals must find it possible to hold the conviction that learning has rewards and that they can take responsibility for their own development.' Responsibility for learning is shared. The educator mediates between the learner, the discipline and the institution. The quality of the learning experience is conditioned by the educator's mediating role. It is easy to cultivate further cynicism and disenchantment in a cynical and disenchanted world. The challenge is to revitalise the ideals of Higher Education and the pursuit of knowledge within a discipline, and have the courage to admit and defend our learned values. Learner responsibility is a joint accomplishment of learner, educator and institution; if we cannot control the environment then at least we can influence how the learner experiences that environment.

REFERENCES

Becker, H (1967) 'Whose side are we on?', *Social Problems*, 3, 239–47.

Bhatia, V K (1993) *Analysing Genre: Language Use in Professional Settings*, Longman, London.

Boshier, R (1976) 'Factor analysts: a critical review of the motivational orientation literature', *Adult Education*, (US), 27, 26–41.

Buttny, R (1993) *Social Accountability in Communication*, Sage, London.

Burke, K (1962) *A Grammar of Motives and A Rhetoric of Motives* (first eds 1945 and 1950), Meridian Books, Cleveland.

Harri-Augstein, E S and Thomas, L F (1991) *Learning Conversations*, Routledge, London and New York.

Iphofen, R (1996) 'Aspiration and inspiration: student motives in adult residential colleges', *Studies in the Education of Adults*, 28, 65–87.

Jarvis, P (1983) *Adult and Continuing Education (Theory and Practice)*, Croom Helm, London.

Lavelle, M, Patterson, P and Iphofen, R (1997) 'On reflection', *Adults Learning*, 8, 267–69.

McGivney, V (1990) *Access to Education for Non-Participant Adults*, NIACE, Leicester.

Purdey, M and Gale, P (1988) *The Adult Education and Training Manual*, Vol. 1: *The Adult Learner and Learning Environment*, Framework Press, Lancaster.

Tremlett, N and Park, A (1995) *Individual Commitment to Learning: Comparative Findings from the Surveys of Individuals', Employers' and Providers' Attitudes*, Dept. for Education and Employment, Sheffield.

Tremlett, N, Park, A and Dundon-Smith, D (1995) *Individual Commitment to Learning: Further Findings from the Individuals' Survey*, Employment Dept., Sheffield.

Uden, T (1994) *The Will to Learn: Individual Commitment and Adult Learning*, NIACE, Leicester.

Watts, N T (1990) *Handbook of Clinical Teaching: Exercises and Guidelines for Health Professionals who Teach Patients, Train Staff, or Supervise Students*, Churchill Livingstone, Edinburgh.

Weiner, B (1991) 'On perceiving the other as responsible', in Dienstbier, R (ed.) *Perspectives on Motivation* (Nebraska Symposium on Motivation 1990), University of Nebraska Press, Lincoln and London.

Wright Mills, C (1940) 'Situated actions and vocabularies of motive', *American Sociological Review*, 8: 904–13.

6

Teaching: Creating a Thirst for Learning?

Phil Race

INTRODUCTION

The perceived importance of student motivation has increased steadily, matching the higher participation rate in Further and Higher Education. When only a small fraction of the population entered Higher Education, it could more or less be taken for granted that students had a strong source of motivation, and would mostly succeed. Now, both drop-out and failure rates give cause for concern. It is argued in this chapter that one of the key causes of this is that an increased proportion of students do not have an autonomous 'want' to learn (or intrinsic motivation), and that we are not always able to substitute for this a strong enough perceived 'need' to learn (or extrinsic motivation). The chapter explores some of the ways in which Higher Education teachers can address both the 'want' and the 'need' to learn in their everyday work activities concerning teaching, learning and assessment. The author argues that the campaign to address and increase students' motivation levels may best be effected by paying attention both to the 'need' and the 'want' to learn continuously through all aspects of large group teaching, small group teaching, resource-based learning, and student support processes.

PROCESSES UNDERPINNING SUCCESSFUL LEARNING

There is a substantial literature about the processes by which students learn effectively. Elsewhere (Race and Brown, 1998), the author has argued that a problem with many of the approaches to describing learning processes has been that the language and terminology used in the literature have been too far removed from the everyday processes engaged in by students and by their teachers. Learning is a natural human activity, and does not require a sophistic-ated vocabulary to describe the fundamental processes involved.

By asking thousands of people direct, straightforward questions about their learning experiences, the author has drawn out the following five factors which underpin successful learning.

- 'wanting' to learn (intrinsic motivation);
- 'needing' to learn (extrinsic motivation);
- learning-by-doing – practice, trial and error, experiential learning;
- learning from feedback – finding out how the learning is progressing;
- making sense of what has been learned – 'digesting'.

The author has proposed (Race, 1994; Race and Brown, 1998) that these processes are involved in an overlapping way ('ripples on a pond' being a suitable metaphor), and argues that they do not occur in a sequential or cyclic manner. The human brain is much more sophisticated than to merely address these processes one at a time, and at any given time all these processes are likely to be involved as learning proceeds. Since two of these factors underpinning successful learning involve motivation, it is worth looking at how everyday teaching and assessment processes can accommodate and enhance them. Moreover, since the other three factors are inextricably linked to motivation, all five factors need to be taken into account in the design of teaching, resource-based learning, and assessment.

RELATIONSHIPS BETWEEN 'WANTING TO LEARN' AND 'NEEDING TO LEARN'

'Wanting to learn' is the most satisfactory state for students to be in. The intensity of the want to learn depends upon several variables, including:

- students' interest in the particular topic being learned;
- students overall wish to succeed in all the subjects being studied;
- students' desire to prove to themselves or to others that they can demonstrate success;
- the extent to which students like, value or respect the teacher of the subject;
- the extent to which students derive satisfaction or enjoyment from resource-based learning materials;
- the amount of encouragement students receive from their teachers;
- the amount of encouragement and support that students receive from significant others in their lives.

'Needing to learn' may also be involved in all the variables listed above, but if the want to learn is strong enough, it is the want that is likely to be the most significant factor driving learning. However, there are often occasions when the need to learn may be stronger than the want to learn. These can include:

- when there is a topic that students don't like very much;

- when something particularly difficult is being learned, but which leads towards other more-interesting or more-important topics;

- when students need to show competence on one thing before being allowed to study what they really want to learn;

- when the pressure to succeed from others (for example family or employers) is sufficient to drive the learning process, even when the 'want' is low;

- when not losing face is the most important driving force;

- when learning is being driven by assessment.

Either or both factors can drive learning successfully. When both factors are present, the position is in some ways optimized, as a strong 'want' to learn is not necessarily sufficient to ensure that students' achievements will be delivered at times, and in ways, that lead them to get appropriate credit for them through assessment processes and instruments.

THE CHANGING STUDENT PROFILE

Silver and Silver (1997) make a substantial case for the scale and extent of change in students in Higher Education as we approach the twenty-first century. Armstrong *et al.* (1997) collect a range of contributions showing the effects of radical change in Higher Education on staff attitudes and motivation, and many of the same factors also affect the motivation levels of students. The impact of an increase in the proportion of mature students in Higher Education is addressed by Newstead *et al.* (1997), who conclude, however, that mature students are a highly motivated group, likely to enrich and make major contributions to university life, and who tend to want their degrees to be the results of their own work and effort, and who tend to succeed in getting good degrees, despite a greater statistical tendency to drop out of Higher Education. Therefore, mature students are not the major cause for concern regarding motivation, and addressing their specific needs is more to do with structures, timetables, and the quality of feedback from tutors, than it is to do with enhancing their motivation levels. The primary concern, therefore, that this chapter will address, is the problems with motivating younger students. There are several factors contributing to the changing attitudes and approaches which students bring to Higher Education. These factors affect the nature and strength or weakness of all of the variables already referred to as underpinning successful learning. The student profile is changing in ways which include:

- the fact that a much broader cross-section of the population participates in Higher Education than was formerly the case;

- the trend towards a degree, or higher degree, being seen as necessary for appointment to employment posts which formerly required no such levels of qualification;

- the growth of consumerism in society, leading to students who have higher expectations that they will be significantly involved in their own experience of Higher Education;

- the wider range of learning experiences that students have already had before entering Higher Education;

- the fact that students have already been involved in the information technology explosion, and are often more comfortable with new media than are some of their teachers;

- a markedly increased wish by students to know exactly what is required of them;

- students demanding to know *why* they should invest their time and energy in learning things, rather than being willing to take for granted that there are good reasons for them doing so;

- increased levels of communication between students, and the fact that more students learn collaboratively rather than in isolation.

All of these trends affect the nature of student motivation. They also affect the ways in which students learn-by-doing, and the way they react to feedback on their progress, and they ways that students move towards making sense of what they are learning. In other words, the changes in the nature of the student population affect all of the variables that underpin successful learning.

LINKS BETWEEN TEACHING, LEARNING, AND ASSESSMENT

The links between teaching and learning have always been complex. The Galileo idea that 'you can't teach a man anything, you can only help him to learn' is often quoted, particularly when teaching seems difficult! Chalmers and Fuller (1997) make some excellent connections between teaching, learning and assessment, linking these processes to the ways that students perceive their own learning, and the way that university teachers perceive the processes of teaching. There is no doubt that some people are much better than others at causing learning to happen, and they are sometimes referred to as good teachers (but often see themselves as facilitators of learning). Indeed, some excellent teachers seem to succeed, while doing anything but what may be seen as focusing on learning, but this is most often simply because in one way or another they manage to stimulate their students' motivation levels.

There are other factors, outside the control of teachers, that are damaging the links between good teaching and effective learning. These factors include:

- more students and less teachers, leading to less chance of teachers getting to know their students, and in turn less opportunities for teachers to stimulate students' motivation levels;

- the higher proportion of the population entering Higher Education, meaning that a more significant fraction of students who lack motivation are involved in the sector;

- changes in the way students are funded, leading to many full-time students also needing to work part-time at least, and sapping their energy for studying, as well as limiting their opportunities to be present at lectures, tutorials or practical work;

- lecturers under increasing work pressure, as they try to teach larger numbers of students than they once did, and particularly as they continue to try to operate the same assessment processes that used to work with comfortable numbers of students;

- increasing tension between teaching and research, with lecturers being exhorted to publish as well as to teach, further reducing the time, energy and enthusiasm they can deliver to their teaching;

- an increased level of bureaucracy in Higher Education, with ever-increasing paperwork associated with course design, learning outcomes specifications, modularization, accreditation of prior learning, credit accumulation and transfer systems – all of which have benefits, but costs in terms of time and energy.

All of these effects can conspire to limit the quality of teaching actually experienced by students, reducing the degree to which even the best teachers succeed in raising students' motivation levels.

Links between assessment and learning are even stronger. Because of students' limited time, reduced motivation, and more demanding expectations, a much higher proportion of students adopt strategic approaches to their learning, and gear their learning as well as they can to the perceived culture of assessment. Lecturers often complain that the most important parts of their students' learning should not be directly linked to assessment, but assessment systems continue to reward those students who adopt strategic approaches. This can, indeed, be turned to advantage if the assessment processes and instruments are re-designed to ensure that strategic students are indeed learning the most important and useful things, and this will be further discussed towards the end of this chapter.

MOTIVATION THROUGH LARGE GROUP TEACHING AND LEARNING

Students can feel surprisingly lonely in large group lectures. When groups are very large, it is quite common for students not to know many of the people sitting around them, and this can reduce their motivation levels. Students see their lecturers for less time than used to be the case, and often lecturers cannot really get to know the students in their lectures. What can lecturers do, in large group contexts, to enhance student motivation? Here are some suggestions.

- Make sure that all the students are clear about the real purposes of each lecture. Intended learning outcomes should not just reside in syllabus documentation, but can be used in large group sessions, where tone of voice, emphasis and body language can all help to translate the intended outcomes into language that students can relate to. When students can see clearly where they are trying to go, their motivation can be enhanced.

- Help students to see the value of the 'need' as well as the 'want'. Not all students will want to learn each topic, but if they can see exactly what the benefits to them will be of investing some time and energy in it, they are more likely to take such topics seriously, and give them their best shot.

- Use large group sessions for learning-by-doing. Getting students involved in tasks or activities *during* large group sessions has significant effects on their motivation. For a start, they often report that 'the time passes much more quickly' than when merely listening to a lecture. Moreover, they try harder to attend sessions, as they discover that if they missed some 'learning-by-doing', it is harder for them to catch up than when they only missed someone's eloquent exposition.

- Use large group sessions to 'spotlight' and 'showcase' rather than to try to cover everything that students are required to learn. Going in deep with important topics is more valuable (and more motivating) for students than trying to use lectures to cover everything.

- Use large group sessions to help students to get as much feedback as possible. This can be feedback from fellow students when doing activities in the session. It is also useful to use lecture times to give large groups shared feedback on work they have done for assessed tasks, talking them through the most common problems, pitfalls, as well as showing them what constitutes 'a good answer'.

- Use large group sessions to help students to make sense of (or 'digest') things that they have already tried to learn. Including question-and-answer episodes in large group sessions can pay dividends. However, it is usually necessary to take positive steps to ensure that students do indeed ask their questions, such as getting them to write 'questions for the next session' on Post-its as they finish the present one. Many students with questions find it much easier to write them than to speak out in a large group.

In the suggestions above, each of the five main processes by which learning occurs are linked to the design of large group sessions. Making such links helps to ensure that motivation levels are on the agenda in all of the design features of the lectures. Of course, there are further ways that some lecturers can raise students' motivation levels, especially where it is possible for the enthusiasm of the lecturer for the topic to be made infectious.

MOTIVATION THROUGH SMALL GROUP TEACHING AND LEARNING

Small group work can be directly structured around three of the central processes underpinning successful learning. Seminars, tutorials and other group activities can be built around tasks that students undertake individually and collaboratively, giving them times and places where learning-by-doing is foremost. Practical, studio and laboratory work (even with large classes) helps students to be part of a smaller, more intimate learning environment than lectures, again with the focus on learning-by-doing. The feedback process is also accommodated, much better in fact than in any other teaching–learning situation, because in small group or practical situations students can receive a considerable amount of peer feedback as well as more authoritative feedback from tutors. The 'making sense' or 'digesting' process is also best accommodated in small group situations. Where students are making sense of things together, there is the advantage that they can often explain things that they have just 'twigged' to each other considerably more clearly than can anyone who has understood them for a long time. For small group work to deliver these benefits to students, those tutoring and planning it need to ensure that student learning is kept to the fore at all times, and that the small group situation does not just degenerate into a continuation of attempts to cover the syllabus. Since the three processes so far discussed are tied up inextricably with 'wanting' or 'needing' to learn, the potential of small group work already allows motivation to be enhanced.

What, more directly, is the potential of enhancing the 'wanting' and 'needing to learn' processes in small groups? When small group work is well planned and facilitated, both of these aspects of learning can be addressed. The more intimate contact between tutors and students in small group situations allows everyone involved to get to know each other that much better than is possible in large groups, and consequently it is easier for tutors to pass on their enthusiasm and interest in their subjects to students, or to take time to explain what the purposes are of addressing those subjects where a 'need' has to substitute for the 'want' to learn.

All told, small group work can play a very significant part in raising the motivation levels of students. Sadly, this potential often fails to be realized in practice. Some of the reasons for this failure include:

- Students often pick up the feeling that small group work is less important than lectures, not least because of the ease with which some tutors cancel small group sessions for all sorts of 'reasons'!

- Because small group work tends to expand on or go deeper into things covered in large group sessions, some students perceive that small group work is only the icing on the cake, and don't give such work the attention that it deserves. 'Oh, it was only a tutorial that I missed' is an all-too-common reaction from students. 'It's worth trying to catch up on a lecture, when I might have missed something crucial, but no-one pays too much attention to the tutorials', they sometimes continue.

- Small group work often does not seem to students to have important learning outcomes of its own associated with it. When, however, important outcomes are clearly 'diverted' away from large group sessions, and it is made clear that these outcomes will be every bit as important as any others *vis-à-vis* assessment, this situation can be rectified.

MOTIVATION AND RESOURCE-BASED LEARNING

Resource-based learning is on the increase for a wide variety of good (and bad) reasons, which include:

- when class sizes have grown rapidly, traditional face-to-face processes in both large and small groups just cannot be managed any more, leading selected areas of the curriculum being 'diverted' to independent learning by students, from learning resource materials;

- the range of learning resource material formats has increased dramatically, now ranging from print-based flexible learning packages to the exciting world of electronic communication and data-retrieval possible through the Internet, computer-conferencing, and electronic mail;

- with so many students having to work part-time at least to see them financially through their time at college, resource-based learning offers a solution for some of their attendance problems, allowing them to work at times and places of their own choosing through selected parts of the curriculum, and at their own pace.

A wide-ranging collection of case studies of the impact of resource-based learning on students and staff in Higher Education has been collected by Brown and Smith (1996). Resource-based learning offers direct development of three of the central processes underpinning successful learning. At its best, it delivers learning-by-doing very effectively, and can be a means of getting detailed ready-devised feedback responses to students on the tasks that they do as they work through a learning package. Both of these can be equally addressed by print-based and computer-based formats. In particular, when the resource materials are studied collaboratively rather than in isolation, resource-based learning can address the 'making sense' or 'digesting' stage as well, with students learning by discussing and arguing with each other.

However, the 'wanting' and 'needing' processes are more difficult to address with resource-based learning. When learning packages are stimulating, the situation is improved. When students lack the 'want' to learn, and with little sense of the 'need' to learn a topic, they can too easily feel that the resource-based learning can be left till later, or even skipped entirely as 'Who will know anyway?'

MOTIVATION THROUGH TUTOR SUPPORT

When there used to be a high level of one-to-one interaction between students and individual lecturers, there is no doubt that motivation was directly enhanced. When tutor support was positive, students' 'want to learn' could be dramatically improved, and the special relationship with tutors could bring out the best in students. Conversely, when the tutor–student relationship was based at least in part on fear or awe or 'not wishing to be found lacking' a strong sense of 'need' could be created in students which proved an effective (if less happy) driving force for their learning.

In some universities, this intimate level of tutor–student interaction continues, and still succeeds. In many colleges, however, with the change in the staff–student ratios of the last decade, it is no longer feasible to have this extent of support from tutors. This can have profound effects on the already low motivation of many of the students who experience this lack of support. With academic staff increasingly under pressure to spend more time researching and publishing, the situation is compounded. Well-trained and caring teaching assistants can provide a substitute, however, but the emphasis has to be on 'well trained' and this is not always achieved in practice.

The principal benefits in terms of enhanced motivation can be thought of as resulting from the significantly personal impetus of the tutor–student relationship, and when this is no longer possible to deliver, other ways of substituting for such a relationship need to be found. This has led to a significant growth in the use of various kinds of mentoring for students.

MOTIVATION AND MENTORING

Mentoring is increasingly being used to bridge the gap caused by more students and less staff. Often, the mentors are students themselves, such as students who are in a more advanced year of a course, and are given the responsibility of helping their less experienced counterparts succeed in selected areas of the curriculum. Mentoring, when well facilitated, can be very motivating both for mentors and mentees. The learning payoff of explaining something to a less experienced student is at least as great for the mentor as for the student on the receiving end.

For mentor support to deliver its potential benefits in raising student motivation levels, everyone involved has to take it seriously. If it is just seen as an optional extra, those students who most need it will fail to benefit at all from it. One of the best ways of giving mentoring higher status is when the mentors themselves receive appropriate credit for it, either in terms of learning outcomes that they themselves achieve and demonstrate through it, or in other ways in which they can gain academic credit for having done it well.

ASSESSMENT: THE ENGINE WHICH DRIVES MOTIVATION?

Earlier in this chapter, the growing trend for students to be strategic regarding assessment was mentioned. However much we may wish that all students would engage in self-development and learning for their own sakes, the fact is that most students now want to know 'What's in it for me?' and 'Why should I bother?'

Assessment can provide 'real' motivators for such students, but often fails to do so due to the following conditions and limitations:

- the amount of assessment is usually too much, and students' learning is over-driven by such assessment;

- the variety of assessment formats is usually too narrow, leading to the skills developed by those students for whom assessment is the prime motivator being too restricted and sometimes quite mundane;

- though assessment can be a strong aid to helping students to learn-by-doing, when almost everything they ever do is assessed, the valuable dimension of learning by trial-and-error is threatened;

- although assessment can be a prime means of helping students learn-through-feedback, and make sense of what they have learned, staff time to provide such feedback is more limited than ever, and the feedback often reaches students far too late – when they have already moved on to other parts of their learning;

- the' fact that assessment formats and instruments tend to concentrate on trying to measure the achievements of individuals relegates student collaborative work to second place, and students are even prompted to disguise collaborative learning and pretend that the outcomes of working together are individual products.

Having expressed some concerns at the way assessment relates to learning-by-doing and feedback, thereby causing secondary effects on motivation, it is worth looking at the primary effects of assessment on motivation. Assessment can be a strong provider of the 'need to learn' but not always very useful at enhancing the 'want to learn'. When students are only learning things so that they are not going to fail assessments, in fact, their natural want to learn can be significantly damaged by the process.

A SPECIAL CASE: STUDENTS ALREADY WITH HIGH INTRINSIC MOTIVATION

Most of this chapter has been concerned with the problems associated with students whose want to learn, or need to learn, requires enhancing or strengthening. While there are numerous actions tutors (and curriculum designers, learning resource creators, and mentors) can take to help improve student motivation, there remain those students whose natural motivation is already high. The effect on them of all these efforts to enhance motivation can be quite counter-productive, even going so far as to make them distrust the validity and origin of their own natural motivation. Those students who already have a strong desire to learn do not need all of this extra pressure on them, which devalues their intrinsic motivation. Care needs to be taken to make sure that such students are treated rather differently, as 'special cases' in fact, and that their own motivation is allowed to direct them naturally without them feeling unduly scrutinized or inappropriately exhorted towards unreasonable efforts. Their situation may not represent the most serious problem facing tutors in Higher Education, but it remains important that the pathfinders among the student population are allowed to stretch themselves naturally.

CONCLUSIONS

Though some academics will continue to hark back to the times when the proportion of the population participating in Higher Education was much smaller, and when the apparent motivation of most students seemed higher, there is much that can be done to address the needs of many of the students who presently need their motivation boosted. There is neither a single 'best way' nor an 'ideal person' to do this. The most productive approach is to try to enhance *all* of the main factors which are known to underpin successful student learning. The present chapter offers some suggestions which may provide starting-points on this mission.

REFERENCES

Armstrong, S, Thompson, G and Brown, S (eds) (1997) *Facing Up to Radical Change in Universities and Colleges*, Kogan Page, London.

Brown, S and Smith, B (eds) (1996) *Resource-Based Learning*, Kogan Page, London.

Chalmers, D and Fuller, R (1997) *Teaching for Learning at University*, Kogan Page, London.

Race, P (1994) *The Open Learning Handbook*, 2nd edn, Kogan Page, London.

Race, P and Brown, S (1998) *The Lecturer's Toolkit*, Kogan Page, London.

Newstead, S E, Hoskins, S, Franklyn-Stokes, A and Dennis, E (1997) 'Older but wiser? The motivation of mature students in Higher Education', in Sutherland, P (ed.), *Adult Learning: A Reader*, Kogan Page, London.

Silver, H and Silver, P (1997) *Students: Changing Roles, Changing Lives*, Open University Press, Buckingham.

SECTION TWO:
Motivating Diverse Students

7

Perspectives on Motivation: The Implications for Effective Learning in Higher Education

Della Fazey and John Fazey

INTRODUCTION

This chapter will consider some of the more recent theories and supporting evidence in the research literature that we might apply to the enhancement of motivation for learning in Higher Education (HE). Three theoretical perspectives are described: the Self-determination theory (Deci and Ryan, 1985), competence motivation theory (eg Nicholls, 1984) and goal orientation (eg Dweck and Leggett, 1988; Duda and Nicholls, 1992). These theories are viewed as complementary, with none in itself sufficient for an adequate explanation of motivation. Two dimensions of self-construct – valence and expectancy – that affect motivated behaviour for achievement are discussed as threads that run through the three theories, providing another way of approaching complex notions of behaviour within the different theoretical framworks.

Recent research evidence, using the Self-determination perspective, is reported and provides information about a small part of the multi-dimensional jigsaw that is students' motivation for study. Throughout the chapter, and in a final section, practical ways of influencing students' academic motivational orientations are highlighted and discussed in relation to theory.

A DYNAMIC, ORGANISMIC APPROACH TO UNDERSTANDING MOTIVATION.

Current theories of motivation are concerned with the factors that affect people's understanding both of the relationship between their behaviour and subsequent outcomes and the selection of appropriate behaviour to achieve desired outcomes (Deci *et al.*, 1991). Motivated activity is central to the survival of all species and is essential for human achievement.

Early theories about human motivation suggested that we are driven to act when we experience discomfort. Few people nowadays subscribe to the simplistic notion that humans are only motivated by the basic need to maintain homeostasis in its biological sense. We eat when we are not hungry and seek shelter when we are not cold and, although we clearly like to be in a state of equilibrium, whether physically, emotionally or cognitively, there is more to human motivation than the reactive behaviours that achieve balance. Appley (1991) argues, however, that equilibration remains a fundamental principle of motivated behaviour in that we continually adapt to situations that threaten us or create dissonance but that we also, importantly, strive to control and shape our environment. Humans are not only acted upon by their environment but are proactively affecting their environment as they have the capacity to anticipate and plan for achievement. This creates a dynamically changing environment. Striving for control – self-actualization (Maslow, 1943), self-determination (Deci and Ryan, 1985) or personal agency (Bandura, 1997) – is an important aspect of motivation that distinguishes us from other animals and contributes considerably to human development and achievement. Bandura (1989, p.418) argues that:

> Human self-motivation relies on both *discrepancy production* and *discrepancy reduction* (Bandura, 1988b). It requires proactive control as well as reactive control. People initially motivate themselves through proactive control by setting themselves valued challenging standards that create a state of disequilibrium and then mobilising their effort on the basis of anticipatory estimation of what it would take to reach them. Self-motivation thus involves a hierarchical dual control process of disequilibrating discrepancy production followed by equilibrating discrepancy reduction.

We view people as active participants in their own development, with a propensity for curiosity, challenge and fun that stimulates behaviour not otherwise instrumentally initiated. First-year undergraduates bring with them to university at least 18 years of unique experiences. The dynamic interaction of such individuals with a HE environment is a complex challenge for all concerned. This chapter emphasizes the need to recognize that understanding why students in HE behave as they do requires an eclectic view of the world, the students and the complex, constantly changing interaction between the two.

VARIATIONS IN THE THEORETICAL DIMENSIONS OF UNDERSTANDING MOTIVATION

Motivational theories relevant to practice in education, employing differing language and constructs, are not necessarily incompatible and are perspectives on the same space or landscape of understanding (cf Marton and Fazey, under review). They offer us a multidimensional approach to understanding student motivation and provide a useful framework for thinking about what can enhance learning in HE.

Self-determination theory

A familiar notion that provides a foundation stone for constructing the framework is that of *intrinsic* and *extrinsic motivation*. Intrinsic motivation provides a stimulus to act which is internally derived whereas extrinsic motivation to act is initiated externally to the individual (Deci *et al.*, 1991). Enjoyment of, and interest in, the activity are often an intrinsic motivator whilst the promise of a reward for participation is likely to be an extrinsic motivator.

Deci and Ryan (1985) used the notion of a continuum of motivational orientations. Intrinsic and external regulation are extremes of internalized reasons for acting with two identifiable elements between the extremes. Deci *et al.* (1991) propose that the four 'types' of motivation, *intrinsic, identified, introjected* and *external,* are typified by the extent to which they provide internalized reasons for acting, with intinsic motivation wholly internalized.

An intrinsically motivated person initiates the activity for personally valued reasons such as interest or enjoyment. According to Deci *et al.* (1991, p.328) intrinsically motivated behaviours are those:

> engaged in for their own sake – for the pleasure and satisfaction derived from their performance . . . they emanate from the self and are fully endorsed . . . When intrinsically motivated people engage in activities that interest them they do so freely with a full sense of volition and without the necessity of material rewards or constraints.

In behaviours that are described as involving identified regulation, although closely aligned with intrinsically motivated behaviours, the reasons for acting are influenced by external sources. For example, a student may choose to study a particular project that is of interest and relevance to them personally but the project is externally initiated as part of the degree programme. The student personally values the learning experience and the outcomes of the research (ie it is internalized), despite it being initiated extrinsically.

Further away from intrinsic motivation, towards the external end of the continuum, is introjected regulation of behaviour. It is often the case that students have to complete assignments which they do not value personally. Their actions are motivated by a recognition that this assignment must be satisfactorily completed but they would avoid doing it if given the choice. The completion of work is distally rewarded (by perhaps passing the module) and that reward is valued, or punishment (which might be loss of face) avoided.

External regulation of behaviour describes the situation where someone can see no personal relevance or value in engaging in the activity but feels that he or she has no choice but to comply. Some students enter HE because it is the next, expected stage in their development and not because they want to learn or because of a particular career aspiration. Their behaviour is externally initiated and controlled with no internalization or 'ownership' of the action. In Self-determination theory, Deci and Ryan (1985) sub-divide intrinsic motivation into non-linear items of the desire 'to know', 'to achieve' and 'to be stimulated'. Extrinsic motivation is calculated from the three motivations in which behaviour is not initiated by the individual, ie identified, introjected and external regulation.

Deci and Ryan (1985) also describe an *amotivated* state in which individuals have no reason for wishing to act – for personal interest, reward or to avoid punishment. They find themselves in a situation which is entirely devoid of any stimulus that encourages participation. Clearly, any student feeling like this about HE would be well advised to look for alternatives.

Competence motivation

The second perspective on reasons for action that we offer is competence motivation. Nicholls (1984) suggests that people choose to act in ways that enable them to demonstrate competence and avoid those in which they are likely to appear incompetent. The self-evaluation of competence, described by Harter (1988) as self-perceived competence when related to an area of a person's life such as academic work, and by Bandura (1989) as self-efficacy when applied to a specific situation such as essay writing, is an important element in an individual's reasons for participating in or avoiding situations.

There is considerable evidence (see, eg Bandura 1989, 1997) to indicate that a high perception of ability for a specific task or situation increases the likelihood that the individual will participate, persist and accept challenge in that situation. Those who perceive themselves to have an inadequate level of ability for the task or situation are more likely to avoid action and challenge. Whilst intuitively this has appeal – we have all experienced students who 'hide' rather than face what seems to them to be an impossibly difficult situation – Dweck and Leggett (1988) offer evidence that the effect of competence as a motivator is mediated by individuals' goal orientations. Goal orientation is presented as our third theoretical perspective.

Goal orientations

Dweck and Leggett (1988), building on previous work by Dweck and Elliott (1983), propose a model to account for differences in individuals' responses to challenging situations. They identified two classes of goals:

1. Performance goals in which individuals are concerned with producing a positive evaluation of their performance (and thus ability).

2. Learning goals in which individuals focus on improving their abilities through mastery attempts.

Adopting a performance goal puts individuals at risk of failure to demonstrate competence and is more likely to lead to the choice of a less-demanding task or avoidance if the task is assessed as being difficult. Making errors and having to expend effort to complete the task are viewed as an indication of lack of competence rather than part of the learning process.

The same task offered to an individual with a learning-goal orientation, however, provides that individual with a welcome opportunity for challenge and improvement of capability. Errors are seen as inherent in the learning process and effort is applied without undermining perceptions of competence or self-esteem. Dweck and Leggett (1988) suggest that the two goal orientations are underpinned by either the belief that ability is a fixed entity (you either have it or you don't – performance orientation) or that ability is incremental and malleable (ability can be acquired through effort – learning orientation). Duda and Nicholls (1992) have applied a similar model of motivational orientation to both sport and classroom achievement behaviours. They identify individuals' motivational characteristics as being task-oriented (cf learning goals) or ego-oriented (cf performance goals). Sarrazin *et al.* (1996) have provided evidence to link the task and ego and learning and performance perspectives and ability concepts. They found that an entity understanding of ability was held by those who are highly ego-oriented. Those with a high task orientation related more strongly to an incremental understanding of ability. Encouragingly perhaps, those who score highly in both task and ego orientations perceive ability to be partly 'entity' and partly 'incremental', providing them with opportunities to claim stability of competence while accepting that capabilities can be improved through effort.

Ames and Archer (1988) propose that the two goal orientations are independent and that individuals can adopt both goals. Duda and Nicholls (1992) suggest that task and ego-orientations are orthogonally related and not bipolar, with those who are able to adopt either a high ego or a high task orientation to suit the situation are more motivationally adaptable. A high ego-orientation with a low task-orientation is risky when individuals are failing either to win or demonstrate a high, norm-referenced ability. Those who are high task-oriented but low ego-oriented may find it difficult to adapt to an environment that is highly competitive.

Bouffard *et al.* (1995) found that college students with a high learning-goal orientation who actively controlled their learning and expended effort to achieve, reported more frequent use of metacognitive strategies and were more motivated than those with a low learning orientation. A performance-orientation was also found to facilitate self-regulation of learning, however, even when the individual scored low on learning-orientation.

Importantly for this discussion, Dweck and Leggett (1988) provide evidence that the learning environment influences the achievement-related behaviour of both learning and performance-oriented individuals and interacts with the predisposition to behave in a particular way.

person–situation interactions are best understood in probabilistic terms, with the situation potentially altering the probability that a predisposing tendency will prevail . . . Where the situation offers no cue favoring either *(learning or performance goals)*, the predisposition should hold sway. If, on the other hand, the situation offers strong cues in favor of either (appreciably increasing its salience or value), predispositions should be overridden.

(Dweck and Leggett, 1988, p.260. Italics are ours)

THREADS THROUGH THE STRUCTURE.

There are clearly many possible reasons for an individual's choice of acting to achieve a goal as these three theoretical perspectives suggest. Two particular threads connecting the theories discussed above, that help us to understand why people choose to act (or not) are:

- the individual's perceived value of the outcome of the potential action and

- the individual's assessment of the likelihood of achieving the desired outcome (see, eg Pintrich and Schrauben, 1992; Weiner, 1992).

Value

Achievement behaviour is more likely to occur if the anticipated outcome of an event is valued by the individual and valued sufficiently highly to overcome barriers to goal achievement. This goal will be different for those who are task, or ego-oriented but may have the same volitional power. On the same task an ego-oriented student will be striving to do better than others whilst the task-oriented student will be focused on personal improvement and learning. Both may be highly motivated and might be classed as intrinsically motivated.

Whatever the goal-orientation of the individual, an internalized reason for acting – one which supports the identity of the self and is congruent with self-beliefs and values – is categorized as intrinsic motivation. A view of the self as the best, or as highly talented in relation to others, however fragile a construct, will be an intrinsic motivator for achievement. More sustainable in the long term, however, is a goal orientation that emphasizes personally controlled, task-focused outcomes that do not rely on the relative success of others. Those who are motivated to avoid punishment or to please others rather than for the value of the activity are more likely to fail to act when the task is perceived as difficult.

The sense of self – of identity, values, beliefs and attitudes – is acquired across a lifetime and modified in relation to experiences. Students arrive in HE institutions with their own well-established framework for behaviour. HE will form their values relating to learning at a higher level within a short but intense period of time and will affect future motivational orientation to learning. Those who are responsible for creating the HE environment have a responsibility to provide a climate that explicitly values learning and personal development.

Expectancy

Expectations about the likelihood of achieving the desired outcome following an action affect the willingness to act. Competence motivation theory clearly states that we choose activities in which we can demonstrate competence and avoid those in which we are likely to appear incompetent, selectively choosing personally appropriate activities. Those who are task-oriented, with a concept of ability as modifiable, are more likely to tackle a 'difficult' task as they will perceive it as a learning opportunity. Those who are ego-oriented will see a 'difficult' task as a potential danger to their self-esteem as they have no control over the norm-referenced outcome. The value of the outcome has to be high for the risk to be worth taking.

Competence motivation theory does not account for the behaviour of those who continue to tackle very difficult tasks at which they persistently 'fail'. The individual's goal must be considered in this instance as it may not be congruent with that of the teacher or observer. Identifying a way forward for such people, to enable them to achieve the externally required outcome, requires individual support and guidance.

Where an intrinsic, rather than an extrinsic orientation exists, that individual is choosing to engage in tasks rather than being required to participate. When the goal is personally chosen it is likely to be achievable as we rarely choose to do something that might damage us. Intrinsically motivated people will have high expectations for success, even when the task appears challenging.

The interaction between value and expectancy

There will be an interaction between these two dimensions of motivation. A highly valued outcome with a high expectation of success is most likely to lead to achievement-seeking behaviours. Low value and low expectations of success are likely to lead to withdrawal or avoidance. Where value is high and expectations for success in the task are low, then dissonance occurs. There are two possible options here for the individual. He or she can reduce the perceived value of the task outcome or address the deficit in competence. The latter is more likely in a task-oriented individual, perceiving that application of strategy or effort can affect ability, than in a high ego-oriented and low task-oriented person who believes that application of effort is a demonstration of limited ability. Students are most likely to apply effort when the goal is personally valued and they assess that it is achievable.

While any motivation to act must be viewed as positive in an overall sense, the extensive research literature on the subject of motivation clearly indicates that some motivational orientations are more prone to break down under stress than are others. Those most resilient in the face of failure are an intrinsic orientation and a task and learning focus. There are two main reasons for this:

1. These orientations involve a personal identification with the goals or activities and do not rely on external stimulii to initiate or reinforce the action. Participation occurs for personally valued reasons that support

underlying self-structures and enhance them. The activities are relevant and salient to the individual with a personal commitment to, and investment in, the actions being undertaken.

2. The activities and their outcomes are controlled (to a large extent) by the individual participant. Unlike those with an extrinsic orientation or with ego or performance goals, task- or learning-oriented individuals and those who have internalized reasons for acting, are able to set their own agendas for success, thus maximizing expectations of a positive outcome to their activities. They do not rely on norm-referencing or external assessment to supply them with a satisfactory outcome to their attempts.

EMPIRICAL RESEARCH INTO STUDENT MOTIVATION

As part of a larger investigation, the motivations for study of 85 randomly selected volunteer undergraduates at the University of Wales, Bangor were measured at six monthly intervals over their first two years at university. Motivation was measured using the Academic Motivation Scale (Vallerand *et al.*, 1992), based on Deci and Ryan's (1985) Self-Determination Theory of intrinsic motivation (IM), extrinsic motivation (EM) and amotivation (AM). IM, EM and their subcomponents as well as AM were compared across time and in relation to age and sex differences.

As Figure 7.1 indicates, first-year undergraduate students were high in IM and EM and significantly lower in AM (p<.0001). These levels were generally stable across time with no significant changes across time in any of the overall motivational orientations (p>0.05). There were no significant sex differences within the orientations and no age differences within AM. EM was significantly higher than IM at Time 2 which might be explained by the proximity of examinations for students (p<.05).

When the subcomponents of IM were analysed (see Figure 7.2) the desire 'to know' was significantly higher (p<.0001) at each test point than the other two subcomponents ('to achieve' and 'to be stimulated') although it decreased significantly over time (p<.03). 'to be stimulated' significantly increased over time (p<.001). Analysis of the EM subcomponents (identified [ID], introjected [IJ] and external regulation [ER]) revealed that ID was consistently significantly higher than IJ and ER (p<.001) (see Figure 7.3). Mature students scored significantly higher than traditional students on IJ and significantly lower on ID and ER (p<.05).

Student motivation, as measured on this scale, appears to be relatively stable and positive. The very low scores for amotivation are reassuring. The high score for EM at first appears to be a negative finding for achievement but, as the subcomponent analysis indicated, this high score was largely attributable to ID at the intrinsic end of extrinsic motivation. Identified regulation is that in which the activity is personally valued but not internally initiated. The consistently higher scoring of identified regulation than of the other two, less internalized, components of extrinsic motivation is a positive finding. Students

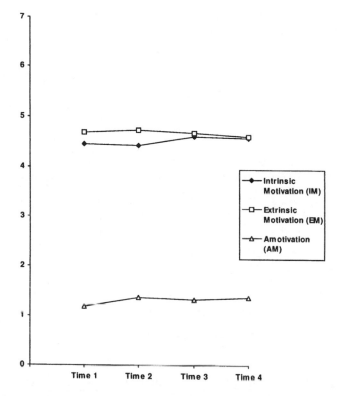

Figure 7.1 *Intrinsic motivation (IM), extrinsic motivation (EM) and amotivation (AM) over two years*

Note: AM is significantly different from IM and EM at all times (p<.0001) and EM is significantly higher than IM at Time 2 (p<.05).

were motivated by a desire to acquire knowledge – an element that remained significantly more important than 'to accomplish' and 'to experience stimulation' across time.

Age differences in the subcomponents of EM were unexpected, with traditional students scoring higher than traditional students in ID and ER but lower on IJ. Mature students have often been academic 'failures' at an earlier age and are wanting to prove that they can succeed academically – a description of IJ motivation. Mature students were consistently higher on IM than their younger peers at the 7 per cent level although this was hypothesized to be a more powerful difference. Older students have made very active and carefully considered decisions to enter HE, often sacrificing well-paid employment for the privilege, and could be expected to score significantly higher than younger students in intrinsic motivation.

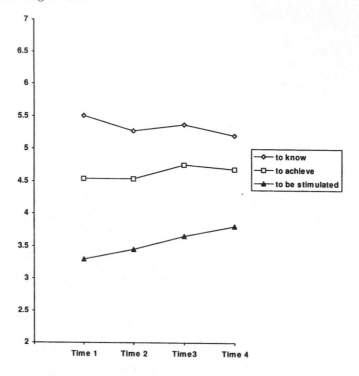

Figure 7.2   *Subcomponents of intrinsic motivation (IM) across two years*

Note: 'To know' is significantly higher than the other two (p<.0001) at each time although it decreases from Time 1 to 4 (p<.03). 'to be stimulated' increases significantly between time 1 and 4 (p<.001).

APPLYING THEORY TO PRACTICE

How can what we know about motivation be applied to the learning culture of the university? There is, of course no simple answer, particularly when it is acknowledged that motivation for achievement involves a dynamic interaction between individuals and their environment with both in themselves presenting a complex structure. This section focuses on three specific elements of the HE environment that, from the theoretical literature, are particularly relevant to motivation and that are largely determined by institutions and the people in them. They are:

● the facilitation of personal control and responsibility;

● the provision of a climate that encourages the adoption of adaptive motivational orientations;

● the promotion of individuals' expectations of success and a value system that will sustain the motivation for life-long, higher level learning.

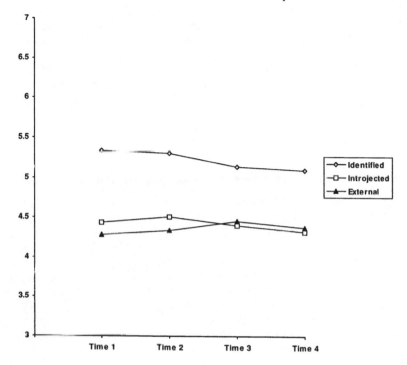

Figure 7.3 *Sub-components of extrinsic motivation (EM) over two years*

Note: Identified regulation was consistently higher than the other two (p<.001).

An assumption in this section (supported by the evidence from the Bangor research) is that students are actually motivated to learn and bring with them an orientation to study that is towards the intrinsic end of the Deci and Ryan (1985) continuum. At Bangor, this positive orientation is generally maintained or enhanced during the first two years of study. Those who are amotivated towards study are not likely to be affected by the motivational climate to any great extent.

Facilitating personal control and responsibility

Providing students with choice and opportunities to take responsibility for their learning has positive motivational effects. It enables students to study personally relevant areas of interest congruent with their sense of self – to be intrinsically-motivated – and to choose topics which they feel are achievable as well as challenging. Perceptions of competence are thus supported, increasing competence motivation and raising expectations for success. This choice can be applied at a number of levels (eg degree programme, module options, assignment choices, flexible submission deadlines, procedures that enable active involvement of students in quality assurance at all levels and appeal procedures).

Institutions must also expect and enable students to take responsibility for their learning. A tightly packed timetable or last-minute information provided by staff about assignments, for instance, will not enable students to manage their own learning and set personal goals. The importance of perceiving that learning is under personal control is also emphasized in goal-orientations, as discussed later (see also a useful discussion about learning goals in Hollenbeck and Brief, 1987). The implications of all this for the staff of universities is that they also have to manage information, advice and guidance effectively in order to enhance student development and learning.

Encouraging an adaptive motivational orientation to study

Both intrinsic and extrinsic motivations enable students to succeed in their studies but an intrinsic motivational orientation is more self-sustaining. While learners cannot be forced to enjoy, be interested in and value every aspect of their studies, an environment which increases the likelihood of this happening will be a more effective learning context. Skilled, enthusiastic, student-centred teachers are essential, as is the involvement of the student in the decision-making of the learning process whenever possible. The element of personal choice is again a feature of this environment, offering opportunities for the student to create self-structured learning contexts.

It is important that students adopt a motivational orientation that focuses on the application of effort to improve performance, even if they also have ego-orientations and performance-orientations in some situations. It seems likely that to be able to adopt either orientation is a valuable asset and leads to adaptive behaviour for achievement (Sarrazin *et al.*, 1996). Constructing environments that encourage task-orientation and learning-orientations requires careful consideration. At national and institutional level, we attach a label to degrees that encourages peer-comparison. Explicit messages, at university, departmental and class level, need to go out to students to persuade them that they can control the outcomes of their learning attempts and that appropriately applied strategies and effort will produce improved results, regardless of the performance of their peers.

A focus on personal improvement of performance, supported by feedback that encourages self-assessment of both achievements and learning deficits, together with opportunities to repeat successes and redeem failures will enable students to adopt a task-orientation to their learning. Student-centred teaching staff can do much to encourage such approaches to study.

Expectation of success and the value of learning

We are convinced by the research that indicates people apply effort to achieve when they anticipate a successful outcome to their attempts (James, 1892; Nicholls, 1978; Harter, 1988; Bandura, 1989; Weiner, 1992). HE institutions need to provide students with opportunities for personal reflection and support for their learning needs at all levels so that they can develop realistic, progress-enhancing self-awareness. Within such an environment, in which constructive feedback about performance plays an essential part, students' perceptions of competence can be nurtured, thus enhancing motivation. Good teaching practices that provide students with constructive feedback and value their attempts at learning are essential in helping students to match their capabilities with the demands of the programme of study and, again, the element of choice and control are important for competence enhancement.

If students are to engage in a lifelong process of cognitive development, they need to value learning. In HE they must be offered intellectual experiences that stimulate, challenge, satisfy and promote curiosity as well as personal satisfaction. The intrinsic desire to achieve a high level of knowledge and understanding and the recognition that the search for these does not end with graduation, the need to develop an ever-widening, eclectic perspective on the world, the ability to apply knowledge and understanding critically to problem-solving, are all elements of the transformation which we aim for in those who are educated at a higher level.

Achieving this transformation requires visionary, enlightened role models who can demonstrate the value, excitement and stimulation of rigorous academic enquiry within a learning context which supports the developing intellectual skills and affective needs of students. The teachers who are on the front line need to have high but realistic expectations of their students and reinforce the notion that capability can be acquired through strategic, focused effort.

The national educational climate has not, recently, reinforced the professional expertise of such higher educationalists. In setting ourselves the goal of providing and maintaining a learning community in a learned setting (a university), we must perceive that we have the individual and collective resources to succeed – we must have an *expectation* of success. Finally, if we *value* the concept of a higher level of education sufficiently then the motivation to sustain our efforts, despite the barriers, will ensure its survival and development.

REFERENCES

Ames, C and Archer, J (1988) 'Achievement goals in the classroom: students' learning strategies and motivation processes', *Journal of Educational Psychology*, 80, 260–7.

Appley, M H (1991) 'Motivation, equilibration, and stress', in Dienstbier, R A (ed.), *Nebraska Symposium on Motivation, 1990: Perspectives on Motivation*, University of Nebraska Press, Lincoln.

Bandura, A (1988) 'Self-regulation of motivation and action through goal systems', in Hamilton, V, Bower, G H and Frijda, N H (eds), *Cognitive Perspectives on Emotion and Motivation*, Kluwer Academic Publishers, Dordrecht.

Bandura, A (1989) 'Perceived self-efficacy in the exercise of personal agency', *The Psychologist: Bulletin of the British Psychological Society*, 10, 411–24.

Bandura, A (1997) *Self-efficacy: The Exercise of Control*, W.H. Freeman and Company, New York.

Bouffard, T, Boisvert, J, Vezeau, C and Larouche, C (1995) 'The impact of goal orientation on self-regulation and performance among college students', *British Journal of Educational Psychology*, 65, 317–29.

Deci, E L and Ryan, R M (1985) *Intrinsic Motivation and Self Determination in Human Behaviour*, Plenum, New York.

Deci, E L, Vallerand, R J, Pelletier, L G and Ryan, R M (1991) 'Motivation and education: the self-determination perspective', *Educational Psychologist*, 26, (3 and 4), 325–46.

Duda, J L and Nicholls, J G (1992) 'Dimensions of achievement motivation in schoolwork and sport', *Journal of Educational Psychology*, 84, 3, 290–9.

Dweck, C S and Elliott, E (1983) 'Achievement motivation', in Mussen, P H (Gen. Ed.) and Hetherington, E M (Vol. Ed.), *Handbook of Child Psychology: Social and Personality Development*, Wiley, New York.

Dweck, C S and Leggett (1988) 'A social-cognitive approach to motivation and personality', *Psychological Review*, 95, 256–73.

Harter, S (1988) 'Causes, correlates and the functional role of self-worth: a life-span perspective', in Kolligan, J and Sternberg, R (eds), *Perceptions of Competence and Incompetence Across the Life-span*, Yale University Press, New Haven, CT.

Hollenbeck, J R and Brief, A P (1987) 'The effects of individual differences and goal origin on goal setting and performance', *Organizational Behavior and Human Decision Processes*, 40, 392–414.

James, W (1892) *Psychology: The Briefer Course*, Henry Holt and Co, New York.

Marton, F and Fazey, J A (under review) 'Understanding a space of variation', *Educational Researcher*.

Maslow, A (1943) 'A theory of human motivation', *Psychological Review*, 50, 370–96.

Nicholls, J G (1978) 'The development of the conceptions of effort and ability, perceptions of academic attainment and the understanding that difficult tasks require more ability', *Child Development*, 49, 800–14.

Nicholls, J G (1984) 'Achievement motivation: conceptions of the nature of ability, subjective experience, task choice and performance', *Psychological Review*, 91, 328–46.

Pintrich, P R and Schrauben, B (1992) 'Students' motivational beliefs and their cognitive engagement in classroom academic tasks', in Schunk, D H and Meece, J L (eds), *Student Perceptions in the Classroom*, Lawrence Erlbaum Associates, London.

Sarrazin, P, Biddle, S, Famose, J P, Cury, F, Fox, K and Durand, M (1996) 'Goal orientations and conceptions of the nature of sport ability in children: a social cognitive approach', *British Journal of Social Psychology*, 35, 399–414.

Vallerand, R J, Pelletier, L G, Blaise, M R, Brière, N M, Senecal, C and Vallières, E F (1992) 'The higher education academic motivation scale: a measure of intrinsic, extrinsic and amotivation in education', *Educational and Psychological Measurement*, 52,1003–17.

Weiner, B (1986) *An Attributional Theory of Motivation and Emotion*, Springer-Verlag, New York.

Weiner, B (1992) *Human Motivation: Metaphors, Theories and Research*, Sage, London.

8

Students' motivation in Higher Education Contexts

Kim Isroff and Teresa del Soldato

INTRODUCTION

We have strong memories of sitting in lectures, feeling sleepy and bored. When we looked around at the other students, some were completely involved in the lecture, others taking copious notes and others were asleep. What are the features of students and learning contexts which influence the students' responses to teaching situations? For example, what are the consequences of bad marks for students' motivation? Do students expect teachers to motivate them? Are there differences in students' motivation between different Higher Education institutions?

This chapter describes a selection of the results of a SEDA-funded project on students' and academic staffs' perceptions of motivating teaching in different Higher Education institutional contexts. The project is studying students and staff at University College London (UCL) and at the Open University (OU). The research project aims to investigate both individual differences and inter-institutional differences.

UCL is a traditional university providing on-campus tuition with full-time students, the majority of whom enter university straight from school. UCL has a very strong research tradition and the admission process is competitive. By contrast, the OU is a distance education institution, with the majority of students being mature, in full-time employment and studying from home using a variety of media. There are no entry requirements apart from wishing to learn. As part of their courses, the OU also holds residential summer schools (OUSS) where students are provided with full-time tuition, normally for one week. This project investigated these three different institutional contexts. Within these contexts, different teaching tactics are used and students bring different features to their learning. In the next section, we review some of the research on instructional motivation.

FRAMEWORKS OF INSTRUCTIONAL MOTIVATION

The teachers' ability to motivate students is sometimes considered a matter of 'talent', beyond the teachers' own control or skills. However, in the past 15 years there has been a strong focus on specifying teaching tactics to provide motivating learning settings. These tactics are applied by expert tutors in order to make the learner 'feel challenged and curious during the tutoring session, ... They also want the learner to leave the tutoring session with a more general sense of challenge and curiosity about the topic' (Lepper *et al.*, 1993). In this sense the application of motivational tactics defines a parallel instructional goal, that complements the instructional goal of having the student merely 'knowing' a topic or mastering a skill. Both goals – helping the student to learn something and helping the student to feel motivated to learn – are deeply interconnected and mutually reinforced. Nevertheless they are distinct and sometimes even compete with each other. For example, providing an easy task to discouraged students may 'delay' the students' apparent progress, although it may help to build the students' confidence to learn in the future. Apart from confidence, as described in this example, other aspects of motivation that can be dealt with by a set of motivational tactics include curiosity, challenge and control. Keller (1983) and Malone and Lepper (1987) provide two frameworks for instructional design based on these categories, among others. In his framework Keller defines four sets of tactics, related to interest, confidence, relevance and satisfaction. Malone and Lepper focused on intrinsic motivation and built a framework based on aspects of curiosity, challenge, fantasy and control. Both frameworks overlap to a great extent in practical terms and we briefly describe the major aspects below.

The learner's curiosity is aroused by tactics that 'surprise' the student, whether it is a sensory surprise or a cognitive surprise. The sensory surprise is stimulated by an unexpected event that is perceived through one of the learner's senses (usually sight or hearing). For example, when a teacher claps hands to attract the learner's attention. Cognitive curiosity is stimulated by situations that challenge the learner's beliefs and existing knowledge structures. For example, presenting a paradoxical result that puzzles the learner, in which case the learner will seek a sensible explanation for such a strange fact that may lead to new areas of the subject domain to be explored. Attracting the students' curiosity is also achieved when analogies are made linking known and unknown topics in the domain, or, in Keller's words, 'to make the strange familiar and the familiar strange' (Keller, 1983).

The 'surprise' factor is also important in raising the learner's sense of challenge. According to Malone and Lepper (1987) students are not motivated by tasks that have their outcome easily predicted, such as tasks that are too easy or too difficult. Thus, instructional activities should provide moderate levels of risk and uncertain outcomes, obtained by adjusting the learning material to an intermediate level of difficulty, according to the learner's ability and confidence. The most important features of a challenging task are that goals should be very well specified (by the system or by the learner) and feedback on whether the goal has been achieved must be clear and, if necessary, must promote goal reformulation. Pursuing a challenging task inspires feelings of competence in many students, but less confident learners may feel defeated rather than stimulated. Malone and Lepper consider this problem when referring to self-esteem as a sub-concept of challenge, whereas Keller constructs a full set of tactics related to confidence.

In instructional environments, the students' perception of self-efficacy affects their choice of activities to be performed – difficult tasks are avoided by less confident learners – and the persistence, or effort, to perform a task – students with a high sense of efficacy are likely to 'work harder and persist longer' (Bandura, 1982). Increasing one's perception of self-efficacy depends on factors beyond simple information, thus praising only (even if emphatic) is not a sufficient factor to raise the learner's confidence, where that is required. Keller suggests that once a less confident learner does a task well, similar activities which are likely to be successful might be set by the tutor. Learner's confidence of success may also be increased if the requirements for success are clearly specified. For instance, a complex problem can be organized in term of simpler sub-goals to be successively achieved.

Keller refers to motivation itself as a matter of choices (of tasks and goals to achieve or avoid) and the degree of effort one applies to pursue the chosen goal. Therefore, personal control over the learning process should be perceived by the learners as actual control over their own success in accomplishing desired goals. In this sense, control-related tactics link responsibility and choice to the task's outcome. Keller suggests a set of tactics to maintain the students' motivation based on the delivery of unexpected and informative feedback and the use of intrinsic rewards, as opposed to extrinsic rewards (such as money, for example).

These frameworks have been studied largely within the context of schools (Lepper *et al.*, 1993) and in the United States. We are interested in how these tactics are applied by teachers in British Higher Education contexts and how they are perceived by students. There are obviously cultural differences between American and British students which could be addressed in further research.

METHODOLOGY

The project methodology involved using questionnaires and interviews to identify the features of the learning contexts which influence the students' motivation. The questionnaire aimed to investigate whether students feel motivated by academic staff, how students perceive their own motivation to learn and which instructional tactics motivate them, in particular related to the four aspects discussed above. The questionnaire had both open-ended and closed questions and this chapter discusses the quantitative results. The questionnaire included background information about the students, for example, age, gender. The students were asked to assess their attitudes towards aspects of motivating teaching on a five-point scale, for example, 'Bad marks encourage me to work harder', 'It is up to academic staff to motivate students'. They were also asked to think about motivating and not motivating teachers and assess how often these teachers used the instructional tactics relating to the frameworks described earlier. An example of this is: How often a motivating teacher 'Lets you decide what work to do'. There were open-ended questions about what students would like their teachers to do to motivate them, what good teachers do to motivate students and what bad teachers do which do not encourage students to learn. These will be mentioned in the chapter as illustrations of the quantitative data.

Table 8.1 shows the number of students questionnaires from each institutional setting, while Table 8.2 shows the age range of the students in the different settings.

Table 8.1   *Number of students*

	UCL	OUSS	OU
Number of students	97	86	48

Table 8.2   *Age range of students*

Age range of students	UCL	OUSS and OU
18–21	64	0
21–30	26	37
31–40	5	53
41–50	0	31
51–60	0	9
Above 60	0	2
Not stated	2	2

From Table 8.2 it is clear that there is a significant difference between the student populations. Some 66 per cent of UCL students were under 21 years old, with only 6 per cent of students being over 30. In contrast, there were no OU students under 21 and 71 per cent of students were over 30 years old. The students were from a variety of disciplines and this may have contributed to the results, but inter-disciplinary differences were not a focus of the research.

RESULTS

This section presents the results from the questionnaires which show clear individual and inter-institutional differences. The data were analysed for all students and with comparisons by institutional context. In some situations, there were no differences between the institutional contexts although pertinent individual differences were detected. Figure 8.1 shows the students' responses

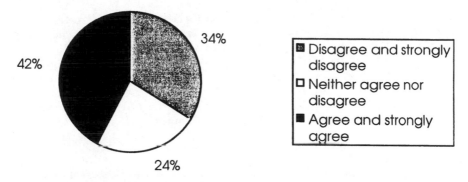

Figure 8.1 *Students' responses to 'Bad marks encourage me to work harder'*

to a question about whether or not bad marks encourage them to work harder. The results show that for 42 per cent of the students, bad marks do encourage them to work harder, whereas for 34 per cent of the students, bad marks do not encourage them to work harder. These show clearly that different students respond in different ways to this particular situation and in this case the result is homogeneous across educational contexts.

A similar result was found when students were asked how often motivating teachers 'Let you decide what work to do' (Figure 8.2). These results show that for some students, motivating teaching does not mean having absolute control of your work (in the sense that the students can decide what work to do), while for others it is desirable to have control over the work that you do. However, for the majority (52 per cent) of students a desirable situation is one in which you sometimes decide what work to do. These results suggest that there needs to be a balance between the teacher and student deciding what work to do.

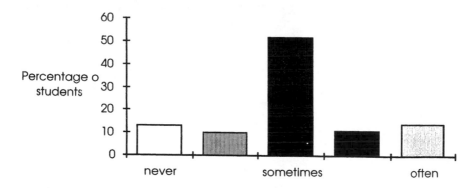

Figure 8.2 *Students' responses to how often a motivating teacher 'Lets you decide what work to do'*

The previous results were ones in which there were no inter-institutional differences. By contrast, Figure 8.3 shows the results of the students' attitudes towards the statement 'I motivate myself most of the time' in which there are significant institutional differences. This shows that OU students feel that they motivate themselves most of the time and this is less true of UCL students. This is borne out by their responses to 'It is up to academic staff to motivate me' where 48 per cent of UCL students agreed or strongly agreed whereas only 22 per cent of OU students agreed or strongly agreed.

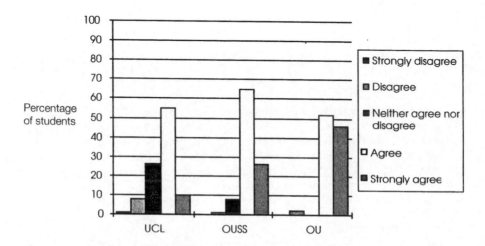

Figure 8.3   *Students' responses to 'I motivate myself most of the time'*

The result shows an inter-institutional difference in students attitudes. Other examples of differences across institutions are shown in Figures 8.4 and 8.5. These two questions investigate students' attitudes about their reasons for studying. Figure 8.4 shows that practically all students from the OU agree with the statement 'I study because I am interested in the subject'. The percentage of students from UCL who disagree with that statement is 8 per cent, which contrasts with 1 per cent of OU students. Figure 8.5 shows a compatible result, whereby 81 per cent of UCL students agree with the statement 'I study in order to get good grades', whereas 63.5 per cent of OU students agree with that statement. These differences indicate that students at UCL are more motivated to get good grades than those at the OU, and that while almost all the students at the OU are motivated by interest, this is not true of UCL students. The results can be interpreted as UCL students being more extrinsically motivated, while OU students are more intrinsically motivated.

It is interesting to notice that sometimes even intra-institutional differences occur. For example, Figure 8.6 shows students' attitudes to the statement 'I find my teachers motivating.' OU students responded differently when they were within the normal distance educational context, to when they were engaged

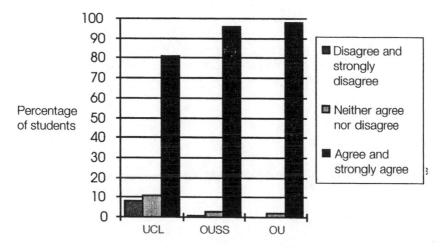

Figure 8.4 *Students' responses to 'I study because I am interested in the subject'*

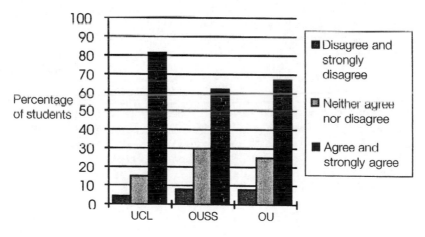

Figure 8.5 *Students' responses to 'I study in order to get good grades'*

in intensive, residential summer school. Some 63 per cent of students at summer school found their teachers motivating, whereas only 35 per cent of OU students studying at a distance found their teachers motivating. This shows that the context does make a difference to the students' motivation. Usually the same tutors teach at summer school as those who support the students for the rest of the year.

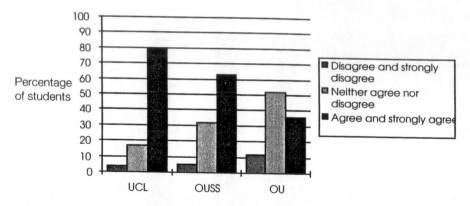

Figure 8.6   *Students' responses to 'I find my teachers motivating'*

CONCLUSION

In terms of students' attitudes to some aspects of the teaching context, there were variations within the student populations. One of the tactics that generates diverse reactions from students relates to bad marks, ie negative feedback. Some students find bad marks encouraging whereas a similar proportion of students find them discouraging. This also has practical implications in terms of the efficacy of whole class teaching. This requires further investigation to determine the particular features of the learning context or the particular student that influence their responses to negative feedback. One hypothesis is that less confident students feel discouraged by bad marks whereas confident students can be challenged by bad marks in a productive way. An alternative to this is that a student's response to bad marks is dependent on their motivation for learning, eg, if a student is motivated by their interest in the subject, a bad mark will not be as relevant to the student as it would be if the student was motivated to study in order to get good grades.

Similar contrasting results were found with respect to deciding what work to do, ie control over their work. There has been much debate about the extent to which students should have control over their work, including advocates of complete control for students and those who believe that only the teacher can make an appropriate choice concerning the sequence of instructional tasks. These results suggests that the majority of students find a balance of control between the student and the teacher motivating.

The results also show that there are clear differences between students in the three institutional contexts. In particular, UCL students feel that it is up to staff to motivate them. This is less true of OU students, who feel that they motivate themselves most of the time. At the same time, OU students seem to be more intrinsically motivated than UCL students, and a significant minority of UCL students are not interested in their subjects. In support of this, the research found that more UCL students are motivated to get good grades than

OU students. This could be because of features of the OU educational setting but it could also be attributed to the different student populations. The OU students in this study, and in general, are significantly older than the UCL students, they generally are in full-time employment and have not studied for several years. In contrast, the UCL students are younger, have generally not had the responsibility of full-time employment and have recently left school. Our school system is one in which teachers do take most of the responsibility for motivating students and the rigid examination system means that students are taught to a particular syllabus without many chances to take responsibility for their own learning. The issue of responsibility for motivating students is an important aspect of Higher Education and has implications for the ways in which teaching and learning occur.

If we believe that our ideal situation is one in which students feel responsible for their own motivation to learn, then we need to think about ways in which we can encourage students, such as those in traditional universities, to motivate themselves and become less reliant on academic staff.

The issue of responsibility for motivating the students was discussed in terms of the differences between the student populations. However, within the same student population, the context has a strong impact on aspects of the students' motivation. The OU summer school students found their teaching more motivating than the other OU students. The key feature of a summer school is the total immersion in teaching and learning over a short period of time. The students have almost continuous contact with academic staff and other students, both socially and academically. The students are given a lot of attention from the staff in order to cope with the extremely demanding academic programme. This is in striking contrast with the normal OU context, where students work largely alone at home, with intermittent contact with staff and other students. It may be that the communication and togetherness engendered by summer school motivate the students.

With the rapid growth of Higher Education in recent years, we have seen an increase in the number of mature and part-time students. There has been little work in examining how these students integrate into conventional Higher Education Institutions with younger students who have generally come straight from school. If the results concerning responsibility presented in this chapter are as a result of the age differences between the OU and UCL students, it is necessary to rethink the way in which we teach in conventional institutions which now combine the two different populations.

REFERENCES

Bandura, A (1982) 'The self and mechanisms of agency', in Suls, J (ed.), *Psychological Perspectives on the Self*, Vol. 1, Lawrence Erlbaum Associates, Hillsdale, NJ.

Keller, J M (1983) 'Motivational design of instruction', in Reigeluth, C M (ed.), *Instructional-Design Theories and Models: An Overview of their Current Status*, Lawrence Erlbaum Associates, Hillsdale, NJ.

Lepper, M R, Woolverton, M, Mumme, D and Gurtner, J (1993) 'Motivational techniques of expert human tutors: lessons for the design of computer-based tutors', in Lajoie, S P and Derry, S J (eds), *Computers as Cognitive Tools*, Lawrence Erlbaum Associates, Hillsdale, NJ.

Malone, T and Lepper, M R (1987) 'Making learning fun', in Snow, R and Farr, M (eds), *Aptitude, Learning and Instruction: Conative and Affective Process Analyses*, Lawrence Erlbaum Associates, Hillsdale, NJ.

9

Age, Gender and Course Differences in Approaches to Studying in First-year Undergraduate Students

Rhona Magee, Ann Baldwin, Stephen Newstead and Hazel Fullerton

INTRODUCTION

The present study is part of a large-scale research project aiming at investigating factors that influence student motivation in Higher Education. This chapter presents selected results from the first phase of this research which asked students to reflect on their approaches and attitudes to studying the last time they were in formal education. A revised version of the Study Processes Questionnaire (Biggs, 1987b) was distributed to first year undergraduates during induction week. In total there were over 600 respondents from a diverse range of disciplines. Age, gender and course registered for were found to have a significant effect on students' approaches to study. There were no significant interactions between these factors. The results are discussed in terms of the methodology of this research area and the implications for Higher Education.

BACKGROUND

Although the study of student approaches to learning has been a research area of interest since Marton and Säljö (1976) first made the distinction between deep and surface learning, there has been increasing interest recently in response to the changing pressures and practices in Higher Education both in the UK and abroad. The demands on Higher Education in terms of increases in student numbers and the simultaneous drop in unit resource have led to changes in the make-up of the student body and the favoured teaching and learning methods. Over the last ten years in the UK the number of mature students (defined as 21 years and over) have increased (Richardson, 1997), and in 1995-6 women made up 51 per cent of the UK student population (Dearing, 1997). In addition, there has been a move towards more student-centred and autonomous forms of learning. These changes make it more important than ever that there is greater understanding about how students approach their learning and what influences their motivation to study.

There are now several methods available to research learning approaches. Marton and Säljö (1976) distinguished deep and surface approaches in students using interviews and reading tasks. Their finding that individuals either approached reading with a view to comprehend the meaning (deep approach) or to memorize or reproduce the text (surface approach) have been confirmed many times. Entwistle has devised inventories to measure deep, surface and strategic orientations (eg Entwistle *et al.*, 1979). A number of versions of the Approaches to Study Inventory (ASI: Entwistle and Ramsden, 1983) have since been developed including a revised version, the RASI (Entwistle and Tait, 1994) and most recently the Approaches and Study Skills Inventory for Students (ASSIST) (Entwistle and Tait, 1997).

Biggs developed a three factor model consisting of deep, surface and achieving approaches (Biggs, 1979, 1987a). According to Biggs, the student's approach to learning is determined by their motives for learning and their accompanying strategies as shown in Table 9.1. For example, students who are learning to get by with minimal trouble, or simply to pass their subjects without aiming high are likely to focus on bare essentials and rote learn them. As well as providing normative data in student populations, these models and inventories have allowed and encouraged researchers to look for and try to explain differences in their students The most popular areas of study have been age and gender differences.

Studies looking at age have generally shown that mature students adopt more desirable strategies, with a tendency for more deep and less surface approaches. For example, Biggs (1987b), having administered the SPQ to over 2300 students at Australian universities and colleges, found deep and achieving

Table 9.1   *Summary of Biggs' (1987b) approaches to learning*

Approach	Motive	Strategy
Surface	Surface motive is to meet requirements minimally; a balancing act between failing and working more than is necessary.	Surface strategy is to limit target to bare essentials and reproduce them through rote learning.
Deep	Deep motive is intrinsic interest in what is being learned; to develop competence in particular academic subjects.	Deep strategy is to discover meaning by reading widely, inter-relating with previous relevant knowledge, etc.
Achieving	Achieving motive is to enhance ego and self-esteem through competition; to obtain highest grades, whether or not material is interesting.	Achieving strategy is to organize one's time and working space; to follow up all suggested readings, schedule time, behave as a model student.

approaches to increase well beyond the age of 40 years while surface approaches decreased. Sadler-Smith (1996) used an alternative inventory, the RASI, and also found the factor age to have a significant effect on approaches to studying. The RASI was administered to 245 business studies students divided into mature (23 or over) and non-mature (less than 23 years). Mature students scored higher on all four deep approach sub-scales than non-mature students. Similarly, non-mature students scored higher on all four surface sub-scales. These findings are consistent with those of Harper and Kember (1986), and Richardson (1995) who all reported that mature students are more likely to adopt a deep approach towards their studies and, conversely, less likely to adopt a surface approach to their studies than their younger counterparts.

Studies exploring gender differences in approaches to learning offer far from a definitive picture, with contradictory findings often being reported. Biggs (1987b) for example, found that males scored significantly higher than females on the surface approach and strategy and on achievement motivation, while females scored higher than males on deep motivation and strategy. Sadler-Smith (1996), on the other hand, having employed the RASI with business studies students reported that males perceived themselves as adopting a deeper approach, whereas females were more surface-orientated. No gender differences were found on the strategic approach. Arguably, one difficulty in reaching conclusions regarding gender difference in approaches to learning arises because of the use of two different measures. Furthermore, Wilson *et al.* (1996) suggest that studies that have found evidence for gender differences are difficult to interpret because of a range of methodological limitations including that of sampling bias. Wilson *et al.* (1996) having overcome some of these methodological inadequacies, by achieving response rates of 98 per cent and 61 per cent and employing students from the same discipline, found no gender differences on the equivalent deep, surface and achieving scales with either instrument.

One of the purposes of the present study was to investigate age and gender differences in approaches to learning in Higher Education, with a view to addressing the sampling limitations apparent in previous studies. The current study employed a data collection process which aimed at as near to 100 per cent response rate as possible.

To date, there appears to have been little systematic investigation into course differences in approaches to learning in Higher Education. This is surprising since earlier studies found that approaches to learning vary as a function of discipline and year of study. Watkins and Hattie (1981) investigated gender, age and faculty differences in the study approaches of students at an Australian university. They found that regardless of gender and age, Art students were the most likely to adopt a deep-level approach to their work, whilst science students were more likely to adopt a surface-level reproductive approach to their work. More recently, Sadler-Smith (1996) took into account the effects of degree discipline when looking at approaches to studying. Five courses were targeted within the same business school at a UK university: business studies, marketing, personnel management, computing and informatics for business, finance and accounting. On the RASI it was found that business studies students were significantly more strategic than computing and informatics for business, accounting and finance and other business-related disciplines. Although this study does, in part, attempt to look at the effects of different disciplines on study processes, it still only incorporates disciplines from the same faculty, which arguably, all have an underlying business component. The current study, therefore, targeted students from six disciplines, one from each of the university's six faculties.

Such research into student motivation will clearly have implications for Higher Education. There is already anecdotal evidence that students are becoming more strategic in their approach to their studies, a somewhat disturbing trend as universities move towards more student-centred learning. There is a need for up-to-date larger-scale studies which can include courses from a variety of disciplines and can provide reliable normative data that reflect the recent changes in the make-up of the UK student population.

The present research project uses a cross-sectional approach, determining motivations of new students in a wide range of disciplines. In addition, a smaller group of students will be given in-depth interviews to determine their motivation in greater detail. These first-year students will be re-assessed at periodic intervals during their first year of university life. This chapter presents selected results from the first phase of this research which asked students to reflect on their approaches and attitudes to studying the last time they were in formal education.

METHODOLOGY

Respondents

A questionnaire designed to assess students' attitudes and approaches to studying the last time they were in formal education was completed by 600 first-year undergraduates. Respondents were drawn from a range of disciplines: geography, psychology, graphic design, education (B.Ed: maths, geography and science), rural resource management and rural estate management (RRM/REM), business studies (BABS) and engineering (B.Eng).

Questionnaires

The participants were presented with a battery of questionnaires designed to examine their attitudes and approaches to studying. The questionnaire was divided into four sections:

1. Demographic information.

2. Reasons for entering Higher Education taken from the ASSIST (Entwistle and Tait, 1997).

3. A modified version of the Study Process Questionnaire (SPQ) (Biggs, 1987b).

4. Open-ended questions exploring factors affecting motivation to study.

The present chapter is only concerned with the results from the SPQ and their relation to demographic variables.

Demographic information

The following demographic information was requested: name, gender, age (18–20, 21–24, 25–35, 36+), course, year, what they were doing in their year prior to coming to university (school or college, permanent employment, temporary employment, other), and what was their most recent formal education prior to coming to university (BTEC/HND, A levels, A levels with year out, Access/ Foundation, GNVQ, other).

Respondents were guaranteed confidentiality. The effects of the two latter variables are not analysed in the present chapter but will be reported in subsequent publications.

Study Process Questionnaire

The SPQ examined the general study approaches that students adopted the last time there were in formal education. This questionnaire was designed to assess the extent to which a student endorses different approaches to learning by identifying the motives and strategies which comprise these approaches. Each item is a self-report statement of a motive or strategy. The questionnaire yields sub-scores on three basic motives and learning strategies which were combined to give general approach to studying scores.

Each of the 42 items on the SPQ are in the present tense. However, as this phase of the present study required respondents to reflect back to their last time in formal education, the items were slightly modified to the past tense. Also, since the SPQ was not developed in the UK, a number of vocabulary items were replaced with words deemed to be more applicable to the present participant population. Respondents were asked to rate each of the statements on a scale ranging from 5 (this item is always or almost always true of me) to 1 (this item is never or rarely true of me).

Procedure

The questionnaires were completed in scheduled sessions during student induction week. The respondents were told that the questionnaire was designed to look at their attitudes and approaches to studying, rather than being told explicitly that it was designed to assess their motivation. Respondents were informed of their right to withdraw from the study at any time.

RESULTS

From the 600 returned questionnaires there was an almost even distribution of males (53.2 per cent) and females (46.8 per cent), reflecting the distribution within the university as a whole. There were fewer mature student respondents than non-mature ones, with 497 responses from the 18–20 yr. category, 47 from the 21–24 yr., 40 from 25–35 yr. and 16 from the 36+ yr. category. The age categories were combined into a non-mature group of 18–20 year olds (n = 497, male = 268, female = 229) and a mature group of 21+ year olds (n = 103, male = 51, female = 52) for all the following analyses. The resulting figure of 17.2 per cent mature students is still slightly lower than the overall figures for the university, which showed that 28 per cent of new entrants in academic year 1996–97 were 21 and over. The number of responses for each of the disciplines targeted are as follows: geography: 151, BABS: 150, psychology: 109, B.Eng: 51, graphic design: 50, B.Ed: 47 and REM/RRM: 42. In some of these cohorts there were prominent gender and age imbalances as shown in Table 9.2.

Table 9.2   *Number of respondents by age, gender and course*

Course	Gender		Age categories	
	male	*female*	*18–20*	*21+*
BABS	94	56	142	8
psychology	27	82	70	39
geography	90	61	146	5
B. Eng	48	3	38	13
graphic design	23	27	36	14
B. Ed	11	36	35	12
RRM/REM	26	16	30	12
Total	319	281	497	103

The motives and strategies given in the sub-scales of the SPQ were combined to give approaches to study and the following analyses were conducted on these combined scores.

Age differences

There were significant age differences across all three of the SPQ approaches. Table 9.3 shows that mature students reported a stronger Achieving Approach, $F(1, 594) = 5.46$, $p<0.05$, and a stronger Deep Approach, $F(1, 590) = 12.94$, $p<0.001$ than non-mature students. Conversely, the non-mature students were more likely to adopt a Surface Approach, $F(1, 594) = 27.62$, $p<0.001$ than the mature students.

Gender differences

When results were combined by *gender*, there were significant differences for Deep and Surface Approaches, but not the Achieving Approach, $F(1, 594) = 2.08$, *ns*. Female students reported that they were more likely to adopt a Deep

Table 9.3 *SPQ approach means and standard deviations by age*

Age categories	SPQ approaches		
	Achieving	Deep	Surface
18–20	41.621	42.276	43.761
	(7.886)	(7.305)	(7.054)
21+	43.735	45.255	39.612
	(10.180)	(8.944)	(8.322)

Approach to their studies, $F(1, 590) = 4.83$, $p<0.05$ than male students. The male students, on the other hand, were more likely to adopt a Surface Approach, $F(1, 594) = 9.26$, $p<0.05$ than the female students, as shown in Table 9.4. There were no significant interactions of *Age* × *Gender* for either the Achieving Approach, $F(1, 592) = 2.35$, *ns*; the Deep Approach, $F(1, 588) = 1.41$, *ns*, or the Surface Approach, $F(1, 592) <1$, *ns*.

Table 9.4 *SPQ approach means and standard deviations by gender*

Gender	SPQ approaches		
	Achieving	Deep	Surface
male	41.521	42.140	43.911
	(8.293)	(7.791)	(7.487)
female	42.509	43.527	42.064
	(8.401)	(7.513)	(7.295)

Course differences

When results were examined by course, there were significant effects for all three approaches as shown in Table 9.5. The Achieving Approach effect was significant, $F(6, 589) = 2.91$, $p<0.05$, with psychology students scoring highest on this measure and B.Ed. scoring lowest. Tukey pairwise comparisons showed that students from Psychology scored significantly higher than both BABS and B.Ed ($p<0.05$). There were no significant interactions between *Course* × *Age*, $F(12,575) = 1.09$, *ns*, or *Course* × *Gender*, $F(6, 582) = 1.66$, *ns*.

The Deep Approach, $F(6, 585) = 8.26$, $p<0.001$, was favoured by students registered for the graphic design and psychology courses. Tukey pairwise comparisons show that scores from psychology students for the Deep Approach are significantly higher than those for all the other courses $p<0.05$. Similarly, graphic design students scored significantly higher than B.Ed., BABS and geography ($p<0.05$) students. For the Deep Approach there were no significant interactions between *Course* × *Age*, $F(6, 578) = 1.34$, *ns*, *Course* × *Gender*, $F(6, 578) = 1.47$, *ns*.

Table 9.5   *SPQ approach means and standard deviations by course*

Course	SPQ Approach Scores		
	Achieving	Deep	Surface
BABS	41.168	41.095	45.067
	(7.660)	(6.666)	(7.372)
psychology	44.380	46.075	40.101
	(8.582)	(8.324)	(7.293)
geography	41.589	42.273	43.101
	(8.093)	(7.052)	(6.766)
B. Eng.	43.353	42.120	43.667
	(8.694)	(8.213)	(7.466)
graphic design	42.417	46.500	41.061
	(9.118)	(7.214)	(6.817)
B. Ed.	39.553	39.872	43.128
	(9.311)	(7.745)	(7.983)
RRM/REM	40.690	42.048	44.762
	(7.393)	(7.644)	(7.978)

The Surface Approach also showed a significant main effect, $F(6, 589) = 5.97$, $p < 0.001$. Tukey pairwise comparisons showed that students on BABS scored significantly higher than psychology and graphic design ($p < 0.05$) students. Geography and RRM/REM were also significantly higher than Psychology on this measure ($p < 0.05$ respectively). For the Surface Approach, *Course* did not interact with *Age*, $F(6, 586) = 1.77$, *ns*, or *Gender*, $F(6, 582) < 1$.

CONCLUSIONS

The study has achieved its aim of providing large-scale data on a UK sample and, in addition, avoids some of the problems of sample bias commented on by Wilson *et al.* (1996). The study was able to examine the effects of course, age and gender on students starting their university careers. This study confirmed the previously found differences in approaches to studying between mature and non-mature groups of students. Here mature students adopted a deeper approach when compared with the non-mature group. Also, the study provides further data on the conflicting patterns previously reported for males and females, with males demonstrating a stronger surface approach than females, and females showing a stronger deep approach than males. Finally, the study has allowed for further investigation of course differences.

There were significant differences in age across all three of the SPQ approaches. Mature students were shown to have a stronger achieving approach and a stronger deep approach than non-mature students. Conversely, the non-mature group of students were more likely to adopt a surface approach to learning. Several suggestions have been made for why these age differences may occur. Harper and Kember (1986) suggested that age differences may be due to:

- mature students being intrinsically motivated;
- younger students acquiring a surface approach in secondary education;
- the prior life experiences of mature students resulting in a deeper approach.

It is clearly difficult to differentiate between the reasons why age differences have occurred so consistently without taking into account other factors which would be expected to influence an individual's motivation to study. Further exploration of the prior educational and life experiences of new students therefore would be particularly useful.

Gender differences have not been as clear-cut as age differences in the previous literature. The present study achieved balanced groups of males and females, reflecting the UK student population, and found that female students were more likely to adopt a deep approach to their studies whereas male students were more likely to adopt a surface approach. There were no gender differences for the achieving approach. In addition, these gender differences were not influenced by the age of the participants. This study provides up to date data on the SPQ within the context of the changing gender balance within Higher Education.

When the results were examined by course, there were significant effects for all three SPQ approaches. For the achieving approach psychology students scored highest and were significantly higher than both BABS and B.Ed. Psychology students also favoured the deep approach and scored significantly higher on this measure than students from all the other courses. Graphic design students also scored highly on the deep approach and significantly higher than B.Ed, BABS and geography students. Data from the surface approach measure support the same pattern of results, with BABS students scoring significantly higher than those enrolled on psychology or graphic design courses. These course differences were not related to age or gender.

These results follow a similar pattern to the findings reported by Watkins and Hattie (1981) in that their course differences also did not interact with age or gender. Since these results are derived from students in a diverse range of specific disciplines, they differ from previous work which has either been restricted to related disciplines (eg Sadler-Smith, 1996) or has combined disciplines into general areas such as Arts and Science (Watkins and Hattie, 1981). However, there do appear to be similarities in some general trends in that Watkins and Hattie reported that Arts students are more likely to adopt a deep approach while Science students favoured a surface approach, these are similar to the differences reported here between graphic design and geography students.

These age, gender and course differences have implications for both this type of research and Higher Education as a whole. In the present study, students were tested in induction week before they started the courses they had registered for. It is possible that the differences identified are emerging from particular prior educational and life experiences, recruitment procedures or application requirements. In addition, Richardson (1997) has suggested that deep approaches are found where students are motivated by relevance, syllabus and interest, whereas the surface approach dominates where individuals are overloaded or over-assessed. Whatever the causes of the influences on motivations to study, staff in Higher Education will need to be aware of and account for these differences during the design and delivery of their courses.

REFERENCES

Biggs, J B (1979) 'Individual differences in study processes and the quality of learning outcomes', *Higher Education*, 8, 381–94.

Biggs, J B (1987a) *Student Approaches to Learning and Studying*, Australian Council for Educational Research, Hawthorn, Victoria.

Biggs, J B (1987b) *Study Process Questionnaire Manual*, Australian Council for Educational Research, Melbourne.

Dearing, R (1997) *Higher Education in the Learning Society*, Report of the National Committee of Enquiry into Higher Education, HMSO, London.

Entwistle, N J and Ramsden, P (1983) *Understanding Student Learning*, Croom Helm, London.

Entwistle, N J and Tait, H (1994) *The Revised Approaches to Studying Inventory*, University of Edinburgh, Centre for Research into Learning and Instruction, Edinburgh.

Entwistle, N J and Tait, H (1997) *Approaches and Study Skills Inventory for Students*, University of Edinburgh, Centre for Research into Learning and Instruction, Edinburgh.

Entwistle, N J, Hanley, M and Hounsell, D (1979) 'Identifying distinctive approaches to studying', *Higher Education*, 8, 365–80.

Harper, G and Kember, D (1986) 'Interpretation of factor analyses from the approaches to studying inventory', *British Journal of Educational Psychology*, 59, 66–74.

Marton, F and Säljö, R (1976) 'On qualitative differences in learning: I. Outcome and process', *British Journal of Educational Psychology*, 46, 4–11.

Newstead, S (1997) *Individual Differences in Student Motivation*, keynote paper presented at Staff and Educational Development Association Conference: Encouraging Student Motivation. University of Plymouth, April 1997.

Richardson, J T E (1993) 'Gender differences in responses to the Approaches to Studying Questionnaire', *Studies in Higher Education*, 18, 3–13.

Richardson, J T E (1995) 'Mature students in higher education: II. An investigation of approaches to studying and academic performance', *Studies in Higher Education*, 19, 309–25.

Richardson, J T E (1997) 'Dispelling some myths about mature students in higher education', in Sutherland, P (ed.), *Adult Learning: A Reader*, Kogan Page, London, pp.166–73.

Sadler-Smith, E (1996) 'Approaches to studying: age, gender and academic performance', *Educational Studies*, 22, 3, 367–79.

Watkins, D and Hattie, J (1981) 'The learning processes of Australian university students: investigations of contextual factors and personological factors', *British Journal of Educational Psychology*, 51, 384–93.

Wilson, K L, Smart, R M and Watson, R J (1996) 'Gender differences in approaches to learning in first year psychology students', *British Journal of Educational Psychology*, 66, 59–71.

10

Learner Autonomy Beyond the Curriculum: Students' Motivations and Institutional Community

Gillian Winfield and Selena Bolingbroke

INTRODUCTION

While other chapters in this volume discuss the important subject of what motivates students towards their studies, this chapter explores students' motivation towards life beyond the curriculum. Those of you looking for ideas to support your teaching might now feel the urge to skip forward to the next chapter. Yet we will be exploring the link between motivation inside and outside the classroom, and arguing that there are educational reasons to consider the role of student representation in gaining and maintaining student motivation. The main body of research discussed in this chapter will be the SEDA-funded research on Students' Motivation to Participate in the Institutional Community that we undertook from October 1996–April 1997. Data from this project are used in conjunction with our perspectives formed from a collective nine years experience working both as Students' Union staff and as researchers in Higher Education.

First, we discuss three current themes within the literature on student learning and explore their inter-relationships, extending them beyond the curriculum to consider the whole institutional community, including all formal and informal interactions between staff and students of the institution. Its importance in student learning is described by Entwistle who sees learning as resulting from 'complex interactions between the characteristics of the students, the nature of the teaching, and the *whole learning environment* provided by the department and institution' (Entwistle, 1992, p. 42, our emphasis). We then go on to present some of our data and discuss their implications for these complex interactions.

TYPOLOGIES OF STUDENTS' APPROACHES TO STUDY

The literature on approaches to study has focused on the curriculum. Categories of approach such as surface or reproducing learner, deep or transforming learner and strategic learner in typologies which differentiate between the ways different learners approach a situation and the quality of learning they gain from it (Entwistle and Ramsden, 1983, Marton and Säljö, 1984, Gibbs, 1992) are used. Approaches chosen by students denote a difference in intentions rather than their ability. A surface approach involves memorizing and reproducing information, while a student using a deep approach will identify key concepts and principles in the subject matter and making links between related ideas. Strategic learners, on the other hand, will choose their approach according to which will be the most successful, given their learning goals and the delivery methods and assessment criteria. Research has explored the inter-relationship between the curriculum content and delivery, assessment methods and such approaches, and it is argued that an overloaded curriculum or closed text examinations could encourage a surface approach to learning (Gibbs, 1992; Newstead, 1997). Elton (1996) argues that this is due to a mismatch between objectives for teaching and assessment. Newstead and Elton both relate the approaches students use to motivation. 'Student motivation is . . . the crucial determinant of how students approach their studies and of how well they perform' (Newstead, 1997, p.1). (See also the previous chapter.)

STUDENT MOTIVATION

To many, the best known work in this area refers to motivation in the workplace. Herzberg *et al.* (1959) introduce us to the idea that there are intrinsic and extrinsic factors that affect motivation. Extrinsic factors are labelled as 'hygiene factors' (negative satisfiers) and include salary and working conditions. Unlike these, in which poor circumstances can lead to de-motivation, intrinsic factors, known as 'motivators', such as responsibility and recognition are 'positive satisfiers' and ensure high motivation. Herzberg focuses on recommendations for management and how they can use this theory to maximize the motivation of their workforce through manipulation of positive satisfiers. Similarly, interest in students' motivation to learn has focused on their experiences on the receiving end of teaching delivery and assessment, which is within the academic sphere of control.

Within all the literature reviewed that uses the distinction between intrinsic and extrinsic factors, there is an implicit assumption that intrinsic motivation is somehow better. Herzberg implies this through the language he chooses. Newstead uses his research on student cheating to show that an extrinsically motivated student, studying as a 'means to an end' is more likely to cheat than a student studying for their own personal development. To academics discussing the motivation of students towards the subject that they have made the main focus of their career, to value the student who shares a love for their discipline seems entirely natural. But these assumptions all fail to recognize that motivation

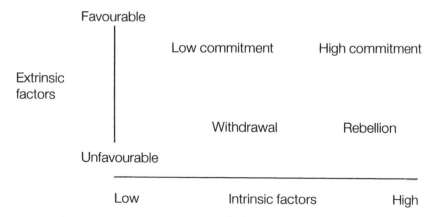

Figure 10.1   *The effect of intrinsic and extrinsic factors on levels of student commitment*

is a personal construct, and what is intrinsic for one can be extrinsic for another (Cryer and Elton, 1990). As Elton argues, we need to consider students' own personal constructs of motivation and accept that passing exams is an understandable goal. Figure 10.1 shows how extrinsic and intrinsic factors work together to lead to states of commitment, withdrawal or rebellion. We found this a useful model for analysis of our own findings.

LEARNER AUTONOMY

Interest in learner autonomy has been raised by theoretical writers such as Boud (1981) and used as a framework for those responsible for maintaining and developing the quality of teaching (eg DfEE Guidance and Learner Autonomy network). This has focused on the way students are empowered in their learning, with issues of the institutional community also explored. Boud (1981) states that the purpose of education is to produce autonomous lifelong learners who are needed to function in society, and defines autonomy in learning as 'the goals of developing independence and interdependence, self-directedness and responsibility for learning' (Boud, 1981, p.8). He states that autonomy can only be fostered by adopting an approach which involves students in decision-making about their learning and gives them some control over their learning environment. Departmental consultative bodies where elected students discuss matters of their concern are an example of how this can be achieved.

Heron's analysis (reported in Boud, 1981) of the locus of power within traditional Higher Education supports this. He argues that choice of mode of assessment, controlled by staff, also highlights the issue of power and its role in developing student autonomy. Heron argues that learner autonomy can only occur if the authoritarian system whereby staff are totally responsible for determining syllabus, teaching method, assessment criteria and students success is overturned. He recommends shifting the balance of power by involving students in all decisions about educational processes, particularly regarding assessment. Elton (1996) suggests negotiated learning objectives, which achieve this power shift, as one way of correcting the mismatch between teaching and assessment objectives that can lead to surface learning approaches.

SYNTHESIS

The three areas of literature overlap, and are sometimes used interchangeably, eg research at the University of Plymouth (Newstead, 1997) on student motivation uses ASSIST, the approaches to study determining questionnaire developed by Entwistle and Tait, to ascertain students' motivation. This shows the assumption that a well-motivated student is learning for intrinsic reasons and will therefore use a deep approach to study. It is commonly presumed that a motivated, autonomous learner will use deep learning approaches and learn 'well'. These presumptions perpetuate the view of the inherently good or bad student and an emphasis on ability as mentioned earlier.

While Boud (1981) and others show how learner autonomy will have a link to their approach to study and their motivation, they stress the importance of recognizing that learner autonomy is a goal rather than something that can be assumed or inherent. Not all students are ready for self-directed learning and that these skills must be taught first. Higgs (reported in Boud, 1981, p.48) writes that autonomous learners do 'whatever learning activities the learners considered would best help them to achieve their learning goals'. Therefore, a course structure and assessment system that reward a surface learning approach will encourage that and an autonomous learner could choose to use such an approach if it will pay off in terms of grades. Taking Heron's critique of power dynamics, unilateral control of staff encourages a surface learning approach and decreases motivation. This shows that the onus is on those structuring and teaching programmes of study to engender deep learning by using teaching and assessment methods that reward it. This requires a shift away from one-off judgements on students' ability or love for their subject to facilitating a process towards autonomy, where students will see the advantages of and be supported in adopting deep learning approaches, whatever their learning goals.

LEARNER AUTONOMY BEYOND THE CURRICULUM

Moving towards learner autonomy requires more than a collection of innovative teaching and assessment methods, and the tendency of the literature we read to focus on the curriculum limits its usefulness in this sense. It is argued elsewhere (Winfield, 1997) that to achieve true learner autonomy as Boud (1981) supports, the curricular and the co-curricular should not be treated as totally separate and distinct. The focus on the curriculum of the student learning literature means it falls short of seeing the students' development holistically and does not fully articulate the implications of learner autonomy for the whole institution.

Student representation is one of the main vehicles used in Higher Education to involve students in decision-making about their learning and gives them some ownership over their learning environment – a requirement for fostering learner autonomy. However, students' experiences outside the curriculum (ie within the whole institutional community) are largely unresearched or encapsulated within theory. However, high levels of motivation are shown by those students who choose to participate in activities outside the curriculum. These activities may affect their own institutional community and might include representation on elected bodies, running the Students' Union or running student organiz ations of common interests or activities. The learning that students engage in outside the curriculum is increasingly recognized.

METHODOLOGY

Previous studies seem to be dominated by the academic perspective; focusing on the curriculum and perpetuating value-laden perspectives about motives by not exploring students' personal constructs of motivation. Our study aimed to look at this from the student perspective and take into account their whole experience of the institution. We hope to provide a contrasting view of student motivation and approaches to study through its qualitative nature. This allows students to talk freely about their motivations and experiences, enabling issues of learner autonomy and institutional community to emerge. Figure 10.2 shows our holistic view of the research subject.

Fieldwork was carried out at Middlesex University and the University of Warwick, both institutions with very different missions. Middlesex, a post-1992 university covering a number of sites, has a modular structure over a semester-ized academic year, and a strong tradition of attracting local and older students to their programmes. Warwick, on the other hand, has a more traditional student population, is not modular and operates over three 10-week terms. These differences were reflected both in our sample and data.

We conducted 30-minute interviews with 29 students across the two institutions, focusing on student representatives on department committees and union representatives elected to leadership positions within union governance. We also interviewed a group we initially defined as non-participants, in order to contrast the motivations expressed. However, this proved to be a misnomer as they all did some activity. The biggest contrast was between those involved as student representatives and others. The data presented in this chapter focus on the interviews with student representatives and the questions about their courses and representation directed to other interviewees. However, many more conclusions were reached from the whole data not directly relevant to the argument we are making here, and for these see our full report (Bolingbroke and Winfield, 1998).

The interviews explored students' own views of their motivation to take part in representative work, how that relates to other aspects of their lives and their experiences of such activity. We devised a grid, based on those used in repertory grid analysis, to help interviewees think about their motivations

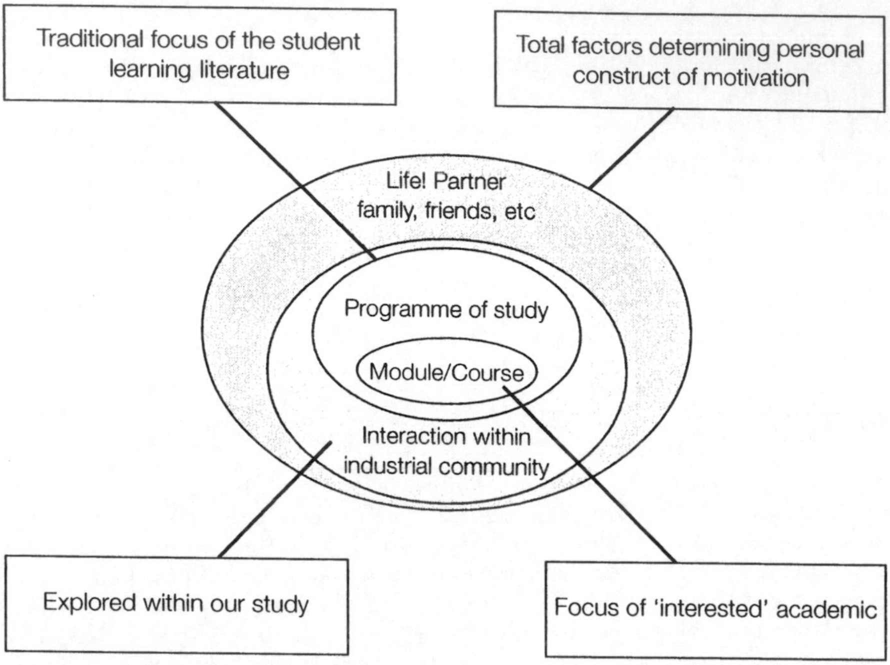

```
┌─────────────────────────────┐              ┌─────────────────────────────┐
│ Traditional focus of the    │              │ Total factors determining   │
│ student learning literature │              │ personal construct of       │
│                             │              │ motivation                  │
└─────────────────────────────┘              └─────────────────────────────┘
```

Life! Partner
family, friends, etc

Programme of study

Module/Course

Interaction within
industrial community

```
┌─────────────────────────────┐              ┌─────────────────────────────┐
│ Explored within our study   │              │ Focus of 'interested'       │
│                             │              │ academic                    │
└─────────────────────────────┘              └─────────────────────────────┘
```

Figure 10.2   *Conceptual representation of the research subject*

generally. They were asked to list motives that would encourage them to do something, then we selected various aspects of their lives to focus on. The grid enabled them to decide how each factor applies to each activity.

Analysing these grids in isolation provides numerical data on motives, but this becomes much richer when analysed alongside the transcript of the interview. We discovered inconsistencies in students' use of the word motivation, and contradictions of the responses given to the grid, administered early in the interview. For a more detailed discussion of the methodological issues see our full report.

FINDINGS

Factors affecting motivation towards being a student representative varied across the two institutions. Middlesex representatives mentioned achievement, social interaction and recognition most frequently, whereas Warwick representatives mentioned challenge, interest and learning something new (Figure 10.3). For both sets of representatives these factors were also the most frequently mentioned in relation to their motivation towards their course (see Figure 10.4). This is not surprising given that their focus of interest was the same in relation to both activities – the course!

Warwick students

Union participants (7)	Course	Position
Challenge	3	4
Interest	3	4
Learning something new	4	4
Career	3	3
Achievement	3	1
Meeting people	2	1
Responsibility	0	2
Rewards	2	0
Enjoyment	1	1
Helping others	1	1
Coercion	1	1
Belief	1	1
Self-worth	0	1
Variety	1	0

Middlesex students

Union participants (7)	Course	Position
Achievement	4	4
Social interaction	3	3
Recognition	2	2
Success	1	1
Responsibility	1	1
Helping others	1	1
Self-satisfaction	1	1
Completing something	1	1
Fulfilling goals	1	1
Change	0	1
Happiness	1	0
Problem-solving	0	1
Panic/fear	1	0
Expectation of something good	0	1
Family/friends	1	0

Rep participants (7)	Course	Position
Interest	2	2
Enacting values	1	3
Enjoyment	1	2
Career	2	1
Achievement	2	1
Rewards	2	0
Using prior experience	1	1
Fulfilment	1	1
Responsibility	0	1
Getting results	0	1
Belonging	0	1
New knowledge	0	1
Inspired by peers	0	1

Rep participants (4)	Course	Position
Social interaction	2	4
Achievement	3	3
Family/friends	3	3
Recognition	2	3
Self-satisfaction	2	2
Happiness	1	2
Injustice	1	2
Career	2	0
Responsibility	0	2
Money	0	1
Panic/fear	1	1
Fulfilling goals	1	0
Personal devotion	1	1
Problem-solving	1	1
Discovery	1	1
Helping others	0	1
Interest in learning	1	1

Figure 10.3   *Motivational factors towards study and participation*

Warwick students

Union participants (3)	Course	Position
Interest	2	2
Enacting values	1	3
Enjoyment	1	2
Career	2	1
Achievement	2	1

Middlesex students

Union participants (7)	Course	Position
Social interaction	2	4
Achievement	3	3
Family/friends	3	3
Recognition	2	3
Self-satisfaction	2	2

Rep participants (7)	Course	Position
Challenge	3	4
Interest	3	4
Learning something new	4	4
Career	3	3
Achievement	3	1

Rep participants (4)	Course	Position
Achievement	4	4
Social interaction	3	3
Recognition	2	2
Success	1	1
Responsibility	1	1

Figure 10.4   *Comparison of most frequently mentioned motivational factors*

At Middlesex, representatives tended to get involved as student representatives for two main reasons;

- no-one else appeared to want the job;
- they identified themselves as strong communicators and thus had the skills to carry out the job effectively.

At Warwick, representatives got involved for related reasons. Many mentioned prior experience at school as making them good candidates, but were less willing to define themselves as skilled for the job.

Interviewees found that their role as a representative was helpful in establishing themselves as part of the departmental community, and appreciated their access to specialist information about their course and the surrounding environment. At both institutions the relationship that representatives had with academic staff was reassuring, especially for those (at Warwick) having difficulty making the transition from school to a more anonymous institution on dual degrees and (at Middlesex) multi-disciplinary programmes of study. 'It puts you into a different light with some of your lecturers . . . as I'm secretary I have to go to all the departmental meetings as well, and I'm known in the department' (Warwick student representative).

All representatives felt that the system was most effective when informal, and problems were most often resolved through representatives speaking directly to staff outside of committee meetings. The enthusiasm and support gained by academic staff for the work that representatives did had a strong influence on how effective they felt their role to be. However, despite the value for representatives of a feeling of belonging within their department, they did not speak of using this access to additional, specialist information about their programme in their representation. We were not able to make a direct link between access to this additional information and motivation towards their study. Student clubs and societies mirrored departments in their functioning as communities. Students often spoke of their difficulties and fears accessing them, yet identified strongly with them once they were established members. In contrast to these smaller communities, union representatives talked of the whole institutional community. Two of the student representatives interviewed had progressed to union involvement, and the others had all come through student societies, suggesting that belonging to a sub-community is an important step to becoming involved at an institutional level.

The student representative structure tended to be viewed as an effective way for students to raise problems and complaints about their programme of study with staff, yet was not seen as a pro-active way of ensuring student input into departmental developments. Moreover, it tended to be used as a reactive body once informal channels had failed to resolve an issue, with most of the non-representatives interviewed reporting that they would go to a friendly tutor first with a problem they had. Having seen tangible changes to their course or department as a result of their actions helped to keep motivation high among representatives. Recruitment of representatives tended to be on a very casual basis and no-one had been involved in an election. One representative, the least motivated and pro-active representative we spoke to, felt she had been coerced into taking on the role.

The informality surrounding this system makes this issue of community particularly important. Representatives told us that they are only effective because their position allows them to build relationships with staff that means problems can be discussed as they arise. The effectiveness of the committee was largely seen as dependent on the attitudes of the department staff, who were described as positive. The notable exception to this was the representative who felt the structure was redundant as staff were so accommodating to any suggestions of change, such matters were resolved before they made it to the committee! However positive this responsiveness may seem, interviewees reported that committees were ineffective regarding issues outside the sole concern of the department, such as library and computing facilities. This is a fascinating illustration of power dynamics between students and staff within an institution. While staff can exercise power at students' behest by agreeing or vetoing departmental policy, they have difficulty influencing institutional policy. Dual degree students and their representatives reported less use of the committee structure due to confusion over how the structure could effectively span two departments.

Time was a factor that was important to all the representatives. At Middlesex time was seen as pressurized and representatives had to carefully balance their time between their course, their representative activities and their part-time jobs. 'There are so many pressures being a student, in a way being a student rep is a pressure you can do without' (Middlesex student representative).

All but one of the students interviewed at Middlesex found part-time jobs financially necessary. At Warwick, while none of the representatives worked, four of them were also heavily involved in a student society or aspect of union governance. Time was still important to these people, in one sense being a student representative was a manageable activity in terms of time compared to their other activities within the university. With one exception, Middlesex representatives were not involved with any other extra-curricular activities within the university. Time was also often mentioned when asked about reality versus expectations of university life. Some interviewees reported an expectation that they would be involved in more activities than they are as a result of under-estimating the time commitment of each activity. 'I was surprised, I'd expected a dynamic environment, passionate discussions in the bar about life!' (Middlesex student representative).

Students who were involved in students' union activities at both institutions felt some frustration in terms of matching their motivation towards these activities and their motivation towards their course. These activities generally involved a greater time commitment and had involved no direct contact with their academic department. However, their general high motivation towards their students' union activities contributed to a positive attitude towards the institution generally. In turn, this helped keep their motivation towards their course relatively high. Students interviewed at Middlesex commented on the particularly high levels of motivation that they felt as end-of-semester assessment deadlines approached. The most frequently mentioned factors of motivation differed between institutions but had similarities among representatives from the same institution.

CONCLUSIONS

Student representatives formed two relatively coherent groups with broadly similar motivations and factors. For other students interviewed there were no discernible patterns. This is likely to be mostly due to the fairly specific nature of the representatives' role, as opposed to the more disparate activities and interests of the union representatives or non-participatory students.

Interest in representation has increased since quality assurance procedures have required students to have input into the running of their course via consultative fora. Initiatives to promote the development of students' trans-ferable skills have also used student representative systems as a way of enabling students to develop skills such as communication and negotiation. However, the experiences of the students we spoke to and the arguments we are making as a result of our analysis show that the importance of representation lies beyond quality or student development, and can have a direct input on learner autonomy and student motivation. Returning to Figure 10.1 we can see that the commit-ment of the representatives we spoke to was high due to positive intrinsic and extrinsic motivation. This also shows the consequences of decreasing motivation – 'rebellion' or 'withdrawal' – states which are interesting to compare with stereotypes of students past and present!

To avoid decreasing motivation, institutional attitudes to representation need to be such that commitment stays high. Ramsden's (1992) conceptualization of the learning environment operating at the different levels of task, teacher, department or course and institution, points out that 'Differences in institutional values and purposes can also influence students learning' due to the 'importance of students' perception of the learning environment in affecting students' behaviour' (quoted in Boud, 1981 p.50). If students are supported and empowered as autonomous learners solely in their academic studies, but their input elsewhere is not valued, a mixed message is being sent at institutional level that will undermine the most enlightened teacher's attempt to motivate. Recognizing a student's need to be part of their institutional community should start in their academic department .

REFERENCES

Bolingbroke, S and Winfield, G (1998) *Student Motivation to Participate in Institutional Community*, SEDA, Birmingham.

Boud, D (1981) (ed.) *Developing Student Autonomy in Learning*, 2nd edn, Kogan Page, London.

Cryer, P and Elton, L (1990) 'Catastrophe theory: A unified model for educational change', *Studies in Higher Education*, 15, 1, 75–86.

Easterby Smith, M, Thorpe, R and Lowe, A (1991) *Management Research*, Sage, London.

Elton, L (1996) 'Strategies to enhance student motivation: a conceptual analysis', *Studies in Higher Education*, 21, 1, 57–67.

Entwistle, N (1992) *The Impact of Teaching on Learning Outcomes in Higher Education: A Literature Review*, CVCP/USDU, Sheffield.

Entwistle, N and Ramsden, P (1983) *Understanding Student Learning*, Croom Helm, London.

Gibbs, G (1992) *Improving the Quality of Student Learning*, Oxford Centre for Staff Development, Plymouth.

Gibbs, G (1994) *Improving Student Learning*, Oxford Centre for Staff Development, Plymouth.

Herzberg, F, Mausner, G and Synderman, B (1959) *The Motivation to Work*, Wiley, New York.

Marton, F and Säljö, R (1984) 'Approaches to learning', in Marton F, Hounsell, D and Entwistle, N (eds), *The Experience of Learning*, Scottish Academic Press, Edinburgh, pp.36–55.

Newstead, S. (1997) 'Individual differences in student motivation', keynote speech presented at Encouraging Student Motivation, SEDA conference, Plymouth, 8–10 April.

Ramsden, P (1992) *Learning to Teach in Higher Education*, Routledge, London.

Winfield, G (1997) 'Student-led not spoon fed: the co-curriculum and student learning and personal development', unpublished paper presented at *Improving Student Learning Symposium*, Strathclyde University, 8–10 September.

11

Does Gender Affect Students' Approaches To Learning?

Kay Greasley

INTRODUCTION

The area of gender and approaches to studying in Higher Education appears to be a relatively new and unexplored field, which is somewhat surprising considering the increase in numbers of female students attending universities (Richardson and King, 1991). This study was designed to take a closer look at whether there is a link between gender and approaches to studying.

The approaches which students may adopt during their university life will almost certainly have an effect on their 'success' academically and indeed in later life. The approaches which a student may adopt fall into three main categories. Firstly there is the *deep approach*. Learners who use this approach tend to have a genuine interest in the subject and want to learn (Marton and Säljö, 1976). The learner is able to interact with the subject and relate to it and the world around them. Second, there are students who adopt a *surface approach* which directs the learner to meet the course requirements by simply regurgitating information. Those who use this approach tend to use rote learning and have no ambition gaining of real understanding (ibid., 1976). The third category is the *strategic approach*, where the main aim of the learner is to achieve the highest grades by utilizing and taking advantage of the Higher Education system (Entwistle and Ramsden, 1983). The students who use this approach know what it takes to get the highest marks. For example they will write what they think the lecturer will want to see, continuously looking for clues for examination and assessment requirements.

It is important to note that a student is not a constant deep or surface learner but will adopt certain approaches at different times. In fact, it could be argued that the most successful learners tend to be those who adopt both a deep and strategic approach as the student who adopts these approaches not only has a true understanding of the subject but also knows how to use this understanding and achieve high marks.

The tool most frequently used to measure students approaches is the Approaches to Studying Inventory (ASI) (Entwistle and Ramsden, 1983). The

ASI offers a convenient way of defining students approaches to learning in different academic departments. As the approaches adopted so clearly influence students' success, it was felt that it was appropriate to use this well established inventory to discover if any differences in approaches could be found between men and women.

Although the ASI has been thoroughly discussed elsewhere (see Chapter 3, this volume), its use in relation to the study of gender differences in Higher Education remains relatively unexplored. Previous studies have identified that gender influences subject choice (Thomas, 1990) with more males choosing science-based subjects, whereas women favour the Arts. Perhaps more importantly, a clear correlation has been found between gender and degree classification with males achieving more firsts and thirds (Chapman, 1996). Of course the explanation for these results may not be linked to approaches to studying but it may well be a possibility.

Recent literature which has attempted to evaluate the ASI and gender has been varied with several authors reaching different conclusions. Meyer (1995) examined structural gender differences of first-year students based on an extended form of the ASI. The author found several differences notably in terms of strategic and deep structures. An earlier study by Meyer *et al.* (1994) demonstrated that again differences can be found between men and women, with men liking deep or strategic learning and showing a preference for operation and comprehension approaches. Women, however, are more organized and not achievement-motivated. Miller *et al.* (1990) also discovered a number of distinctions between gender and approaches to learning. Women were found to be more intrinsically motivated, strategic in approach, and scored highly on fear of failure and surface approach. Males were also shown to have preferences, including extrinsic motivation, deep approach and achievement motivation.

Other schools of thought assume that there is a connection between gender and approaches to studying, but this connection is best proved through qualitative methodologies rather than formal questionnaires. Richardson and King (1991) examined previous literature of gender in Higher Education and concluded that questionnaires did not produce consistent or valid results as a number of methodological problems were evident. However, the authors did find that when qualitative methods were used, distinct developmental schemes were found in male and female students. Other studies, while accepting that differences between gender and approaches to learning are plausible, have found no clear evidence to support this theory (Richardson,1993; Wilson *et al.*, 1996).

The fact that there are so many different attitudes towards the idea of a relationship between gender and learning would indicate in itself that the area is worthy of further investigation. The fact that much of the literature supports that there is some form of a relationship may point further exploratory studies towards more qualitative methods which may help explain the relationships between gender and approaches to learning.

METHODOLOGY

The inventory used in this study is the full version of the Approaches to Studying Inventory which provides quantitative data. The ASI consists of 64 items in 16 subscales, grouped under four main headings, these being meaning orientation, reproducing orientation, achieving orientation and styles and pathologies (Entwistle and Ramsden, 1983).

To provide further anecdotal evidence for the study, focus group questions were used to provide the opportunity for students to discuss their thoughts freely rather than in the confines of a questionnaire.

A random sample of students were used from BTEC to postgraduate courses. The gender split of the students sampled was reasonably equal with men accounting for 51.4 per cent and women accounting for the remaining 48.6 per cent, thus providing a fairly good representative sample of students. The students who took part in the survey were informed that their responses were confidential and anonymous in an attempt to ensure a freer response to the questions. They were also asked to complete further details about themselves, eg gender, age range, ethnicity, etc. This questionnaire was administered to 300 Business and Management students.

The initial design of the questionnaire insisted that the students needed to be supervised and to ensure that the questionnaires would be completed the students were asked to complete the questionnaire individually. The students were then divided into groups of five and participated in a 20-minute discussion of the focus group questions which were either recorded on tape or noted down by a supervisor.

The taped discussions of the focus group questions were then listened to and the transcripts of the conversations were analysed. Individual responses on the focus group questions were also analysed so that common themes could be identified and any interesting quotes were noted for further reference. These qualitative data are then used to support quantitative results found in the ASI.

ASI and gender significant results

Table 11.1 illustrates all of the significant results themed into subscales. The results are described in terms of chi-square, level of significance and the gender preference.

The results in Table 11.1 show that there is a clear relationship between gender and the variables. These results will now be analysed using qualitative data gained from the focus group questions and observation of the chi-square results.

DISCUSSION OF FINDINGS

As can be seen from Table 11.1 there are a number of interesting findings which point to the fact that significant relationships are present between gender and approaches to learning. Hopefully this discussion will help to clarify the nature of the relationship and perhaps provide some reason as to why they exist.

Table 11.1 *Gender significant results*

Questions	χ^2	Significance	Gender
Deep approach I often find myself questioning things that I hear in lectures or read in books	10.5	.03279	M
Relating ideas I try to relate ideas in one subject to those in others whenever possible	11.8	.01874	F
I need to read around a subject pretty widely before I'm ready to put my ideas down on paper	13.0	.01133	F
Intrinsic motivation My main reason for being here is so that I can learn more about the subjects which really interest me	9.9	.04173	F
I spend a good deal of my spare time in finding out more about interesting topics which have been discussed in classes	12.2	.01575	F
Surface approach Lecturers seem to delight in making the simple truth unnecessarily complicated	15.2	.00429	F
I usually don't have time to think about the implications of what I have read	19.1	.00075	F
Often I find I have to read a thing without having a chance to really understand it	14.6	.00572	F
Fear of failure The continual pressure of work-assignments, deadlines and competition often makes me tense and depressed	11.1	.02501	F
A poor first answer in an exam makes me panic	31.9	.00001	F
Having to speak in tutorials is quite an ordeal for me	12.1	.01653	F
Extrinsic motivation I suppose I am more interested in the qualifications I'll get than in the course I'm taking	11.7	.01998	M
Strategic approach One way or another I manage to get hold of the books I need for studying	13.1	.01061	F
Achievement motivation I enjoy competition: I find it stimulating	10.0	.04056	M

Note: p ≤ 0.05, df =4.

Fear of failure

When examining the table perhaps the most striking set of results are those which fall under the heading fear of failure, with women favouring this type of approach, supporting the findings described by Miller *et al.* (1990). A fear of failure is fairly self-explanatory as it simply means that students are more preoccupied with the fact that they might fail rather than the subject content. Under this heading the students were questioned with regard to workload pressure, poor first answers in exams and speaking in tutorials, all of which appeared to affect females more than males as they feel reluctant to air their views during tutorials, particularly when more vocal students are present. One female student noted, 'You always get somebody that completely takes over and you don't get a chance to say anything'. This is an area that women seem to feel quite strongly about as often they find the environment is not conducive for them to speak, for example, 'lecturers should show an interest in your opinion and if they don't they are just domineering', 'this is the way it is and you have no say over it'. This is perhaps an area where lecturers and academic departments could make improvements by lecturers encouraging students to share ideas rather than competing to see whose idea is best.

If one looks at the results it can also be seen that there is a high likelihood of a relationship between gender and responses to a poor first answer in an exam. This may mean that women are more adversely affected by examinations than males.

The fact that women have a high fear of failure can have many implications: first, it may influence the fact that males achieve a greater proportion of firsts and thirds (Chapman, 1996). The reasoning behind that assumption is quite simple as women have a high fear of failure and so are unlikely to take risks. To quote one female student, women 'hold back on ideas in case they are wrong'. Generally, to achieve a first-class degree risks have to be taken and, obviously, the failure or success of these risks would account for the high number of thirds and firsts gained by males.

Second, it may have an effect on relating ideas as women like to read about a subject before writing their ideas down. This could be because they need to feel certain of what they are saying to avoid any possibility of failure. Third, women were found to have a high strategic approach (Miller *et al.*, 1990) when it came to getting hold of books they needed. Again, this may be because they are reliant on other sources to support their views and are reluctant to put their own views forward without supportive evidence.

Surface approach

Another area where females scored highly is the surface approach. Students who use this approach tend not to be successful students as they simply try to memorize information without any real attempt to understand the subject. Again, these findings are supported by earlier work which found that women preferred a surface approach (Severiens and Ten Dam, 1994). Academic departments are influential in the approach a student adopts and features like overload of work, exams and lack of freedom in learning can encourage a surface approach. Here it can be seen that workload plays an important role, with women frequently not having time to think about their reading, this is clearly indicated by one female student, 'You don't concentrate on new info as you just want to do your assessment'. The impact of an overload of work on learning approaches has been identified by Ramsden and Entwistle (1981), as a promoter of surface approaches, but it can be seen to affect women more than men in this sample. If women and men are to be encouraged to use a deep approach perhaps there should be a reduction in the number of assignments and changes should be made to the type of assignments.

The findings also indicated that females thought lecturers enjoyed making the subject complicated; this is neatly commented on by a female student, 'when lecturers think that using the most complex language will impress the student rather than delivering the message'. If females feel intimidated and overworked, it is quite likely that a surface approach will be adopted. As females show a tendency to favour a surface approach, one may suspect males will show a preference for a deep approach and from looking at Table 11.1 it can be seen that there is a statistically significant relationship with males favouring this variable, which asked if they questioned things that they heard or read in books. Miller *et al.* (1990) discovered the same relationship, with men favouring a deep approach.

Motivation

A definite distinction can be found when examining motivation through the ASI as females show a preference for intrinsic motivation whereas males prefer extrinsic motivation. Again, the findings are supported by other authors, eg Miller *et al.* (1990), Severiens and Ten Dam (1994). As males are extrinsically motivated, they are more motivated by qualifications they will obtain than the course they are studying. This is unlike women as they are intrinsically motivated and therefore want to learn for their own personal satisfaction. This is positive news for women as it indicates that women want to learn for their own interest, looking for 'lots of learning opportunities that then motivated me to go away after the lesson to continue my studies'. This is something that can be built on as female students are at university mainly to learn about subjects that interest them and like to pursue their interest in their own time. This is perhaps an area which needs to be encouraged not just to utilize women's interest but to try to encourage males to realize that picking a course simply because of the qualification it will provide is not a good basis for learning. This may, however, be an ambitious plan as it is difficult to alter someone's motives, as some students are quite clear as to why they are here, 'I am here to achieve the objective of completing the qualification.' Achievement motivation was found to be popular with men, as they appeared to enjoy competition, finding it beneficial to their learning experience. Severeins and Ten Dam (1994) identified the same findings with men approving of achievement motivation.

CONCLUSIONS

This chapter describes an investigation into gender and approaches to learning, using both quantitative and qualitative methods, that is, the ASI and focus group questions. The chapter was based on a questionnaire given to a sample of Business and Management students from a number of different courses and years.

The study showed a number of differences between men and women in their approaches to learning. One of the most striking is the high fear of failure which women seemed to have, responding positively to all of the questions asked under this subscale. A high fear of failure certainly does not benefit the academic performance of women in their studies as they are reluctant to voice their opinions and are often weighed down by work. The result is supported by the focus group evidence which strongly pointed to the fact that women have a high fear of failure.

When questioned about finding the books they need, a high strategic approach was found to be preferred by females. It could be argued that this is related to the high fear of failure females have, as they are unwilling to be forthcoming in their views unless they have evidence to support them.

As might be expected from the earlier results, females and males differ in their preference to the surface approach, with females heavily favouring this type of approach. A surface approach can be encouraged by an overload of work as the students do not have the time to really understand the topic and are simply trying to get by. This can obviously affect all students but in this study it seems to have a more negative effect on women. Women also found not only did they feel overworked but they felt that the lecturer enjoyed making the subject unnecessarily complicated. Again this will have a negative effect on the level of understanding gained.

Females, however, do seem to have a particularly positive attitude towards intrinsic motivation, learning for themselves rather than just for the qualification. The fact that they are intrinsically motivated may be taken as an indication that in the right environment more effective learning approaches may well be adopted by women.

The results discussed in the chapter mainly focus on women for the simple reason that women showed more preferences than men. However, certain male preferences can be drawn from the study. Extrinsic motivation was shown to be favoured by males as they appear to be more interested in job opportunities and qualifications than the course itself which may prevent the male students from realizing their full potential.

Males were also found to prefer a deep and achievement approach to learning which has been argued to be the most effective combination of approaches in terms of achieving a good qualification.

As clear preferences for both men and women can be drawn, it is evident that some type of teaching and learning strategy needs to be formed to combat the negative approaches to learning and to promote the positive approaches. It is evident from these results that certain features which encourage a surface approach and a high fear of failure affect women more negatively.

Therefore, if academic departments do encourage surface and fear of failure approaches they are not only discouraging the full learning potential of all students but of female students in particular. It is therefore important that academic departments instigate policies that encourage a deep approach to learning to allow all students to realize their full potential.

REFERENCES

Chapman, K (1996) 'An analysis of degree results in geography by gender', *Assessment and Evaluation in Higher Education*, 21, 293–311.

Entwistle, N and Ramsden, P (1983) *Understanding Student Learning*, Croom Helm, London.

Marton, F and Säljö, R (1976) 'On qualitative differences in learning, 1 – outcome and process', *British Journal of Educational Psychology*, 46, 4–11.

Meyer, J H F (1995) 'Gender-group differences in the learning behaviour of entering first-year university students', *Higher Education*, 29, 201–15.

Meyer, J H F, Dunne, T T and Richardson, J T E (1994) 'A gender comparison of contextualised study behaviour in higher education', *Higher Education*, 27, 469–85.

Miller, C D, Finley, J and McKinley, D (1990) 'Learning approaches and motives: male and female differences and implications for learning assistance programs', *Journal of College Student Development*, 31, 147–54.

Ramsden, P and Entwistle, N J (1981) 'Effects of academic departments on students' approaches to studying', *British Journal of Educational Psychology*, 51, 368–83.

Richardson, J T E (1993) 'Gender differences in responses to the Approaches to Studying Inventory', *Studies in Higher Education*, 18, 3–13.

Richardson, J T E and King, E (1991) 'Gender differences in the experience of higher education: quantitative and qualitative approaches', *Educational Psychology*, 11, 363–82.

Severiens, S E and Ten Dam, G T M (1994) 'Gender differences in learning styles: a narrative review and quantitative meta-analysis', *Higher Education*, 27, 487–501.

Thomas, K (1990) *Gender and Subject in Higher Education*, SRHE and Open University Press, Buckingham.

Wilson, K L, Smart, R M and Watson, R J (1996) 'Gender differences in approaches to learning in first year psychology students', *British Journal of Educational Psychology*, 66, 59–71.

12

Layers of Motivation: Individual Orientations and Contextual Influences

Linda France and Liz Beaty

INTRODUCTION

The following comment was made back in 1980 and demonstrates that motivating students has for many years been an important issue for researchers of student learning:

> When teachers in higher education discuss their problems a fairly frequent complaint is that students are not motivated. Teachers who say this explain that students lack an urge to work independently, applying themselves only if external pressures are exerted. When invited to give examples or expand their comments, they may add that students these days are not interested in the courses they have selected but simply 'want a qualification and a good job'.
>
> (Beard and Senior, 1980, p.1)

Eighteen years on, lecturers are still grappling with the issue of student motivation, or the so-called lack of it. The more cynical still might say that students are not as motivated as they used to be and that the current changes taking place in Higher Education are creating a different type of student, but it is also true that motivating students is not simply a problem associated with present-day problems in Higher Education, rather, it is something that is a natural aspect of formal educational systems.

The pressures, demands and the overall experience of being a student today are, however, very different to those of 20 years ago. In considering student motivation, it is also important to acknowledge and understand the nature of their particular experiences.

There are many different reasons why students decide to enter Higher Education. In recent years, with growing student numbers and a more diverse intake, these reasons may be more complex than 20 years ago. What students want from their university experiences will affect how they relate to their studies.

This relationship also changes over time, as students become accustomed to the university and what it offers. The picture is a complex one, made up of different layers and various influences. In order to encourage student motivation, it is important to understand these orientations, the aims and purposes that individual students identify as having an influence in their being at university. A clearer understanding of orientations can help us to see how these impact on and influence students' approaches to their studies, what is likely to motivate them and what will lead to a more rewarding experience in terms of their learning.

This chapter explores the different types of orientation to learning that students have and the impact of this on their motivation. Based on case studies of students in the 1970s and in the 1990s, we explore how far the typology of orientations from the 1970s still holds true for today's students. We take the view that it is important to understand students' individual orientations to learning, on the one hand, and the influences of the university and wider environment, on the other, in coming to a clear view of the motivational context for students in the late 1990s.

ORIENTATION TO STUDY

The concept of motivation has been used to explain variations in how students study. However, there are problems with the use of this concept. First, the term 'motivation' has been used in so many different ways, there is lack of precision in its meaning. Second, it has been used as an explanation of behaviour, which may not take account of the conscious control learners have over how and what they study. Motivation can be seen as a drive, with students viewed as essentially being driven by factors without their control. Similarly, some goal-direction theories tend to view students as responding to stimuli, not actively constructing their own behaviour patterns. More recently goal-direction theories have incorporated a view of the individual agency in relation to the context (Newstead, 1997).

The concept of orientation was developed to take account of the purposes that students described for their own studies (Taylor, 1983). Orientation is defined as 'all those attitudes and purposes which express the student's individual relationship with a course and the university' (Beaty *et al.*, 1997). Learning orientation is the collection of purposes which form the personal context for the individual student's learning. From the point of view of orientation, success and failure are judged in terms of the student's fulfilment of their own aims. Orientation does not assume any trait belonging to the student; it is a quality of the relationship between the student and the course, rather than a quality inherent in the student, and so may change over time. The analysis of orientation therefore does not set out to typify students, rather, it sets out to identify and describe types of orientation and to show the implications of different types of orientation for the approach a student takes to learning.

A study of students' orientations to learning at Surrey University in the 1970s, (Taylor, 1983) identified four distinct types of orientation. These were *academic orientation*, where the student's goals were to do with the academic side of university life; *vocational orientation*, to do with getting a job after university; *personal orientation*, to do with their own personal development, and *social orientation*, where the student's goals were to do with the social side of university life. The first three types of orientation could be divided into two sub-types according to whether the student was directly interested in the content of the course or whether they were studying the course merely as a means to an end. These sub-types were labelled *intrinsic* and *extrinsic*, respectively. Taylor found that concerns that students had while studying at university were intimately connected to the type of orientation they had and these two factors helped to make sense of the amount of effort the student gave to different aspects of the course and the university life, ie what motivated them (see Table 12.1).

Table 12.1   *Student's learning orientation*

Orientation	Interest	Aim	Concerns
Vocational	Intrinsic	Training	Relevance of course to future career
	Extrinsic	Qualification	Recognition of qualification's worth
Academic	Intrinsic	Intellectual interest	Choosing stimulating lectures
	Extrinsic	Educational progression	Grades and academic progress
Personal	Intrinsic	Broadening or self-improvement	Challenging, interesting material
	Extrinsic	Compensation or proof capability	Feedback and passing the course
Social	Extrinsic	Having a good time	Facilities for sport and social activities

Source: Beaty *et al.* (1997).

Our research on the first-year experience at the University of Brighton has considered how far this typology can be applied to students in the 1990s. The three case studies below have been selected to illustrate the different orientations and the bearing these have on their approaches to learning.

Ben: Vocational (intrinsic/extrinsic) – social

Ben set his heart on a particular profession. His next-door neighbour back home was a role model and source of encouragement. He knew exactly which course he wanted to study, as his neighbour had said that the department had a good reputation in the field. Ben was seriously committed to working hard. He knew exactly what he wanted from the degree and selected his modules carefully in order to steer a career pathway for himself (vocational intrinsic). He was set on achieving a good degree classification, in order to help his job prospects (vocational extrinsic), 'well personally I aim to go out with a minimum 2.1 degree – I mean that's my target over the years'.

Although his main concerns were with the course, Ben also wanted to combine this with a good social life. 'Um, basically to study hard during the day and, like, enjoy yourself at night'. Ben had succeeded in this respect and was getting involved in DJ-ing at local clubs and was enjoying this new student lifestyle (social).

Wendy: Personal (intrinsic)

Having left school with few qualifications, Wendy had been out to work for a few years. She was frustrated by its unchallenging nature and wanted to do something 'more her'.

'I decided to give up the job and be really, really brave. Every day I used to go in and think "what the hell am I doing here?" It's appalling, I shouldn't be here, I should be doing something more creative, I want to do something more me!'

She was not sure what she wanted to do after the degree, but was glad to be 'getting out of the rut' of her job. Wendy wanted to enjoy herself and get a good degree and gain lots of experiences and get studying 'out of her system'. She saw coming to university as 'like coming to a good job every day'. She found it stimulating and a way of broadening her mind. In terms of her approach to learning, Wendy spoke about how each lecture challenged her to question her opinions on things. '(learning is about) getting a feel for ideas, broadening your mind, not being so blinkered . . . my opinions change with practically every lecture, I discard the old one, put it down for a little while'.

With this personal orientation Wendy was looking to gain self-development from her studies. She enjoyed learning that challenged her current way of thinking and got frustrated when pieces of work were not stimulating and appeared to be there just for the sake of it.

'An exam. That was a joke really, it was just too easy – I can't really see the purpose in us having it because it doesn't go towards our degree, I think it's just to make us all turn up one day (laughs). No, it was really simple and we all passed, no problem . . . But I hope next time it will be more like, more challenging and you can feel like you've really done something (laughs).'

Ellie: Social – Academic (extrinsic)

'I just assumed it would be the same as A level, um, I really like studying and that's why I wanted to come to university from when I was really little, I always wanted to come and I enjoy doing it.'

Ellie came to university with an open mind and university was the next progression after A level (*academic extrinsic*). She wasn't sure what she wanted to study but took advice and followed in the footsteps of her mother and grandfather. She came to university to have fun and to meet lots of people (social). 'I thought it was going to be excellent, I knew that, and I knew I was going to have an awful lot of fun, meet lots of new people and I hoped that the course was going to be enjoyable, etc and I was just really looking forward to coming.'

Ellie's social life often proved to get in the way of her studies and she was constantly struggling to find the right balance.

'Yeah, I like that (laughs) [the social life], yes that's caused my problems I suppose because in the end I was enjoying myself too much really, I think (laughs). Enjoying the social life a bit too much and putting the work off and then that caused a few of the problems, I suppose, most of them anyway. But no, I definitely enjoy it. It's weird, my life's changed so much. It's just, um, I just really like student life, it's good.'

A NEW ORIENTATION

The case studies suggest that the typology of orientation still applies to students today. However, we also identified an additional orientation which was not fully described in the typology which appeared to be important to these students. We have called this 'independence orientation'.

When asking the students what they hoped to gain from their time at university the students referred frequently to the following set of factors: becoming more independent, finding out about life, gaining greater confidence, maturing and developing as a person, getting away from home and having a fresh start. The frequency with which these factors occurred in the interviews indicated that there is a new or previously undefined orientation. These factors refer to issues of self-development and becoming a new, independent person as a consequence of their experience of coming away to study as university.

It's about broadening my experience to get the most out of life – both academically and socially... But I don't think university is just about your career, it's about building yourself up as the person you are, and learning about the world and what life is all about. There's quite a lot in there.

(Holly)

> I'll have new hands-on experiences . . . it's made me a different person already . . . it will turn me into an adult, more mature, sensible, a more complete person.
>
> (Ellie)

> Living away from home I'll grow up, rely on myself. It's helped making friends . . . starting from scratch.
>
> (Edward)

This new orientation should not be confused with social orientation. The social orientation is about enjoying life as a student, having a good time, whereas these students are talking about meeting new people and overcoming the hurdles of living away from home for the first time and the impact that has on the way that person views themselves as an adult. They see this in terms of their own development, not in terms of a new social life and the opportunities to go out 'clubbing and pubbing'. Nor is it to be confused with intrinsic personal orientation as the factors that these students refer to are independent of the course content or specifics, they apply to the wider student experience of life at university. While for the personal orientation it is the course which is providing the context for broadening experience, for these students it is the other aspects of student life which provide the context, the orientation is essentially therefore an extrinsic type.

For some, it appeared that the degree was just an incidental vehicle on which to travel in order to visit all these other experiences. This is not to say that their degree was not important to them, but rather their motivation to study at university was rich, complex and entangled with this craving for wider development. University offered the opportunity to mix with a wider selection of people from all over the country and indeed, the world, the opportunity to live and experience life in a town rather than a rural village, the opportunity to face new experiences and to come into contact with things you might otherwise have been sheltered from. The students saw these aspects of coming away to university as very important in terms of their own personal development and the new outlook on life that it gave them.

As with all orientations, the independence orientation has an impact on how students approach their study. We found that there was a tendency to concentrate their effort on the course assessment requirements, ensuring they had covered the bare minimum, in order to get through, but also to keep up with their peers. 'Finding the right balance between social life and study' was often referred to as an important aspect of student life. Students strategically worked out where effort was needed in order to achieve the desired result, ie a good social life without jeopardizing the grades.

> Coming here and thinking you can have a pretty good social life as well as doing the work – it's just trying to find that balance – I remember talking about that earlier, which I hadn't got right at the beginning but it's getting there. Like I still have my door open, but I can now say to people, you know, 'get out' sort of thing, 'I'm working'.
>
> (Holly)

This new independence orientation produces concerns to do with personal development and life skills; something not necessarily explicit within Higher Education.

DISCUSSION

The identification of this new orientation is important in understanding students' motivation for studying. First, it puts the focus firmly on the student experience as a whole, rather than seeing course-based studies as the foreground with everything else to do with life as a student as unimportant. For students with this orientation, university life would not offer the same chances for development if they were to live at home and study at the local university. It is the essence of the experience of being away from home and with very different people which motivates these students. They are learning, but not focused only on their courses of study. Rather, their learning is experiential and based around the life they are leading and the company they share this life with. As an education, the university is offering a broad experience but it appears that the more focused requirements of a course are being given a secondary place. In this scenario, it is not surprising that students appear to tutors to lack motivation. In fact, their attention and effort towards learning are directed at other aspects of their lives. It is important to note, however, that students rarely have only one orientation and that most students who show this independence orientation will also have an academic or vocational orientation too.

'Lecturespeak' and the language of skills and competence

Researchers have pointed out the importance of the social environmental influence, or what Malcolm Parlett calls 'milieu'. 'Students are profoundly affected by the immediate environment in which they work . . . the academic context, the whole network of beliefs, assumptions, organisational goals, rewards, constraints and penalties that form part of it.' (Parlett and Dearden, 1981, p.151). What lecturers say appears to have an impact on students in the form of 'lecture speak', ie where students seem to use lecturers' words rather than their own. In the case study interviews, there are occasions where students reiterate what appeared to be messages from lectures, for example, on the importance of extra reading. It is not clear from our interviews at what point this becomes part of their own perceptions of what learning is about. The interviews do demonstrate, however, students grappling with understanding what is required of them in relation to their own goals.

The students' peer group also played a major part in their perceptions of what university life is all about. Messages about what counted as adequate effort were important influences on their motivation. For example, second-year students comments that 'the first year is a doddle - you only need to get 40 per cent to pass' or comparisons of grades with their fellow students 'it's okay, I got 60 per cent and most of the others got in the 50s, so I'm doing okay'.

As well as being influenced by their lecturers and peer group, students are also profoundly affected by the wider socio-political climate within which they are studying. In analysing our case study material, we have been impressed by the language that students use to describe their experiences at university, in that they use words and phrases which are an essential part of the wider debate about Higher Education. In the present climate, a new vocabulary based on the issue of skill acquisition has emerged – the language of 'competence', 'core skills', 'personal transferable skills', and so on has shifted the attention from the subject specific to the more generic attributes that a student can expect to develop while studying for a degree. Our case study students see the benefits of equipping themselves with these broader skills, therefore making themselves more employable in the future. Perhaps it is not surprising that, when there has been so much debate about the nature of Higher Education that students should see the value of university in new ways.

In the 1970s students coming to university could believe that the competition had ended with A levels. Now they were entering a part of the education system which guaranteed them, if not a particular job, then almost certainly a high position in the job market. They knew that, on graduating, they would be members of a small group looking for professional positions and were guaranteed a good salary. Today's students are guaranteed very little. There are many more of them and the job market is not as buoyant. The call for graduates has grown but the type of job graduates find is often not of as high status as it was in the past. So what are students to think about their university experience? Very few will go on to further study and many do not believe that they will gain a good job simply by graduating. Their search for a different meaning for their time at university is well founded. To see Higher Education as a broadening opportunity may well be a functional motivation for the times.

In order to encourage student motivation, we need to understand the orientations that students have and the context within which they are studying. Individual lecturers can affect student motivation but they have more chance of doing so if they start with a deeper understanding of the experience of being a student in the late 1990s.

Encouraging student motivation is more complex than the relationship between the individual lecturer and their students. We are more likely to have a positive influence on motivation to learning if we understand the subtle interplay between a student's orientation and the context of university life. Students come to university with their own orientations, this meets peer group pressure, the university milieu and the wider political context. Understanding motivation requires acknowledgement of these contextual layers.

REFERENCES

Beard, R and Senior, I 1980 *Motivating Students*, Routledge and Kegan Paul, London, p.1.

Beaty, L, Morgan, A and Gibbs, G (1997) 'Orientation to learning', in Marton, F, Hounsell, D J and Entwistle, N J (eds), *The Experience of Learning*, 2nd edn, Scottish University Press, Edinburgh.

Newstead, S (1997) 'Individual differences in student motivation', keynote speech presented at Encouraging Student Motivation, SEDA conference, Plymouth, 8–10 April.

Parlett, M and Dearden, G (eds) (1981) *Introduction to Illuminative Evaluation. Studies in Higher Education*, SRHE, Guildford.

Taylor, E (1983) 'Orientation to learning: a longitudinal study of students on two courses in one university', unpublished PhD thesis, University of Surrey.

SECTION THREE:
The Impact of University Practices on Motivation

13

The Effect of Stressors on Student Motivation: A Report of Work in Progress at Sunderland Business School

Gail Thompson

INTRODUCTION

It has become fashionable in recent years to blame stress for a wide range of problems in the workplace, most notably absenteeism, underachievement, and even serious ill health. Nevertheless, most of us would readily acknowledge that we work best under a certain degree of pressure, so when does 'pressure' become 'stress', and why is it that the same pressures can motivate one person to work to the best of their abilities, and yet cause another to feel that they cannot cope? A study is under way at Sunderland Business School to investigate these issues in the context of student learning experience. This chapter discusses the current findings as they relate to student motivation.

THEORETICAL BACKGROUND

Researchers in this field have long acknowledged the two faces of stress. In the 1950s Selye defined 'negative' stress as *distress*, and 'positive' stress, (what we

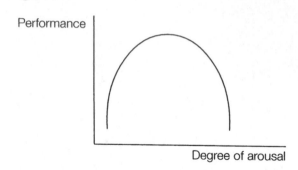

Performance

Degree of arousal

Figure 13.1   *Idealized representation of the Yerkes–Dodson Law (source: Fisher, 1986)*

might consider in layman's terms to be the 'pressure' that makes us work better), as *eustress* (Selye, 1956). As long ago as the early 1900s, the relationship between degree of stress and performance of an individual was described in the Yerkes–Dodson Law (Yerkes and Dodson, 1908). Here, the relationship is expressed as an inverted 'U'-shaped curve which describes how performance first increases, peaks, and then declines with increased arousal (see Figure 13.1).

So it appears that it is possible to be under-stressed. Clearly, to achieve optimum performance in individuals, we need to expose them to the right amount of pressure . If we consider how this might apply to students, we must exert enough pressure to motivate them to work to their best ability, but must ensure that they are not pushed over the peak, when their performance is likely to deteriorate rapidly. Exposure to high levels of stress can lead to serious consequences, not only for the student, but also for the university itself. The most obvious examples here are the increased resources required to manage referrals and the financial consequences of high drop-out. In a study by Fisher and Hood, it was reported that 9 per cent of all students questioned had considered leaving university because of stress (Fisher and Hood, 1987). Although less well established, research also suggests that exposure of students to too little pressure could have similar consequences.

What complicates the problem is the fact that the Yerkes–Dodson curve can shift to the left or the right for different individuals. In practical terms, this means that, given the same amount of pressure, some people will become over-stressed very quickly, whilst others will remain insufficiently stimulated to work to their potential. With the huge diversity of students that we have in the majority of universities today, it is a much greater problem to find just the right level of pressure than it is in organizations with a more homogeneous student population, say, for example, in a medical or dental school (where, incidentally, most of the existing research into student stress has been carried out).

To add to the problem, the individual nature of people's perception of stress makes it a difficult subject to research. Nevertheless, there are a number of common denominators that can be used to identify key stressors. It is widely accepted that stress is created by an imbalance between *demand* or environmental pressure, and the *capacity* to meet demand. One model presented by McGrath

(1974) proposed that a person who feels that adaptation to a new situation is within his or her capacity would be expected to feel less stressed than someone who feels unable to meet that demand. Thus, a person with high capabilities might be able to cope with a broad range of environments without feeling stressed. This theory has implications for the many students who now enter Higher Education from a non-academic background and with non-traditional or lower entry qualifications. These types of students may be less likely to feel that the demands of Higher Education are within their capabilities, and may suffer stress as a result. Nor should we ignore here the student at the opposite end of the spectrum, the high achiever who had been expected to secure a place at an 'old' university, and for one reason or another didn't make it. They may feel resentful of having to 'make do' with a place at a so-called new university, may face pressure from parents or peers because of a perceived lack of achievement, and may consequently feel that they do not fit into their new environment.

Life change is another widely researched cause of stress. The changes associated with moving to university usually cause significant social disruption for the student, and it has been argued that this can lead to and maintain raised anxiety (Fisher, 1994). Fisher proposed that life change leads to a reduction in control that an individual has over his or her lifestyle. It is widely documented that a person who perceives that he or she has no control over a situation is more likely to become stressed. In this situation, even small and seemingly insignificant events can become stressful. Indeed, Lazarus has argued that 'daily hassles' can be more damaging than major events (Lazarus and Folkman, 1984).

Finally, stress levels can be affected by workload, and this has two opposing aspects. Work overload is perhaps the most predictable cause of stress, but this itself has two elements which have been described by researchers. 'Quantitative' overload occurs when an individual has *too much* work to do, and 'qualitative' overload occurs when the work is *too difficult* (Cooper et al., 1988). Work underload is the second problem we must consider. Cox has described how ill health can result if an individual is not sufficiently challenged by work. (Cox, 1980).

I have discussed earlier how individuals can be affected quite differently, despite the fact they are under the same pressures from the environment. This individual response results largely from how a person copes with stress. Coping is strongly linked to an individual's personality characteristics, but an important factor which impacts upon a person's ability to cope with stress is the emotional and social support he or she receives from people around them. Numerous studies have shown that people who have many social ties (spouse, friends, relatives and group membership) live longer and are less likely to succumb to stress-related illness than are people who have few supportive social contacts (Cohen and Willis, 1985). This opportunity for social support is greatly reduced in the modern Higher Education environment; modularization has removed the consistent peer-group support associated with traditional degree teaching sessions, staff-student contact is strictly limited, and many students fill their non-study time with one or more jobs, thus limiting their opportunity for socializing or family contact, and increasing time pressures.

There is much published work identifying sources of stress among students and attempting to measure their effect, but most has been carried out in the US, and has mainly focused on specific groups of students (for example, ethnic minorities). Little research has sought to identify the effects of stress in the diverse student population that we have today in the UK, with its non-traditional Higher Education environment as found particularly in some of the 'new' universities. There are many features of this new and still-changing environment which suggest that it is likely to be stressful to students. While most universities cater for the damaging consequences of extreme stress by providing counselling and other support services, it seems certain that there are many students who are suffering unnoticed the effects of under- or over-stress, and are not achieving their potential because of it. My study attempts to investigate this issue.

THE SUNDERLAND STUDY

A study is under way at Sunderland Business School to identify the effects of stress on student learning and the university experience. The first part of this study took place during the 1995–96 academic year. This used the Middlesex Hospital Questionnaire (Crown and Crisp, 1966) to measure levels of stress and identify any patterns in its occurrence. Three hundred full-time undergraduate students completed the questionnaire. The survey was administered during core lecture sessions in order to capture data from all courses and levels. The study found that while most students exhibited what might be considered normal levels of stress, there were significant numbers showing indications of very high levels. In addition, as predicted, some students showed extremely low levels of stress. The data also showed a number of interesting patterns in the stress levels. These have yet to be investigated further.

The second phase of the study, initiated during the 1996–97 academic year, is seeking to identify the key stressors as perceived by the students themselves, and to determine what effect these have on learning and the university experience. In-depth interviews have been carried out within 25 students from all levels. Mature and overseas students were included in the sample. The interview schedule was constructed around the common denominators of stress, ie *change*, *control*, *person–environment fit*, and *workload*. It also investigated the effects of stress and coping methods.

Although many positive influences on motivation were identified, only those key findings from the interviews that related to negative influences on student motivation are reported here. It is planned to develop a full-scale survey from the findings which will lead to a quantitative analysis.

Change

Two aspects of change were investigated during the interviews: whether the change (to university) has been planned for, and whether the reality of the change met with the students' expectations. Both of these aspects have been established as important factors in determining how stressful the change will be.

All but two of the students interviewed had planned to come to university, most stating that they saw it as 'natural progression'. The two students who had not planned to come to university felt that they had been coerced into coming by tutors and family. Both exhibited discontent with all aspects of university life, and said that they frequently considered leaving the course. One, a final-year student, said that he still felt like this, even though he knew he only had a few weeks left at university. The other, a first-year student, was planning to leave at the end of the current semester.

The most significant responses came when the students were asked how the reality of university had differed from their expectations. Thirteen respondents felt that the academic staff were different from what they had expected, and 17 students said that the work was different.

The majority of the views expressed about the staff centred on the issues of support and personal contact. Students were surprised and disappointed that they did not have the same level of personal contact with tutors that they had previously at school or college. 'I thought they'd be a lot more user-friendly. Some lecturers are very remote and back off. It makes me feel frustrated sometimes, although I'm used to it now.'

Of the students claiming that the work was different from what they had expected, only one thought it was harder than he had anticipated, and many felt that it was easier: 'I managed to do my first assignment in no time, and I got a grade 12 for it. I wondered how I'd managed to get that grade when I put so little effort into it.'

Many of the students, particularly those with an A-level background, reported that they had found the student-centred system difficult to get used to, and were not prepared for working on their own initiative. It took them most of the first semester to appreciate that they did not have as much free time as their timetables seemed to indicate!

There were some interesting responses when students were asked how the differences made them feel when they first joined the university, for example:

> It would have kept me interested if the work had been harder. It didn't motivate me to work harder.

> At Christmas, I think that everything got on top of me, and I thought about leaving for a while. I felt that I couldn't continue. I was putting three times the amount of work into my language [module] and neglecting my other work. I don't think I was enjoying it as much as I thought I would.

Four students said that the unexpected differences that they encountered when they first joined the university had made them feel like leaving their course, although only one was still planning to leave.

Control

Two issues, *lack of information* and *group working*, stood out as being areas where students felt that their personal control was being eroded or weakened, leading to anger, frustration, and anxiety in many cases.

More than half the students interviewed felt that they did not have sufficient information about individual modules to make informed choices. More importantly, most felt that they were not given enough information about assignments, despite the fact that all assignments at the Business School are issued with detailed learning outcomes and assessment criteria. The main gap appeared to lie with the interpretation of these criteria. The students felt that they needed some personal guidance and reassurance that they were working along the right lines, and the opportunity to talk through their ideas on an individual basis. Typical comments were:

> We need more information. More teachers talking to you as an individual, rather than as a whole group. Make us feel that we really count. Simple things like that – but it's the simple things that count.

> I think we need a bit more contact than we're getting. I feel as if we are only half-heartedly involved in a subject, we aren't really immersed in it.

Group working produced similar feelings of loss of control and uncertainty, but there was a marked polarity in the comments the students made. On the one hand were those students who wanted to take control, but felt frustrated because they had to bow to others' opinion:

> There are a lot of people who won't do any work, but if you try to get something done, putting forward ideas, the others think that you're trying to take over. There's a lot more conflict in it.

> I feel angry when I have to work in a group. It's very stressful.

At the other end of the scale were the students who felt frustration because they could not contribute as much as they would have liked. There seemed to be varying reasons for this; some students felt too insecure to make a contribution, and, interestingly, several overseas students said that they felt excluded because of language or cultural differences:

> I don't want to say anything because I'm scared of giving the impression that I'm stupid. I don't want people to say that my ideas don't count.

> As an overseas student, if I'm in a group with British students they talk more quickly and easily than I can, and sometimes I don't understand what they are saying, so I feel isolated. They use terms that I don't understand. I just listen, because I think that they don't want to tell me.

Person-environment fit:

Under this heading, students were questioned on how well their needs were met by the university resources. Four categories of resources were looked at: *staff*, *facilities*, the *local surroundings*, and *peers*. On the whole, responses in this category were positive, particularly in relation to the campus facilities. Several students commented that it was the standard of the facilities that had made them choose Sunderland over other Business Schools. Significant comments did, however, emerge from the investigation of the staff–student relationship. Thirteen of those questioned felt that they had received insufficient support from the academic staff. Most of the negative comments related to the inaccessibility of staff, particularly when help with assignments was needed. Students talked about some staff 'not having time for them', or 'not being bothered' to help them. This one issue aroused the strongest feelings throughout the interviews:

> It's demotivating and frustrating.

> They don't care, and that makes me angry and upset. I *want* someone to care.

> They don't want to get close. They keep away from you as much as they can. It makes me feel a bit pushed-out. That's one of the reasons why I'm so unsettled.

Workload

On the whole, the majority of students found both the quantity and level of the work 'manageable'. A small minority found it either too difficult or too easy, but all of those who found it too hard had found a way to cope. It was those students who found the work too easy, particularly in the first year, who voiced the greatest concerns, feeling that they weren't motivated to do well, and consequently were not prepared for the jump in the level of work between the first and second years:

> I want it to be harder. If the work is so easy, I won't feel as if I've accomplished anything.

> I want a feeling of being under pressure.

> I would love to feel motivated by the work like I did last year [at college]. I would love that feeling again. It gives me an adrenaline rush.

WHAT DOES THIS TELL US?

Although this study was designed to investigate stressors, the links with student motivation are clear. When we consider the feelings and opinions voiced by the students on many of these issues, we can see that there are some things that are discouraging them from doing their best, and reducing their enjoyment of the university experience. The key issues, I feel, are those of control and person–environment fit, for these generated the strongest feelings in the students I interviewed. Of course, there are clear parallels here with the traditional theories of motivation; anyone familiar with the Hawthorne experiment (Mayo, 1953) will appreciate that individuals work better if they have some control over their work and feel that they are a valued member of the working environment.

Fundamental to all of this, and the theme that ran through all areas of the interviews, was the staff–student relationship. The students talked about not feeling in control because they did not get enough information or help from some staff; of feeling frustrated because those staff did not have enough time for them; angry when a member of staff was offhand; and demotivated when they realized that a member of staff did not know who they were or what they had achieved. There was an overall sense that some staff did not care about them *as individuals*, and this made many of these students try less hard or become down-hearted.

The findings are particularly perplexing when we consider the support infrastructure that exists within Sunderland Business School to help students with the very problems that seem to be causing the complaints. All students have time-tabled sessions with a 'Study Group Tutor' (weekly in their first year, and fortnightly thereafter). This is a member of the academic staff who acts as a mentor for the student throughout their time at the university. In study group sessions the students are given help on such things as understanding the university systems and regulations; module choice; study skills; applying for placements, and so on. The same member of staff also acts as the students' personal tutor, and can be contacted at any time to provide pastoral support. Academic support is provided for many modules in the form of surgeries, where students can drop in to ask for individual help on specific problems. (This support is in addition to the scheduled lectures, seminars and tutorials for the module.) Although these systems are available and adequately resourced, neither system is extensively used by the students, which would indicate that they feel that they do not need the additional support. This, of course, contradicts the findings of the current study.

This contradiction might be partially explained by a finding which emerged when I pressed the students further on the issue of staff–student relationships. In almost every case, it seemed that their attitude towards the staff had been formed as a result of one or two isolated incidents, often very early in the students' university career. Final-year students recalled in detail the hurt and anger they felt when a member of staff had treated them in a way that they felt was unfair, perhaps in their first semester at university. Although the majority of students conceded that most staff were helpful and approachable, these isolated bad experiences seemed to have overshadowed the positive points, and often made students much more reluctant to approach any staff member subsequently.

Any member of academic staff working in a busy university will appreciate the significance of this issue. I am sure that everyone will recall at least one time when they have snapped at a student simply because he was the umpteenth one to knock on the door that morning to ask the same question; or hurried an assignment brief because there was a meeting to go to; or told a student to 'come back later' and then felt annoyed when the student hasn't returned. Even the most dedicated lecturer has moments like these. They seem insignificant to us at the time, but it would appear that they may be more significant to the students involved.

Most of the students I spoke to expressed a sympathetic understanding for the pressures that lecturers were under, but still found it difficult to cope when they did not get the individual attention they desired. Some students explained that the situation was largely due to the expectations that they brought with them from school or college, where they were typically in much smaller groups and where the tutors had much more time with them; they simply had not been prepared for the very different situation that they found at university.

With all of the increasing pressures and demands on lecturers today it could be argued that there is no way that we can avoid this situation – we simply do not have time to give individual attention 'on demand' to every student. But perhaps it is a vicious circle; if the students are not achieving their full potential and are becoming demotivated, it increases the pressure on staff. Dealing with demotivated students is stressful in itself, but having to set repeat assignments, do additional marking, and teach more classes because of repeats is only making matters worse.

This issue of not giving students individual attention also seems to be affecting what I would term the 'under-stressed' student. By this, I mean the students who report finding the 'level one' work too easy, and who become demotivated as a result. It seems that these students' needs are not being fully met in our efforts to bring everyone up to the same level during the first year of the course, and it could mean that we risk losing some of our more able students because of this.

This study has raised a number of important issues that have implications for student motivation and achievement, quality, and staff development. Although the sample was small, many similar comments were raised over and over again by different students, and were voiced with strong emotion. Most significantly, it suggests that the staff–student relationship is still the key to providing students with an enjoyable and successful university experience, despite the developing culture of student-centred learning and the increasing use of technology in Higher Education today. But, it seems from my discussions that students do not necessarily want or need more formal classes – what they need most is to be treated as individuals and to feel that someone *cares* about their progress. At Sunderland Business School the systems put in place to try to meet these needs do not seem to be fully successful, largely because of the students' reluctance to use them. *Why* this is so needs to be fully investigated, but the expectations that students bring with them to university, and the first interactions that they have with staff seem to play a part. Perhaps there needs to be some education on both sides of the equation, to give both staff and students a better appreciation of the other's perspective.

What *is* clear is that a solution does need to be found, because the students' current feelings of anonymity and isolation seem, in many cases, to be leading to frustration, anger, demotivation and stress. Measurement of just how widespread these feelings are, and the effect they are having on the student population, will form the next part of my study, to be reported at a later date.

REFERENCES

Cohen, S and Willis, T A (1985) 'Stress, social support, and the buffering hypothesis', *Psychological Bulletin*, 98,

Cooper, C L, Cooper, R D and Eaker, L H (1988) *Living with Stress*, Penguin, London.

Cox, T (1980) 'Repetitive work', in Cooper, C L and Payne, R (eds), *Current Concerns in Occupational Stress*, John Wiley, Chichester.

Crown, S and Crisp, A H (1966) 'A short clinical diagnostic self-rating scale for psycho-neurotic patients', *British Journal of Psychiatry*, 112, 917–23.

Fisher, S (1986) *Stress and Strategy*, Lawrence Erlbaum, London.

Fisher, S (1994) *Stress in Academic Life: The Mental Assembly Line*, SRHE and Open University Press, Buckingham.

Fisher, S and Hood, B (1987) 'The stress of the transition to universty': a longitudinal study of vulnerability to pychological disturbance and homesickness', *British Journal of Psychology*, 78, 425–41.

Lazarus, R S and Folkman, S (1984) *Stress, Appraisal and Coping*, Springer Publishing Company, New York.

Mayo, E (1953) *The Human Problems of an Industrial Civilization*, Macmillan, New York.

McGrath, J (1974) *Social and Psychological Factors in Stress*, Holt, Rinehart & Winston, New York.

Selye, H (1956) *The Stress of Life*, Longmans, Green & Co, London.

Yerkes, R M and Dodson, J D (1908) The relation of strength of stimulus to rapidity of habit formation', *Journal of Comparative Neurological Psychology*, 18, 459–82.

14

Undergraduate Research Projects: Motivation and Skills Development

Martin Luck

INTRODUCTION

Research projects are a component of final level undergraduate study in many universities. Their value as a means of studying a specialized subject in depth is well recognized but there is little agreement as to how they should be incorporated into the curriculum and the academic reasons for doing so. The wider implications of project work as a learning tool are seldom discussed and the reasons why students might find them valuable are unclear. Anecdotal evidence indicates that individual universities and departments set their own agendas; details of time, format, resources, expectations and individual responsibility are seldom compared. Exposure to research rarely features in discussions of graduateness and there are no recognized standards for this aspect of Higher Education among institutions.

The aim of this chapter is to consider the value of undergraduate research and to promote discussion of this quiet feature of university education (Luck, 1997a). It can be argued that the experience of research offers the student a great deal more than just a detailed knowledge of his or her main subject. For many, the project is a crucial point in their academic and personal development. It is also a route to the acquisition of transferable skills, useful in seeking employment and in later professional life. A key question, therefore, is: are we properly motivating our students to recognize the full value of their research projects?

THE NOTTINGHAM EXPERIENCE

The author's Faculty has used research projects as a key element in its degree programmes for many years. The project occupies one quarter of student time (45/180 credits) over the final three semesters and is considered a defining element of the course. Students frequently expend disproportionately large amounts of effort on their projects, often producing work of publishable quality.

133

Curiously, conversations with Faculty colleagues revealed an almost total ignorance about how our use of undergraduate projects compares with that in other parts of the university. Similarly, although they expressed much pride in their own approach, colleagues could offer only hearsay evidence about how it compared with that of other institutions in related fields.

In beginning to overcome this lack of information, and with the additional aim of wishing to promote best practice, a survey was carried out on project use within the University of Nottingham. The outcome is a case study covering seven faculties: it contains factual information but also provides a useful reference with which to gauge academic attitudes and strategies.

THE SURVEY

Questionnaires were sent in (1995–96) to each of the 59 departments in seven faculties. A research project was defined as *a piece of research or other extended study, carried out in the final level of study, involving the acquisition and critical assessment of new information and usually resulting in a printed report*. Questions dealt with the formal arrangements for project work and its credit rating, departmental strategies for supervision, methods of assessment, resources, perceived student attitude and motivation, academic effectiveness, and educational and professional value. Some 83 per cent of departments, representing 54 bachelor degree courses, responded (see Table 14.1). Research projects, normally compulsory, were used in 75% of these. (The lowest apparent use (8/16) was in Medicine, but specialist departments in that faculty do not teach final-year undergraduates in the sense described in the questionnaire.)

Credit ratings ranged from 10 to 45 (where a 3-year, 6-semester degree = 360 credits). Regulations for project study, presentation and assessment were invariably set at departmental level, a fact also reflected in the variation in credit ratings within faculties. Projects were largely individual assignments although groups of up to 5 were reported. Academic staff most usually supervised 2–4 project students each per year.

Supervisors invariably perceived student motivation to be 'excellent' or 'very high' and made other comments reflecting extremely positive attitudes on both sides. All referred to the high educational and professional value of the project element of their courses. Several had documentary evidence from employers or external examiners to support this view. Many felt that the value of projects was insufficiently recognized in terms of departmental resources and that projects were run in spite of severe constraints on academic time.

An outstanding feature of the survey responses was the widespread recognition that projects lead to transferable skill development. Respondents listed a wide range of skills which project students might acquire (summarized in Table 14.2). The reporting of skills was largely discipline-neutral, that is to say, it was not possible to subdivide or skew the lists by Faculty. The exception to this was Process Skills, several of which were, as would be expected, limited to but common among the science and engineering faculties.

Table 14.1 Research projects in undergraduate teaching at the University of Nottingham. 1) Summary of questionnaire responses

Faculty (Number of departments)	Response (%)	Project use (% of courses)	Compulsory: Optional	Credit rating Mode (range)	Group size Mode (range)	Students–staff ratio Mode (range)
Arts (13)	69	67	5:1	20 (10–40)	1	2 (1–16)
Engineering (8)	88	89	8:0	30 (20–40)	1 (1–4)	2 (1–6)
Agricultural and Food Sciences (3)	100	100	3:0	45	1	2 (1–8)
Law and Social Sciences (8)	90	89	6:2	40 (10–40)	1 (1–3)	5 (1–10)
Medicine (17)	94	50	9:0		1 (1–5)	1 (1–6)
Nursing and Midwifery (1)	100	100	3:0	40	1	3
Science (7)	71	100	4:1	40 (10–40)	1 (1–2)	4 (2–5)
All	83	75	38:4	10–45	1 (1–5)	2–4 (1–16)

Table 14.2   *Research projects in undergraduate teaching at the University of Nottingham. 2) Transferable skills acquired by students, as reported by supervisors (categorized by MRL)*

Process skills	Presentational skills	Management skills	Personal skills
Problem formulation	Language	Project planning	Independence
Assessing information	Data presentation	Setting objectives	Self-confidence
Sifting of evidence	Oral communication	Project management	Self reliance
Problem solving	Report writing	Progress review	Self-discipline
Library searching	Word processing	Time management	Self-enquiry
Use of literature	Desk-top publishing	Working to deadlines	
Data analysis		Working with others	
Developing arguments		Person management	
Attention to detail		Coping with crises	
Numeracy			
Literacy			
Computing skills			
Laboratory skills			
Safety			
Good laboratory practice			

In summary, the survey shows that research projects are a common feature of undergraduate courses at Nottingham but that regulations and formats are decided locally. Students appear to be highly motivated for this aspect of their degree programme. Academic staff place high value on the project as an educational tool and believe that valuable transferable skills are acquired.

The information generated in this local survey provides the basis for a wider discussion of research as a tool in undergraduate education. Although further information is needed, there is room for a comparison of approaches, between disciplines as well as institutions, and for the dissemination of good practice. The debate can be joined under four headings, as follows:

1. Reasons for using projects.

2. Student motivation.

3. Project design and management.

4. Defined student-visible outcomes.

Reasons for using projects

It is not at all clear that academic staff spend much time considering why research projects are included in their courses. Course review and restructuring are usually evolutionary rather than revolutionary; opportunities for a complete re-think are rare and it is often easier and less disruptive to follow precedent.

Nevertheless, some very positive reasons for introducing students to research are reported:

- *Encouraging focused, in-depth study:* this is the most obvious value of the research experience. The project is one the few elements of a packed undergraduate course where depth is allowed at the expense of breadth. It is likely to be a new experience and students may be surprised at the intensity and single-mindedness required of them.

- *Integrating teaching and research:* the relationship between teaching and research may be intuitive to academics since their profession encourages them to engage successfully in both. Evidence submitted to Dearing (NCIHE, 1997, 8.7 and 11.2) confirms the impact of scholarly activity and research on teaching as a distinctive feature of Higher Education. Students benefit by being taught by staff with a working knowledge of the current limits, trends and uncertainties of their field. Whether students appreciate this relationship, particularly at stages of study where they are being encouraged to accumulate knowledge, is doubtful. By asking students to engage in research, we are encouraging them to recognize the link between the two activities.

- *Introducing research concepts and methods:* This is an inevitable feature of the research experience, although its long-term value to the student is less apparent. Most students do not have a research career in prospect, although there are undoubtedly some for whom the project is a decisive moment in making up their mind (for or against). So for most students the experience of research must be advantageous in other ways. Dearing recognized this advantage, recommending that vocational courses such as medicine 'remain firmly embedded in higher education institutions in a research environment' (NCIHE, 1997, 10.20).

- *Developing an appreciation of the limits of confident knowledge:* knowledge acquired at school and in earlier parts of the undergraduate course is often presented as objective and factual (most student textbooks are sold on that premise). Academics know, however, that most of what is imparted is subjective, uncertain, value-laden and constantly open to revision (Sharp and Howard, 1996). Exposing students to the methods by which new knowledge is acquired is an effective way of making them appreciate this. The advantage in later life should be that the graduate is in a better position to evaluate new information.

- *Developing personal, transferable skills:* as pointed out in the context of the Nottingham Survey, the research project is seen as a very significant route to the acquisition of transferable skills. These skills are, in addition, the subject-specific skills needed for the project itself and which may or may not have lasting value. The transferable skills are the real prize (Purcell and Pitcher, 1996; Yorke, 1997) and would alone be enough to justify the inclusion of research in a degree course.

- *Tangible outcome:* departments may have non-educational reasons for encouraging student research. According to Nottingham colleagues, the effort and resources expended on undergraduate projects are seldom repaid in terms of RAE-valid outcome. Nevertheless, there was evidence in the survey that students contribute significantly to the departmental research effort. Student projects were commonly used as pilot work or to 'test the water' before further resources were committed. A few departments reported that student work led to a publishable outcome, although this was almost always as a small part of a larger study. Within vocational courses, especially in applied science, engineering and design-related fields, students may contribute to the completion of commissioned work.

Student motivation

Nottingham staff were unanimous in finding students highly motivated for research work. The reasons why students are motivated are less clear and it would be necessary to consult them directly. Nevertheless, several types of student motivation can be suggested and defined in the context of undergraduate project work (see Table 14.3).

Table 14.3 *Types of student motivation for research project work*

Type of motivation	Characteristics applied to research project
Extrinsic	Required for satisfactory completion of the course Mark may carry high weighting or determine degree class Institutional culture sets pressure to do well in research Project topic or specific skills may be related to career aspirations
Intrinsic	Seen as natural development of interest in the subject area Reflects a personal goal to contribute to knowledge Opportunity for personal involvement with and ownership of the subject Means of expressing independence and self-confidence
Achievement	Allows demonstration of personal achievement and competence Opportunity for exploiting time-management and organized study skills Means of setting and responding to personal challenges Peer competition based on personal rather than institutional challenge

It would also be useful to know whether students share, in general, the supervisors' reported impression that high levels of enthusiasm are maintained for the duration of the project. Presumably not all students find their project work constantly stimulating. Projects are not always successful and the quality of supervision varies. These are areas where additional data are needed.

Student interest can be engaged and maintained in a number of ways (see Table 14.4) and the identification of best practice in these areas would be one of the major benefits of a wider discussion both within and between institutions.

Table 14.4   *Approaches to encouraging undergraduate interest in research project work*

Approach	Practice
Staff attitude	Emphasis on limits to current knowledge during formal teaching Staff make themselves accessible to students Students made aware of staff research interests Students encouraged to attend departmental research seminars Students made to feel that their research is real and valuable
Departmental culture	Vertical communication between new and existing project students Research staff encouraged to be involved in student projects Project students contribute to departmental seminar programme High visibility of completed dissertations within department Recognize student input to published material
Management strategy	Encourage student input into choice of topic Clear strategy for allocation of students to supervisors Clear definition of supervisor's role Provision of clear guidelines for dissertation Specific modules teaching research and presentation techniques Allocation of specific resources for project work

Project design and management

Students are likely to be motivated by success and demotivated by lack of it. The success of the project depends on student commitment and ability but also, crucially, on sound design, effective management and good supervision. It is evident that undergraduate research needs to be handled in a completely different manner from post-graduate research. The following characteristics of project students need to be recognised in particular:

- Their time is very short and they are doing other things concurrently.

- They have had little time to assimilate fully the earlier, background parts of their course.

- They may lack self-confidence and be unsure of their academic abilities.

- They may be uncertain of their interests and not necessarily committed to a research career.

These features can strongly influence the way in which projects are designed and managed. For example, there needs to be a clear assessment of risk and the consequences of failure. With little opportunity for repeating work that gives an unsatisfactory result, it becomes essential that the project has intrinsic value (knowledge gained, methods used, improved understanding, etc) beyond its outcome. In other words, the risk must be borne by the supervisor rather than the student. At the same time, however, the student needs to feel that their research is real and to understand that uncertainty of outcome is one of its defining characteristics; a project which is guaranteed to work will lose much of its excitement and interest.

It is not uncommon for departments to offer specific training in research methods as part of the undergraduate course. Such modules often include discussions of research philosophy where matters such as uncertainty and risk can be introduced. In some cases, training modules are extended into the design phase of the project itself and students are required to provide a detailed analysis of the topic, their investigative approach and the resources required.

The introduction of such a module expresses, on the part of the department, a commitment to research and a strong belief that it forms a valuable part of student experience. It also means that time for other areas of the curriculum is squeezed. This can be a particular problem in vocational areas or where the demands of external course accreditation need to be fulfilled. Unfortunately, perhaps, there is no agreement about the extent to which degree courses should be designed around research nor whether 'graduateness' implies some experience of it. It is interesting to note that the University of Sydney incorporates 'an appreciation of the requirements and characteristics of scholarship and research' among the specified knowledge skills of its graduates (NCIHE, 1997, Appendix 5, Annex 4).

Defined student-visible outcomes

While academics may appreciate the educational value of exposure to research, as discussed above, students themselves, especially as they enter this stage of their studies, are less likely to be aware of what they can expect to achieve. Additional motivation can be given by defining the possible outcomes of the project from the outset. Such transparency may also affect the students' choice of topic, their work strategy and their approach to problems. Four types of outcome can be defined:

1. *Intrinsic:* this may include:
a   subject-specific knowledge or experience gained by studying the topic in depth;
b   a tangible product (eg a construction, plan, model, computer program, etc);
c   specific training of vocational value.

The extent to which any of these is applicable is highly discipline-dependent.

2. *Dissertation:* the Nottingham survey defined project work in terms of a printed outcome and it is evident that the formal dissertation is an almost universal end-point for student projects. Word processing and some form of loose or hard binding are invariably specified. For most students, the dissertation is the largest and most detailed item of written work they have yet produced. Available technology means that they have total control over production, as well as writing and content. They therefore have the opportunity to produce a document of professional quality which may, in itself, be motivating.

3. *Publication:* as discussed above, the survey revealed much departmental variation in the extent to which student research work is of publishable value. Departments will therefore take individual approaches as to whether they explicitly encourage their students on that basis. The author's experience is that prospective students frequently ask whether a project's results are likely to be published, evidently seeing this as a motivating possibility. More importantly, perhaps, the fact that they ask the question is indicative of some appreciation of how progress in academic scholarship is achieved.

4. *Skills:* it is becoming increasingly common for the documents describing university modules to identify the transferable skills which a student might expect to acquire by following them. Dearing strongly recommends that this is universally done (NCIHE, 1997, Recommendation 21). With research project modules, given the diversity of topics, methods and approaches even within a single subject area, this can be difficult to do other than by using vague statements of intent. Nevertheless, as the Nottingham survey clearly showed, supervisors are convinced of the tremendous skill development potential of research projects. Opportunities need to be found for using skill development potential to motivate students and also to encourage staff to build this element deliberately into project design. At best, students would use the range of skills on offer as a criterion for selecting the type of research they wish to undertake.

On the matter of transferable skill recognition, the author's Faculty has piloted a Certificate of Skills based on the research project experience (Luck, 1997b). This does not solve the problem of *a priori* skill specification but it does create a motivating expectation on the part of the student and causes them to be aware of skill development as their work proceeds. The Certificate is generated at the time of dissertation submission and lists the skills, categorized according to Table 14.2, which the student and supervisor mutually recognize as having been developed or enhanced as a result of carrying out the work. The certificate is qualitative rather than quantitative (levels of skill achievement are not assessed) and is designed to encourage the student to make explicit recognition of his or her own personal development. The certificate can be appended to the CV or used as supporting evidence for job applications. As such, it enables an employer to see beyond the title of the dissertation towards the real experiences and potential of the candidate and should provoke productive discussion at interview.

CONCLUSION

Academic staff and course designers have several excellent reasons for wishing to expose undergraduate students to the experience of research. Student motivation appears high although the reasons for this have yet to be determined at first hand. It is also likely that further discussion between institutions and departments will identify additional ways of promoting student interest. Students need to be encouraged to recognize the extrinsic as well as the intrinsic value of their project work and, particularly, to recognize research as a vehicle for the acquisition of valuable transferable skills.

REFERENCES

Luck, M R (1997a) 'Undergraduate research projects as a route to skill development', *Capability*, 3, 2, 21–4.

Luck, M R (1997b) 'Undergraduate research projects: what are they worth?' *The New Academic*, 6, 1, 23–4.

National Committee of Inquiry into Higher Education (the Dearing Report) (1997) *Report of the National Committee*, HMSO, London.

Purcell, K and Pitcher, J (1996) *Great Expectations: The New Diversity of Graduate Skills and Aspirations*, Higher Education Careers Service Unit, Manchester.

Sharp, J A and Howard, K (1996) *The Management of a Student Research Project*, 2nd edn, Gower, Aldershot.

Yorke, M (1997) 'The skills of graduates: a small enterprise perspective', *Capability*, 3, 1, 27–32.

15

Multidisciplinary Student Teams Motivated by Industrial Experience

Paul Wellington

INTRODUCTION

Professional education in fields such as engineering and business should not only focus on the content of that discipline but also must develop graduates with appropriate knowledge, skills and attitudes, together with the ability to apply them to the types of functions likely to be encountered in the workplace. The projects discussed in this chapter are aimed at developing broad-ranging student skills by motivating them in realistic simulations of the industrial and business environment.

The process of product development is one of the most challenging functions of graduates from technical and business courses. New product design and manufacture must meet market demand at an appropriate price, but rarely have tertiary courses attempted to ensure that their graduates develop the skills needed to perform well in such processes.

In 1996, six teams, containing seven to ten students from marketing, design, industrial engineering and accounting at Monash University, worked on projects offered by local manufacturers. The students were mainly third years, hence bringing substantial expertise in their discipline to bear. Each problem had significant elements of product design, process selection, materials handling, cost accounting and market research, thus offering challenges to students from each discipline. This chapter reviews the motivating aspects of these projects and considers the resulting benefits to the students and ultimately to their future employers.

STATED LEARNING OBJECTIVES

Students were given the following list of objectives (Wellington, 1996):

- To formulate, through group interactions, solutions to business problems which require the integration of design, manufacturing and marketing solutions.

- To separate engineering, accounting and marketing problems into solvable elements; to explore solutions mindful of the influence each discipline area has on the other.

- To demonstrate understanding of manufacturing design and the possible need for redesign.

- To exhibit committee chairperson, secretarial and recording skills.

- To negotiate responsibilities within a group to ensure effective project management.

- To organize communication systems to ensure effective project management.

- To compile, present and defend a syndicate report on the project.

- To assess personal and peer performance in achieving individual and group objectives.

- To value the complexity of issues and range of people affected by the introduction of new products and technology.

- To appreciate the degree of involvement necessary in the decision-making process in a typical industrial situation from disciplines including planning, marketing, finance, design, processing, quality, legal and human resource management.

To effectively meet these objectives, students needed to not only apply the knowledge developed in other subjects, but also to develop a new range of team and problem solving skills. By structuring the projects to reflect current theories of industrial best practice, such as using multidiscipline teams for concurrent engineering new products, student motivation and hence performance, should be optimized.

THE NEED FOR TEAM SKILLS IN INDUSTRY

In the increasingly complex industrial environment of the 1990s, New Product Development (NPD) is seen as essential for companies to remain competitive and profitable. Floyd *et al.* (1993) emphasize the increasing trend to 'concurrent engineering' which involves all relevant departments working simultaneously on design, manufacturing and marketing, which they claim enables improvements of between 30 and 60 per cent in NPD cycle time, as well as improving quality and decreasing costs. They point out that cross-functional design arms need skills including marketing, research and development (R&D), design, manufacturing, testing and quality. They go on to identify barriers to communication stemming from inter-departmental rivalries and inappropriate company reward structures. Parsaei and Sullivan (1993) also discuss the benefits and difficulties with concurrent engineering, indicating great benefits can accrue from multidiscipline teams provided problems such as jargon and different personal views of the world can be overcome.

Bertodo (1989) stated that the training programme implemented at Austin Rover for young graduates cost over £10 million annually to supplement formal education, which was 'largely preoccupied with the enhancement of narrow technical expertise, to the detriment of wider attributes'. He discussed other approaches 'with the aim of increasing the pool core people familiar with both the technologies and practices of the business, beyond the engineering functions, ie finance, marketing, merchandising etc'.

The Monash projects give undergraduates the opportunity to experience cross-functional team work in a concurrent engineering approach to new product development, hence achieving the knowledge and confidence to participate in such situations in industry with little need for further training.

EDUCATIONAL BENEFITS FLOWING FROM PROJECT WORK

Kjursdam (1993) discussed findings of 20 years' experience of project-based courses at the University of Aalborg in Denmark, where he claimed that their team approach enhanced communication and interpersonal skills, application of theory to practice and developing graduates who 'had no problems with economics or statuary conditions, or in working with specialists from other areas'. This is contrary to the findings of Beswick *et al.* (1988) who found that graduates from Australian universities felt their more traditional courses should have better prepared them in developing 'self-awareness and confidence, industrial relations and people-management and management of cost and resources and understanding of the place of engineering in the broader business context'. Albrecht (1994) and Kuczynski (1996) identified lack of skills in accounting and marketing graduates respectively, including communication, decision-making and leadership skills, problem solving and working with other disciplines.

Wellington (1989) described how engineering and marketing students applied their skills to the design, development, construction, promotion and funding of a solar-powered vehicle that was subsequently entered, with significant success, in an international competition in 1990. The success of the entry was substantially due to the dedication and enthusiasm of each group of students encouraged by the positive interaction between the mechanical and electrical engineers and marketeers. The projects discussed in this chapter ensure that these benefits will continue, and by optimizing student motivation, high achievement in multiple skills becomes possible.

MOTIVATIONAL THEORIES RELEVANT TO PROJECT WORK

Pintrich and Schunk (1996) discuss various theories of motivation in education with the following being most relevant to large group problem-based learning. They emphasize that group motivation is optimized when having a clear goal to attain, feeling efficacious about performing well, having positive outcome expectations, attributing success to ability, effort and strategy, and receiving relevant and prompt feedback. They quote Slavin (1983a, b) who found that group motivation differs from individual motivation as a result of the group and reward structures. He found co-operative work often leads to better perform- ance than individual work but an appropriate incentive structure must be in effect, and individual accountability must be identifiable and independently rewarded. The Monash projects have required each student to undertake responsibility for different aspects of the project and peer assessment ensures that rewards are given independently.

They also outline Ford's Motivational Systems Theory (1992), from which they derived implications for teachers (facilitators) which included:

- goal activation – projects must encourage students to attain their own goals;
- goal salience – goals must be clear and a student must know what is expected;
- multiple goals – should lead to greater success;
- goal alignment – goals should be aligned with each other, not in conflict;
- feedback – must be relevant and prompt;
- optimal challenge – tasks should be difficult and challenging but not excessive;
- reality – self-efficacy will develop from achieving skills seen as 'real'.

In the Monash study under discussion, the course has been structured to encompass these objectives although goal salience must be derived by the students with the guidance of the industry partners and academic supervisors, not provided in explicit detail.

Pintrich and Schunk cite the comment of Ames (1992) who found that tasks should be structured to highlight short-term goals which will help students feel efficacious about goals, hence interim reports are important. They also discuss the concept of locus of control (Rotter, 1966) who claimed that an internal locus, which allows students to feel they are in control of their own destiny, is essential to high motivation as compared to an external locus in which they feel controlled by others. They also discuss studies of student interest in the topics on which they work, specifically citing Krapp *et al.* (1992) who suggested interest could be personal, situational or a 'psychological state' in which personal and situational interest reinforce each other. The interest inherent in the Monash projects has largely developed from the industrial situation rather than prior personal interest in the product.

Argyle (1989) discusses intrinsic motivation in the work place, indicating that most people want to do intrinsically interesting work that may involve solving difficult tasks leading to increased competence, which is further enhanced by receiving positive feedback. He discusses achievement motivation, found commonly in managers or skilled workers, motivated by the likelihood of recognition by others and a boost of self-esteem by success, which conform to need for esteem and self-actualization as proposed by Maslow (1954).

Thomas *et al.* (1996) emphasized the need for assessment to be relevant to objectives, and claim that process objectives should be evaluated by observation, not by written exams. Hence, they proposed that the students should be assessed by clients, peers, the students themselves and their supervisors. The existing study contains elements of each of these, weighted to reflect the learning objectives (Brown-Parker *et al.*, 1997).

The Monash projects are structured to provide a real challenge which will require students to apply existing skills and to develop new skills to achieve a goal which they themselves set and for which they are responsible. Interim deadlines are set and prompt detailed feedback is given. The outcomes of the group are seen and assessed by the other members of their group, their supervisor and the company. The students will also develop self-confidence by working effectively in a simulated work experience with other disciplines and on real problems, especially if they are successful.

ESTABLISHING AND ORGANIZING THE MULTIDISCIPLINE PROJECTS

For the design and engineering students, these projects were compulsory, while for marketing and accounting students, they were electives. Six teams were established with five industrial engineering, one industrial design, one or two accounting and marketing students being a typical composition.

The projects investigated the feasibility of the companies developing a product for a new market. The products were a 4-litre plastic pail, a 1 500-litre plastic tank and rubber anti-vibration mounts. Market research to determine the size and type of market and a realistic sales price, design of a new product to meet the appropriate regulations and evaluating the capital expenditure for manufacturing that product, were required. The manufacturing process was costed to determine potential profitability and hence whether the company should go ahead.

Each team established schedules for members to undertake the role of chairperson and minutes secretary over the course of the semester, and projects were divided into similar sized components with each member selecting an area of responsibility (Wellington and Thomas, 1997).

Figure 15.1 gives a graphical representation of the separate stages of the project, the responsibilities of each discipline, and the decision-making process.

In Figure 15.1, the six numbers identify the following:

1.   The disciplines involved.

2.   The work described in the first interim report.

3. and 4.   The work leading to and selection of the preferred concept featured in the 2nd interim report.

5.   The detail development discussed in the draft final report.

6.   The final presentation and report.

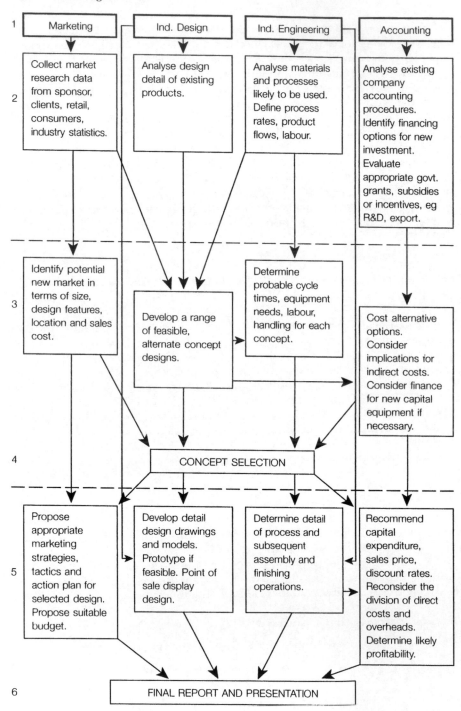

Figure 15.1 *Analysis of group responsibilities and decision-making*

The arrows indicate the sequence of decision-making and interaction between disciplines at various stages while the dotted lines indicate the major intermediate deadlines when interim reports are submitted and feedback is given.

Each group held formal meetings weekly which were observed by the supervisor who awarded marks for contributions by each student. The meeting was formally chaired and minuted, with each student rotating through both roles in which they were also assessed.

The groups prepared two interim reports; the first in week five and the second in week ten of the semester. Copies of each report were sent to the relevant host company, who, in many cases, provided useful feedback. The individual contributions in each report were assessed.

A final report and formal presentation of their recommendations were made by each group to members of their sponsoring company at the end of semester. These were assessed by both the company (with some moderation) and supervisors, amounting to 50 per cent of the total marks.

OUTCOMES

The assessment of the students by their peers and supervisors showed good correlation and has been discussed elsewhere (Brown-Parker *et al.*, 1997). The majority of students received higher marks than in more traditional subjects, partly as a result of the companies and supervisors emphasizing the professional standards expected, resulting in most impressive team efforts from five of the six teams. While critics may query the results, the combination of company, supervisor and peer assessment based on both direct observation of meetings and presentations and written reports, generally showing high correlation, has overcome many problems encountered in assessing group work.

FEEDBACK FROM THE COMPANIES

While the companies were quite impressed by the reports and presentations, they indicated key areas to be improved. These included justifying all recommendations by detailed cost analysis and market surveys. The engineering students were advised to quantify their observations and explore all feasible processes, not just one or two possibilities. The marketers needed to explore all areas of product use and buyer preference so as to define the exact market requirements, and should have found alternative means of obtaining critical information if their first approach was unsuccessful. The accountants were advised to attempt to fully understand the company's accounting system and consider all relevant cost factors, including government grants and incentives for R&D.

ANALYSIS OF STUDENT FEEDBACK

Student feedback was obtained from individual reports, in which they commented on what they had learnt, the way in which their group had performed, ideas for improvements to the project organization, and their attitude to peer assessment. The main points emerging from this evaluation were:

- The multi-disciplinary nature of the project was strongly endorsed, with 42 of the respondents indicating a positive attitude, one hesitant and only three finding it of little benefit. The student enthusiasm seems to contain elements of gaining a more comprehensive view of the problem than would occur in narrower based teams, as well as the feeling that they are experiencing processes likely to become more important as their careers progress.

- Value of industry contact – 25 students made positive comments about the value of the industry experience and having been involved in a real world project.

These comments came uniformly from students in each discipline. There were 17 responses which expressed a degree of frustration that the sponsoring company did not provide as much information as the students had desired. In some instances, the information was not available, the right questions were not asked of the right people or the company was unprepared to provide commercially sensitive information. A number of students also realized that often the information was simply not known, and they had to use innovative thinking to find a solution.

- Some accounting students found that their company used unfamiliar systems, which, along with abbreviated procedures and approximations, provided a significant lesson in dealing with real-world situations. In one company, students discovered a communication breakdown between production and accounting, leading to incorrect data for cost calculations. This was an excellent example of one type of problem which these projects are aimed at addressing.

- The formal meeting structure – 38 students expressed enthusiasm about their introduction to formal meetings, although ten students, mainly in the less successful teams, had reservations about the implementation in their particular group.

- Skills developed – 22 students commented that they believed that the project enhanced their communication skills and 16 students indicated development of other organizational skills including planning, co-ordinating and motivating others. A number of mainly accounting and marketing students with no prior project experience commented on the unanticipated difficulties in gathering information and dealing with the unstructured nature of 'real' problems.

- Division of the problems – 9 students highlighted the skills that they had developed in learning how to subdivide a large, unstructured problem into components of similar importance and then to ensure that each facet was the responsibility of one member of the team.

- Peer assessment – 30 of the 35 students who commented on this issue were in favour of the notion of peer assessment, but many thought that its administration could be improved.

CONCLUSIONS

The real world of business and industry is continuously changing and innovative educational methods can ensure that graduates are adequately prepared. By participating in multi-disciplinary project teams, students develop a broad range of interpersonal and communication skills and insights into issues outside their own area of responsibility.

The scope for larger teams to address the multiple facets of real problems has allowed more comprehensive solutions to such problems to be found, leading in turn to increased feelings of achievement and self-confidence. The reality and optimal challenge of the problems, coupled with direct feedback, were also appreciated by the team members. The division of such projects into clear areas of responsibility allowing each student to set their own goals and be assessed, both formally and informally, on their ability to meet those goals, helped develop a high level of responsibility among most students.

The types of products investigated prompted little inherent personal interest, but the student comments indicate that the interest generated by the situation was highly motivational. The success the teams had in meeting their goals was obviously derived from the commitment and effort of most students. The standard which the students achieved, could not be taught or developed in traditional lectures and tutorials, but only as a result of the motivation developed by the teamwork and the perceived reality of the problems investigated.

ACKNOWLEDGEMENTS

These projects were only made possible by the enthusiasm and dedication of the staff of Monash University involved who included: Ms Linda Brennan and Ms Irene Powell (Marketing), Mr Brian Clarke (Accounting), Mr Ted Kayser (Industrial Design), Dr Lin Ma and Mr Don Shen'dan (Industrial Engineering), Mr Ian Thomas (Teaching Services) and Dr Judi Brown-Parker (Professional Development).

REFERENCES

Albrecht W S *et al.* (1994) 'An accounting curriculum for the next century', *Issues in Accounting Education*, Fall 1994, pp.401–25.

Ames, C (1992) 'Classrooms: goals, structures, and student motivation', *Journal of Educational Psychology*, 79, 409–14.

Argyle, M (1989) *The Social Psychology of Work*, Penguin, London.

Bertodo, R (1989) 'Human resource deployment for design excellence', *Proceedings of the Institute of Mechanical Engineers, international conference, ICED '89*, Vol. VI, pp.39–56.

Beswick, D, Julian, J and McMillan, C (1988) *A National Survey Of Engineering Students And Graduates: Review of the Discipline of Engineering, vol. 3*, AGPS, Canberra, Appendices, pp.39–106.

Brown-Parker, J, Thomas, I and Wellington, P (1997) 'Peer assessment of student performance: measuring congruency of perceptions in a multidisciplinary team', *Research and Development in Higher Education*, 20.

Floyd, T D, Levy, S, Wolfman, A B (1993) *Winning the New Product Development Battle*, IEEE Engineers Guide to Business, IEEE, New York.

Ford, M (1992) *Motivating Humans: Goals, Emotions, and Personal Agency Beliefs*, Sage, Newbury Park, CA.

Kjursdam, F (1993) 'Evaluation of project-organised engineering education', *European Journal of Engineering Education*, 18, 4, 375–80.

Krapp, A, Hidi, S and Renninger, K A (1992) *The Role of Interest in Learning and Development*, Hillsdale, NJ.

Kuczynski, A (1996) *Marketing Graduates Lacking Skills*, Australian Professional Marketing Training Institute, St Leonards, Australia.

Maslow, A H (1954) *Motivation and Personality*, Harper, New York.

Parsaei, H R and Sullivan, W G (1993) *Concurrent Engineering*, Chapman and Hall, London.

Pintrich, P R and Schunk, D H (1996) *Motivation in Education: Theory, Research and Applications*, Merrill, Prentice Hall, Columbus, Ohio.

Rotter, J B (1996) 'Generalised expectancies for internal versus external control of reinforcement', *Psychological Monographs*, 80 (1, Whole No. 609).

Slavin, R (1983a) *Cooperative Learning*, New York, Longman.

Slavin, R (1983b) 'When does cooperative learning increase student achievement?' *Psychological Bulletin*, 94, 429–45.

Thomas, I D, Hadgraft, R G and Daly, P S (1996) 'Issues related to the use of peer assessment in engineering courses using a problem-based learning approach', *Proceedings of the third East–West Congress on Engineering Education*, Gdynia Maritime Academy, Gdynia Poland.

Wellington, P (1996) *Preliminary Information for Multidisciplinary Industry Based Projects IND 3322 and AIKT 3631*, Monash University, Melbourne.

Wellington, R P (1989) 'Competition develops organizational skills', *Proceedings of the Institute of Mechanical Engineers, ICED '89*, Harrogate, UK, Vol. 2, pp.1027–38.

Wellington, R P and Thomas, I D (1997) 'Engineering and business students cooperate on industry based projects. Paper presented at the first Asia Pacific forum on engineering and technology education', Monash University, Melbourne, 6–9 July 1997.

16

Motivational Perspectives and Work-Based Learning

Debbie Keeling, Eleri Jones, David Botterill and Colin Gray

INTRODUCTION

This chapter explores the role that motivation plays in promoting Work-Based Learning (WBL), emphasizing organizational–individual relationships, appropriate support structures and the need for effective communication. WBL is important within a wider framework of LifeLong Learning (LLL), which enjoyed a high profile throughout 1996 – the European Year of Lifelong Learning (Department for Education and Employment, 1996). LLL impacts on traditional perspectives of UK education, emphasizing the importance of credit for recognition and accreditation of learning achieved in educational establishments, work, community or home, and necessitating a fundamental review of delivery and the role of educational technological support. A wide range of open and distance learning and WBL schemes have been established, promoting access to education and facilitating progression, eroding temporal and geographic constraints. LLL, and promotion of a knowledge economy, require a new vision of education extending beyond traditional boundaries to embrace a range of experiences within a coherent framework for post-16 education, acknowledging diversity of educational achievement and providing for individual learners.

WBL, defined as 'learning linked to the requirements of people's jobs . . . (a) learning for work (b) learning at work and (c) learning through work' (Seagraves *et al.*, 1996, p.6), is diverse, ranging from formally delivered courses and in-house training to informal opportunities (eg mentoring, work-shadowing, job swaps and departmental exchange). WBL emphasizes continual social and technological changes facing organizations and the key role of personal development in organizational stability and success (Arnold *et al.*, 1991; Department of Employment, 1992).

To exploit WBL as a resource for individuals and industry alike, the dynamics of the learning setting need exploration, including the impact that the organization itself has on the individual. Arguably, the key to WBL success, while supported by education–industry partnerships and government funding, is the individual employee. Regardless of the extent of WBL opportunities, benefits must be recognized by individuals for learning to take place and organizational benefit from knowledge acquisition and application to accrue.

Individual participation in, and learning from, WBL will be heavily influenced by motivational perspectives. An individual should value WBL as a useful resource, addressing individual and organizational needs, if they are to exploit opportunities fully. Learner motivation is identified as an essential prerequisite to effective learning in traditional educational settings (Slavin, 1991) and training at work (Goldstein, 1986). The learner must be 'ready to learn' (ie have the necessary ability, motivation and attitudes to learning) or learning will not take place (Goldstein, 1986) and must be properly resourced so that he or she does not have to cope with a plethora of demotivating issues, eg financial and temporal constraints (Slavin, 1991). Furthermore, motivation must be sustained to promote application and contextualization of knowledge appropriately (Walberg and Vguroglu, 1980). Attempts to acquire or apply new learning may fail if conflicting pressures are inadequately managed (Marx, 1982). However, despite the potential importance of motivation in WBL little research has as yet investigated this issue.

Environmental factors also impact on WBL. A supportive learning environment must recognize fundamental learning principles and contextualize learning to enhance knowledge transfer from training room to work setting (Goldstein, 1986). Training should be based on clearly established aims and objectives derived from a systematic job/skills/task/person analysis and must be effectively evaluated to inform future training (Arnold *et al.*, 1991). Although findings focus on formal training and traditional student–instructor delivery modes, there are important lessons for WBL with its wider range of learning paradigms. Indeed, in traditional educational settings environmental variables are differentially related to various aspects of motivation (Knight, 1991), indicating the potentially complex inter-relationship between environmental and individual factors. This chapter explores employee views of their learning environment and its impact on their perception of, participation and success in, WBL. A sound learning environment at work should promote WBL credibility and validity through: communicating employer commitment to WBL 'from the top'; resourcing learners appropriately; making WBL opportunities explicit; cultivating an ethos and culture that respects learning and is 'ready to learn' (Brennan and Little, 1996; Work-Based Learning Network Conference, 1996). Problems may arise from: WBL competing with the commercial focus and workloads; organizational structures reducing flexibility; inadequate resourcing; a lack of understanding by the organization and the individual about the commitment demanded by WBL.

WBL research has focused on operational issues, although some has considered the learning environment, indicating the need for provision of an emotionally, practically and politically supportive environment by all stakeholders – trainees, trainers, mentors, colleagues and line managers (Brennan and Little, 1996). Other studies have demonstrated organizational and individual cost–benefits (Department of Employment, 1992; Work-Based Learning Network, 1996). Employers benefit from the salience of WBL to the organization and pragmatic application of knowledge to organizational problems. WBL can be an integral part of, and enhance, employee development plans. However, there are inevitably costs, not least financial. Employees benefit through personal development and gaining occupationally relevant knowledge, enhancing work performance and promotion prospects. Costs to the employee may be financial or result from conflicting temporal pressures.

Currently no coherent theory underpins our understanding of the role of motivation in WBL. Findings from research in traditional and work settings have important implications for the implementation of WBL schemes, indicating the need to identify individual and environmental factors and their complex interactions. Furthermore, not only formal, but also informal, aspects of WBL must be recognized as there are important differences in individual recognition and perception of each. Adult education (AE) researchers have argued that an individual must be aware of the available educational resources if they are to take advantage of them (Cookson, 1986) and this must certainly apply to WBL where implicit learning opportunities may go unrecognized.

It is important to establish the definition of motivation within this project as the abundance of motivational theories can confuse (Landy and Becker, 1987) and make inter-study comparison difficult. These theories can be categorized as: needs; values; goal setting; behaviour, and may be complementary falling along a continuum addressing various parts of a single process (Aamodt, 1991; Locke and Henne, 1986 (see Figure 16.1).

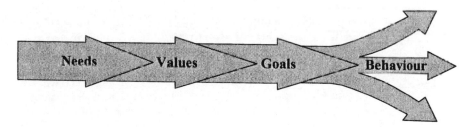

Figure 16.1 *The motivation process*

Source: Locke and Henne, 1986

Motivation is thus defined as a multi-staged process encompassing needs, values, goals and behaviour where each stage amplifies inter-individual differences. To fully understand the role of motivation in WBL we must consider organizational and individual perspectives of these elements. Although these factors have not been extensively studied in the WBL literature, the AE literature confirms their importance (eg Cookson, 1986; Courtney, 1992; Darkenwald and Merriam, 1982) and it seems reasonable that they should apply to WBL. AE models also indicate the importance of environmental conditions to participation in WBL, including: financial issues; geographical constraints; peer or family influences; awareness of environmental opportunities. As the employer creates the learning environment for WBL there may be important motivational influences arising from the complex employer–employee inter-actions (Argyle, 1989; Coates, 1993; Steers and Porter, 1991) and the creation of WBL opportunities, facilitating WBL participation through removing barriers to learning and explicitly demonstrating 'respect for learning' and 'readiness to learn'.

This study seeks to promote understanding of motivational perspectives in WBL by exploring:

- employee definitions of WBL in terms of the extent of recognition of formal and informal aspects and perceptions of WBL support structures and communication;

- motivational issues against a framework of: needs; values; goals; behaviour.

METHODOLOGY

Due to the lack of previous research in this area, this study is exploratory in nature. Work-based focus groups (five groups of 4–8 people) were used to identify factors that influence individual participation in WBL. Participants were drawn from companies within the financial sector in Cardiff and held similar hierarchical positions within their organizations. The financial sector was targeted as it is developing in Cardiff, with the relocation of several large international companies. This sector continually faces new operational and technological developments to maintain competitiveness and productivity and has an on-going need for efficient and effective training. Promoting formal and informal WBL opportunities is vitally important to such companies, offering organizationally relevant training and efficient use of everyday experiences.

Focus group discussions explored: individual definitions and recognition of formal and informal WBL opportunities; individual perceptions of learning needs; the value placed on WBL; learning goals and participation in WBL; individual perceptions of organizational goals and the learning environment and its effect on WBL, including the structure of WBL schemes.

The Learning Diagnostic Questionnaire (LDQ) was used to identify individual scores on three scales: knowledge and skills (knowledge about the learning process and the ability to learn from experience); attitudes and emotions (attitudes towards learning from experience and emotional robustness to 'bounce back' from failure and try new things); working environment (the extent to which the learning environment generates learning opportunities) – predisposing factors for the promotion and facilitation of WBL (Honey and Mumford, 1989). Individual perspectives of WBL are compared with LDQ scores to identify the effect of individual predisposition to learning.

The results are discussed involving two key areas: the definition, recognition and participation in WBL; the individual motivation process.

RESULTS

Although individual definitions of WBL were diverse, initially formal courses (both internal and external) dominated, for example, 'Work-based learning is learning that has something to do with your work . . . including . . . management training and technical training, . . . project management skills, time management training and PC training'. This has serious implications for exploitation of informal opportunities, which may be taken for granted or not recognized and the potential learning diminished. Following further discussion, however, a number of everyday experiences were identified from which individuals had been able to learn and apply learning to new situations, for example, 'People [are] moving to newly formed business units or across functions so . . . there has to be . . . 'one-to-one' training . . . like, "this is how we do this".' Here the value of talking to colleagues and observing skills 'on-the-job' was emphasized. Individuals were asked to identify examples of WBL that they participated in, a selection of which are presented in Table 16.1.

Table 16.1 *Examples of formal and informal WBL opportunities*

Formal WBL	Informal WBL
Technical training (especially IT)	Software applications through daily exposure to usage
Management training	One-to-one desk training on functions
Language training	Telephone requests and irate customers
NVQ, eg level 3 in customer care	Line manager explaining errors and how to address problems
Certificates relating to various financial associations	Work-shadowing
Counselling skills	Team meetings

WBL is clearly diverse and the utilization of formal *and* informal aspects of WBL underlines its potential importance in the workplace, indicating that focusing just on one or other, as in previous studies, is unjustified. Individuals more readily gave examples of formal training received than informal WBL opportunities, reflecting the initial definitions of WBL offered. This issue is critical and requires exploration by organizations as non-recognition of informal WBL represents lost opportunities. The importance of recognizing educational resources as a prerequisite for participation has been noted (Cookson, 1986). Therefore, it is important not to overshadow informal opportunities by focusing largely on formal aspects and diminish potential learning. The examples of WBL given indicate the need for a balance of formal and informal opportunities. Organizational responsibility to ensure that all stakeholders are aware of the full potential of WBL must be clearly identified to achieve success.

INDIVIDUAL MOTIVATION PROCESS

Figure 16.1 is used as the basis for organizing findings relating to the individual motivation process.

Needs

The needs that individuals perceived as being addressed by WBL can be broadly categorized into two key areas: personal development (confidence building; networking; enhancing career profile); and work development (increasing specific knowledge; development of task-specific skills; enhancing work performance), and is consistent with the AE literature. Boshier (1977) suggests that individual participation in AE was based on location on a psychological continuum ranging from 'life chance' to 'life space'. 'Life spacers', like Maslow's 'self-actualisers', participate in AE to 'express' themselves (Maslow, 1954). 'Life chancers' participate because of the need to acquire knowledge, skills or attitudes in order to cope with social, psychological or vocational aspects of their life. The needs expressed in this study, not unexpectedly for WBL which often focuses on inadequacies in specific work-related areas, lie closer to the 'life chance' pole of the continuum than the 'life space' pole.

Furthermore, individuals described situations consistent with life-cycle theory where triggers, eg organizational realignments or restructuring, prompted individuals to learn, promoting adaptation to circumstantial changes and new roles and responsibilities. Indeed, it is essential that such developmental responses are supported if the organization is to maintain stability.

However, employee perceptions of organizational systems for identifying needs were not entirely positive. Organizations were viewed as implementing company-wide training policies that often ignored individual needs, were too general and sometimes inappropriately applied. Although individuals understood the difficulties faced by organizations, they felt that specific departmental training needs should be considered and effective communication systems should exist between departments and the training section to promote need identification and WBL implementation.

One starting-point is appraisal, which was viewed positively as an opportunity to discuss individual needs with line managers and negotiate appropriate training plans. However, significant barriers to effective appraisal included: lack of finance to support requisite training; and attitudinal differences between line managers in approaches to learning. Furthermore, there was a perceived contraposition between organizationally driven training and individual needs negotiated via appraisal and regardless of individual needs. An employee may attend a course simply because somebody from the department was required to participate.

Individuals perceive that various needs are being addressed by WBL, however, the particular approach adopted by the organization may be inappropriate with serious implications for participation in, and the success of, WBL affecting job performance and satisfaction. Indeed, Argyle (1989) has suggested that the scope of a job, eg variety of task, level of responsibility and opportunities for development, can seriously influence such factors.

Values

Despite an initial bias towards formal WBL, employees clearly place great value on informal WBL as more relevant to specific job tasks and offering greater opportunity to promote knowledge transfer in the work-place. However, organizations were perceived as valuing formal WBL more highly than informal, and that rather than recognizing the potential learning from informal WBL the organization simply viewed this as 'doing the job'. Hence, there was no system for recognising learning achieved in this way. Additionally, organizations were viewed as encouraging participation on formal courses to enhance the company profile through 'numbers on courses' and not for their specific educational benefits. Clearly, this perceived bias adversely affected the value placed on formal WBL by individuals and may have exaggerated the value placed on informal WBL in reaction.

Organizations would be advised to explicitly demonstrate recognition of the value of informal and formal WBL to achieve full benefit. Learning opportunities must be explicitly recognized and valued organizationally to be exploited seriously by individuals. Although the value placed on learning may be affected by numerous factors, eg social status and former educational attainment (Darkenwald and Merriam, 1982), for WBL organizational influences are likely to adumbrate. Individual values for WBL seemed to be affected by perceived organizational values and in turn crucially influence employee commitment to WBL. Organizations would benefit from systems to evaluate the efficacy of formal and informal WBL and to demonstrate encouragement for participation in and success from WBL.

Goal setting

Individual goal setting was based on appraisal, where individual training plans were negotiated and appropriate resources targeted, including in-house and external courses or via individuals with specific expertise within the company. Individuals perceived organizational goals to be identifying and implementing company-wide courses and specifying the number of individuals involved. Several issues may seriously hinder the attainment of these goals, particularly the organizational system for implementing WBL and the commitment portrayed to employees.

An organizational focus on formal WBL led to a range of courses being offered on either a voluntary or compulsory basis. Voluntary courses consistent with individual training pathways were subscribed to, although sometimes the range of courses was inadequate or particular courses were over-subscribed. However, the majority of employees viewed compulsory courses negatively, perceiving that employees were often sent on courses simply to 'make up numbers' rather than relevance. This approach seemingly confirmed individual perceptions of low organizational commitment to WBL and hence under-exploitation. Consequently, employees rejected organizational goals, seriously affecting goal attainment as in other educational settings (Cross, 1981). Goals must be realistic for an individual to invest time and energy requisite for success.

Organizational goal setting procedures seemingly violate a number of recommendations to promote goal attainment including: specificity; challenging but attainable; feedback mechanisms; participation by all stakeholders (Argyle, 1989; Goldstein, 1986). These recommendations seem appropriate as employees perceived appraisal positively through its establishment of individual salience by negotiation. Organizational training drives were perceived negatively as they involved little or no negotiation and were imposed 'from above'. However, WBL within these organizations may already have broken down at the 'values' stage as discussed above.

Pragmatic issues: supports and barriers

Several practical considerations also influenced participation in WBL, examples of which are given in Table 16.2. One of the most common barriers was the cost of courses and books. Where organizations offered subsidies, there was evidence of greater participation and enthusiasm to participate. Another major obstacle was the requisite time, particularly for formal WBL courses, to complete the required study. Individuals sometimes were reluctant to make this commitment, particularly when it encroached on quality time allocated to family or leisure. Informal learning was neglected through competitive pressures on time, individuals being too busy to reflect on potential learning experiences or spend time demonstrating skills to colleagues. Furthermore, individuals were often not released as colleagues were unable to cover the work-load. However, organizations recognized these problems, to varying degrees, and worked to overcome them, by providing financial help and study leave. While such pragmatic issues seem self-evident, their impact on participation must be seriously considered by organizations promoting WBL.

Table 16.2   *Examples of environmental supports and barriers to WBL*

Supports	Barriers
Financial supports for courses and rewards for successful completion	Initial payouts for registration, compulsory book purchases
Time off work granted, exam study leave	No or little time off given for study
Work-load reduced, supported by colleagues or line manager	Work-load not reduced, no support from colleagues or line manager
Mentor (internal) or tutor (external) support (company visits or help lines)	Lack of mentor or tutor support, telephone help lines not sufficient
In-house courses or external courses held on-site	Long distance, one-day courses

Learning Diagnostic Questionnaire (LDQ)

Scores ranged widely on LDQ's 'knowledge and skills' and 'attitudes and emotions' scales. However, certain relationships were identified between scores and individual perceptions of WBL. Individuals with higher scores on the 'knowledge and skills' scale showed more involvement in WBL, particularly formal courses, and more awareness of those with whom they can discuss development issues and problems. Individuals with higher scores on the 'attitudes and emotions' scale were more positive about WBL, enthusiastically highlighting positives and glossing over negatives. Despite individuals with high scores on both these scales encountering similar obstacles, they seemed better equipped to overcome them and did not let them hinder personal development.

Individuals in the same organization, however, obtained similar scores on the 'work environment' scale. All scores on this dimension were low to medium suggesting that the organizations studied were either not offering a wide range of learning opportunities or not communicating such opportunities to their employees. Large individual differences in uptake and motivation towards WBL may be influenced by differences in 'knowledge and skills' and 'attitudes and emotions' scores, emphasizing the importance of these factors. The work environment score is a useful performance indicator for organizational commitment to WBL.

CONCLUSION: A MODEL OF INTERACTION

A model of motivation in WBL must address interactions between organizational and individual factors. The work setting creates the learning environment for WBL, and is instrumental in creating opportunities and barriers to learning. Three issues are highlighted. First, effective organization–employee communication is essential to the motivation process to promote WBL and align individual needs and WBL opportunities, communication gaps lead to organization–employee dissonance and, ultimately, a lack of uptake and success of WBL. Second, individuals perceive that organizations under-exploit the potential of WBL projects, eg through ineffective cascading or dissemination, and hence individuals often undervalue WBL as an effective resource for themselves and the organization. Third, a supportive environment is vital, not only to overcome barriers, eg time constraints and financial burdens, but more positively to encourage exploitation of available opportunities.

A unifying model of WBL is proposed (Figure 16.2) which emphasizes individual and organizational contributions to each phase of motivation in WBL, from identification of needs and ascribed values through goal setting to behavioural outcomes and success or failure. The organization and the individual interact at each stage, the focus groups clearly demonstrating the organizational influence on the individual. Successful WBL requires congruency of organizational and individual perceptions at each stage, hence the inclusion of arrows representing the phased input of both organization and individual. These inputs may in reality represent communication lines

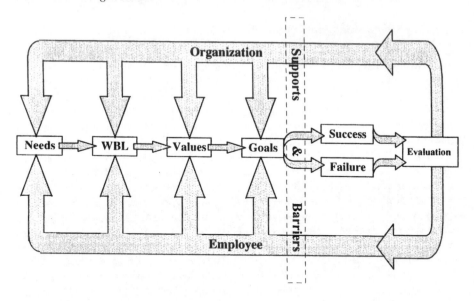

Figure 16.2   *A model of motivational perspectives in WBL*

between the individual and the organization and any breakdown may seriously impact on the success of WBL.

However, WBL is not just about participation or non-participation. Arguably most jobs have an element of experiential learning and individuals often participate in compulsory courses, rather, it is a case of effectively recognizing and exploiting learning opportunities. However, individual differences in the exploitation of WBL opportunities may relate to differences in: the definition and recognition of WBL; needs; values ascribed to WBL opportunities; ownership of training goals. The 'knowledge and skills' and 'attitudes and emotions' scales of LDQ may be important in distinguishing such differences in approach. Organizations need to seriously consider these factors, perhaps adopting a 'study skills' approach like traditional educational establishments.

It should be noted that these findings are based on individual perceptions and further research will seek to establish actual congruence and dissonance of individual and employer perspectives which may emanate from breakdown in communication between the organization and the individual. The larger the organization, the more problematic is the implementation of WBL schemes that cater for individual learning needs and there may need to be some trade-off between individual and organization-centred approaches.

Motivational perspectives are important in WBL as they enhance our understanding of the design and uptake of WBL schemes. Motivation in WBL is a process where organizations and individuals interact, synergistically or antagonistically, to affect participation. Such interactions can encourage growth and self-development through establishing mutual benefit, however, they can seriously hamper the effectiveness of WBL. Organizations are advised to explore these dynamics, particularly to evaluate communication channels and their effect on individual perceptions of WBL, to inform and enhance the formal and informal training structures that encourage uptake and promote the success of WBL and achieve mutual benefit. The key to the success of WBL is the employee who can be facilitated by effective employer–employee partnerships and inter-communication.

REFERENCES

Aamodt, M G (1991) *Applied Industrial/Organisational Psychology*, Wadsworth Publishing Company, California.

Argyle, M (1989) *The Social Psychology of Work*, Penguin, Harmondsworth.

Arnold, J, Robertson, I and Cooper, C (1991) *Work Psychology: Understanding Human Behaviour in the Workplace*, Pitman Publishing, London.

Boshier, R (1977) 'Motivational orientations revisited: life space motivation and the education participation scale', *Adult Education*, 27, 2, 89–115.

Brennan, J and Little, B (1996) *A Review of Work-Based Learning in Higher Education*, Quality Support Centre, London.

Coates, C L (1993) 'Motivation theories' lacklustre performance: identity at work as explanation for expended effort', *ETTI*, 31, 1, 26–30.

Cookson, P (1986) 'A framework for theory and research on adult education participation', *Adult Education Quarterly*, 36, 130–42.

Courtney, S (1992) *Why Adults Learn: Towards a Theory of Participation in Adult Education*, Routledge, London.

Cross, K P (1981) *Adults as Learners*, Jossey-Bass: San Francisco.

Darkenwald, G and Merriam, S (1982) *Adult Education: Foundations of Practice*, Harper Row, New York.

Department for Education and Employment (1996) 1996 European Year of Lifelong Learning, http://www.transcend.co.LIFELONG_LEARNING/eyll.html

Department of Employment (1992) *Learning Through Work*, HMSO, London.

Goldstein, I L (1986) *Training in Organisations*, 2nd edn, Brooks/Cole Publishing Company, California.

Honey, P and Mumford, A (1989) *The Manual of Learning Opportunities*, Peter Honey, Berkshire.

Knight, S L (1991) 'The effects of students' perceptions of the learning environment on their motivation in language arts', *Journal of Classroom Interaction*, 26, 2, 19–23.

Landy, F J and Becker, W S (1987) 'Motivation theory reconsidered', *Research in Organisational Behaviour*, 9, 1–31.

Locke, E A and Henne, D (1986) 'Work motivation theories', in Cooper, C L and Robertson, I (eds), *International Review of Industrial and Organisational Psychology*, Wiley, Chichester.

Marx, R D (1982) 'Relapse prevention for managerial training: a model for maintenance of behaviour change', *Academy of Management Review*, 7, 433–41.

Maslow, A H (1954) *Motivation and Personality*, Harper, New York.

Seagraves, L, Osbourne, M, Neal, P, Dockrell, R, Hartshorn, C and Boyd A (1996) *Learning in Smaller Companies: Final Report*, Educational Policy and Development, Stirling.

Slavin, R E (1991) *Educational Psychology: Theory into Practice*, 3rd edn, Prentice Hall International Inc, Englewood Cliffs, NJ.

Steers, R M and Porter, L W (1991) *Motivation and Work-Behaviour*, 5th edn, McGraw-Hill, New York.

Walberg, H J and Vguroglu, M E (1980) Motivation and education productivity: theories, results and implications', in Fyans Jr, L J (ed.), *Achievement Motivation: Recent Trends in Theory and Research*, Plenum, New York.

17

Learning as an Aesthetic Practice: Motivation Through Beauty in Higher Education

Alan Bleakley

INTRODUCTION

Contemplating early retirement from the hurly-burly of education? Or perhaps already sniffing the push, as a result of managerial 'rationalization' of resources, and looking for a career change? Then perhaps we could take Iain Sinclair's (1997, p.11) advice from the highly educational *Lights Out for the Territory*, a post-modern guide to some of London's more unsettling subcultures: 'Dog training, surveillance, security: those are the growth areas, that's where to sink your redundancy packet.' Disconcertingly, Sinclair's tongue-in-cheek 'growth areas' may already describe the territory of Higher Education – as it becomes infected by a behaviourist revival; follows a top-heavy assessment and evaluation programme underpinned by a paranoid, surveillance-led 'quality assurance' mentality; and exhibits an institutional obsession with security, in which health and safety concerns seem to create more interest than intellectual risk.

MOTIVATION AND AESTHETICS

Educational psychology's treatment of the relationships between motivation, learning and academic performance for Higher Education students could be seen as the tilling of an already overworked, even sterile, field. Indeed, orthodox educational psychology has offered little of real significance and value that has improved upon McKeachie's (1961) research in the early 1960s connecting motivation specifically with performance in Higher Education contexts: that extroverts, who find it relatively difficult to concentrate, perform less well than introverts in standard assessments; that students with a high need for achievement perform better than those with a low need for achievement; that students with a high need for power perform better in learning environments in which they can exercise such power; that students with a high need for affiliation perform better in more collaborative learning contexts; and that intrinsic motive is more effective in the longer term than extrinsic reward.

There is nothing counter-intuitive about these findings. They not only confirm common sense, but also continue to serve to illustrate what is banal about much educational psychology. However, they disguise a major dilemma: that it is notoriously difficult to predict how any one motive may apply to any one learning context. A standard text (Hoyenga and Hoyenga, 1984, p.414) rehearses this dilemma: 'What would you tell teachers who wanted to maximise the learning of the students in their classrooms? . . . the kind of classroom atmosphere that is "best" for one student may turn out to be "worst" for another.' Further, 'The complexity of human motivation . . . means not only that different people may have different motives for doing exactly the same thing, but also that the same person may have different motives for the same behaviour at different times' (ibid., p.416).

Current studies of motivation in education may suffer from the more general complaint noted by Chris Shilling (in Ball, 1995, p.267) that 'educational studies are in a state of "intellectual stagnation"'. Something seems to be missing from the field, is neglected, or perhaps even systematically repressed. This missing element may be the aesthetic dimension to motivation. Shilling's complaint can be reformulated: educational studies are not so much in a state of stagnation as anaesthesis, that is, dulled. To remind ourselves about genuine desire for learning, we might shelve our journals of educational psychology and return to Plato.

Socrates' defence of beauty in Plato's *Symposium* describes the love of wisdom as a form of beauty, and inextricably binds wisdom (or learning), beauty and eros. Learning can be both beautiful and erotic. How then do we account for a contemporary condition in which, for a significant number of students, learning constitutes not a *philia* but a *phobia*; not a turn-on but a turn-off, not a passion but a bore, and for some even a dread? That we can systematically turn a young child's burning curiosity and desire to learn into a young adult's disenchantment and fear of failure constitutes a cultural crisis, fuelled by a deep distrust of aesthetic values, and a privileging of the 'technical–rational' (Schon, 1991). Dictated by politicians and accountants rather than lecturers and students, this culture of instrumentalism has nevertheless infected the latter groups, so that even they have begun to converse in what Stephen Ball (1995, p.267) describes as 'the bland, technical and desolate languages of policy science and policy entrepreneurship' – languages that have no regard for 'a love of the beautiful' (ibid.) with regard to theory. Higher Education appears to have abandoned interest in aesthetic and in imagination, consequently suffering from a lack of aesthetic sensitivity, as it exorcises beauty, wit, elegance and style from its concerns.

We shy away from talk of love, eros, sensuality, passion and desire in learning – not the ephemeral personalizing of passions between teachers and students, but the lifelong passion and erotic desire for, and the sensual appreciation of, learning itself. We have come to defend ourselves against such implications of eros through instrumental reason, technical strategy, desiccated theory and practice, and the commodification of education – its new grounding in business enterprise. In the face of this severance of learning from eros and beauty, is it any wonder that we have to re-invent theories and strategies of 'motivation' to recover or release the repressed eros, to explain the loss of vigour, body and passion in education? As it follows the lead of the training culture, Higher Education is now about 'earning a living' rather than 'learning a living'. Politicized economic values now offer the major key, relegating aesthetic, religious, social, and even theoretical, values to supporting roles.

MOTIVATION AND BEAUTY

'Motivation', which entered the English language in the mid-seventeenth century, means to move something to action. Its original reference is to motion: to movement of the limbs, of body, of muscle. This frames motivation as incitement, spur or stimulus – extrinsic motive. Educationists usually see extrinsic motives as less powerful than intrinsic factors such as curiosity, interest and 'desire', a term in use in the English language at least a century before 'motive'. 'Desire' means something wished for, and refers directly to matters of the heart, returning us to aesthetics. Learning by heart has been confused with learning by rote, but the former, as a 'thought of the heart' (Hillman, 1981), once grounded learning in the passionate excesses of imagination.

Such aesthetically sculpted passion has been driven underground in the post-modern world of Higher Education, with its programmes, goals, competences, and unconditional championing of instrumental reason. The latter provide the very conditions for the discouragement of motivation through desire, setting up contexts that bore or fail to involve, offering an an(ti)-aesthetic or numbing. A common response to such numbing is the attempt to turn education into entertainment. This, however, fails to address the issue of the repression of that which brings the senses, and attentive close noticing, into play in learning – the presence of beauty. 'Aesthetic', literally meaning 'sense-perception', refers to the quick in-breath one draws in awe or wonder: a gasp taken as one's attention is held. Hence Thomas Aquinas' notion that 'beauty arrests motion'. And, if we are to follow Keats, 'What the imagination seizes as beauty must be truth.'

Beauty traditionally tends to be described through frames of high rhetoric: ideals, truths, or transcendent forms. This leads to an abstraction of beauty, severing it from the realm of the senses and the root meaning of 'aesthetic'. Where beauty is raised up to heights, it tends to be seen as merely prettifying, rarified, and then surplus. What is dark, deep and unsettling (sensuous, and commonly felt) can also be beautiful, or moves us into the territory of the meeting between beauty and terror, the sublime. Plato (*Phaedrus*, 250b), who is often held guilty of abstracting beauty as a transcendent principle, actually says that beauty is present in what is 'the most manifest to sense', and Plotinus sees beauty as an act or practice – an effort of close noticing, a sensate awareness. Hilary Armstrong (Read and Armstrong, 1987, p.69) suggests that for all Neoplatonists beauty is 'the vividness and directness of sense-awareness at its most intense'. Beauty is then linked to attention, and here is its most powerful connection to learning and motivation. Herbert Read (ibid.) reminds us that beauty's antonym – the ugly – has the same root in Romance languages as 'dull', 'stupid' and 'senseless'. Beauty counters the senseless and the dull, or stupidity. If beauty is simultaneously both what and how we sense, intelligently, then beauty can also be described as an aesthetic *practice*.

FACTORS THAT DISCOURAGE MOTIVATION

Rather than offering a *via positiva*, trotting out functional tips on how to motivate students, we might follow a *via negativa*, summarizing what works against motivation – factors that could be said to be discouraging to student motivation precisely because they dull, anaesthetize, or deny beauty.

A culture of instrumental reason, governmentality and surveillance

The legacy of Enlightenment thinking – instrumental rationalism – remains the dominant force in educational thinking, despite the thorough critique of the Frankfurt School (Bronner, 1994), the assault on the status of 'truth values' by post-structuralist thinkers (Lyotard, 1984), and the reading of liberal humanist 'emancipation' as itself a discourse of discipline (Foucault, 1977). Typical strategies to encourage student motivation, such as the promise of autonomy, can be seen, however, to offer a dissimulation: a means of conveniently shifting control and surveillance from the institution to the individual through 'learner responsibility' (self-discipline). Also, the overriding emphasis upon extrinsic performance dulls us to the importance of the tacit dimension to learning (that we know more than we can say, or do) (Reber, 1993). What can be observed and measured (the behavioural and instrumental) is privileged over the intuitive, which is repressed and returns in a distorted form – as learners' irrationalities or symptoms that ironically may hinder effective performance.

Our view of motivation and its relationship to learning continues to be effectively defined by Max Weber's thesis developed at the turn of the century, that suggests a causal link between the Protestant ethic and the spirit of capitalism – that capitalistic entrepreneurial activity and Protestantism are mutually supportive, exemplified by the culture of 'performance'. Indeed, we can be said to have entered a new wave of puritanism in education, signalled by the 'back to basics' campaign. While we uphold 'achievement' as an educational goal, whose subsets include competence, mastery, effectiveness, and the will to power (defining the spirit of capitalism), we place puritan restrictions upon such achievement. Learning is not to be pleasurable, aesthetic, intense, excessive or extreme, but functional, sensible, and confined to what counts as 'valid' knowledge, conforming to what Georges Bataille (1993) has characterized as a 'restricted' economy. Excess is not simply quantitative, but qualitative: intensity and complexity are vital elements in an aesthetic learning that might unhook education from its Protestant bias through a counter-reformation of desire.

Mechanical, unimaginative teaching

The puritan mentality seems also to deny the development of style and 'artistry' (Schon, 1991) in teaching, so that we are content with unimaginative and functional (explicitly non-aesthetic) approaches. Lack of imaginative teaching may be explained as: first, lecturers unable to work their way out from an Aristotelian legacy that categorizes rather than imagines knowledge, and rigidly follows the academic ritual of explaining the phenomenon prior to appreciating it (thus displacing the phenomenon from its sensuous presence to concept). Second, lecturers trapped in a cult of facts, unable to imagine their discipline as mythological, as story-telling, thus losing a potential audience. Third, lecturers caught by a mechanical notion of their jobs, or a technological imagination of their roles: not as inspiring intellectual, aesthetic and affective models, but as managers of a system.

The 'information age' – a denial of eros and aesthetic in teaching and text

Where teaching and learning are imagined more mechanically or functionally, as programmatic, so their potential eros is dried up, and all concerned lose heart. Through the 'information revolution', we have come to confuse 'sexiness' of information with eros in learning. Sexy information (packaged as 'edutainment' or 'infotainment') is seductive but transparent, where sound byte replaces imaginative scholarship, and business metaphors dominate. Such late capitalist discourse has sinister reaches. Jeremy Seabrook (1996, pp.186–7) points out that:

> Market values, applied with relentless vigour to the outer circumstances of our lives, also invade and colonize the spaces within, so that even our most intimate relationships and profound involvements with others are now governed by emotional and psychic economics. We interrogate our human associations to discover whether or not they are profitable.

The generation, storage and retrieval of a deluge of information now managed by computer technologies are both astonishing and worrying. We have created a cult of information without an imagination of this information, that generates sickness: information *philias* and addictions, showing a lack of discrimination; or *phobias*, following despair in the face of literal overload. Information is privileged as 'fact' rather than 'story' – technically rather than poetically. So-called 'objective', hard-nosed information is treated as if it were free from social, cultural and historical construction and representation, and celebrated for its virulent resistance to metaphor. Academics believe that they are writing non-fictional accounts substantiated by 'objective' research, but their work can be re-framed as fiction in a social–realist genre. Jerome Bruner (in Geertz, 1997, p.22) has recently devoted himself to the study of subject-learning as the sharing of cultural narratives, and now characterizes education as:

not simply a technical business of well-managed information processing, nor even simply a matter of applying 'learning theories' to the classroom . . . It is a complex pursuit of fitting a culture to the needs of its members and their ways of knowing to the needs of the culture.

Bruner has re-visioned the subject-matter of educational psychology as a study of competing narratives, in the process radically reformulating the locus of a satisfactory motive for learning, which is no longer seen as intrapersonal (Bruner's previous championing of intrinsic motives), but as discursive and dialogical, a product of shared narratives. As Clifford Geertz (ibid., p.23) suggests, education at all levels is about telling stories in how we maintain and transform culture, although we 'would hardly know it from standard educational theory, trained as it is upon tests and recipes'. Geertz suggests that Bruner's new 'cultural psychology' is 'radical, not to say subversive' (ibid., p.24). However, what Bruner says is necessary but not sufficient, stopping short of a conclusion concerning aesthetic worth – that if we are going to re-vision education as the sharing of narratives, then let us make sure that the stories are good, or pass as decent literature. Aesthetic – or its pathos in sublimity – is primary to compelling narrative.

Environmental numbing

There appears to be little effective dialogue between designers of interiors in educational institutions and those who work in them. As James Hillman (1986, p.78) suggests: 'The conditions of our psyches . . . reflect the interior of our rooms. There are relations between our habits and our habitations.' Where we learn may be as important as how and what we learn. Recall the typical classroom that is over- or under-heated, fitted with harsh fluorescent ceiling lighting, reinforcing the Enlightenment fantasy that illumination equates with revelation, and that shared illumination produces a sense of democracy. The reality, however, is more akin to Iain Sinclair's (1997, p.6) description of 'the flickering interference of strip lighting that reduces humans to a species of desktop cacti'. Harsh lighting (especially coupled with 'open plan' environments) also makes for an atmosphere of surveillance or interrogation, denying the intimacy and mystery created by subdued lighting with its play of shadow and light. As for its effects upon motivation and learning, the ceiling lighting forces our heads down in depressive posture, paradoxically into an interiority, so that we no longer notice, or care to notice, the noxious exterior world. The ceiling itself, made from tacky acoustic board, will usually be wholly functional, carrying the wiring or the plumbing and seeming to attract on-going repair (mechanics) rather than appreciation (aesthetics). It will then be denied its form as an object of beauty – a tapestry or hanging (the root meaning of the word 'ceiling'). Such environments normalize (under the guise of efficiency), and lower tolerance for the mediocre through a numbing, subduing aesthetic resistance.

Environment is probably the most neglected aspect of motivational conditions for effective learning. Herzberg's and Maslow's classic work-related studies relegated such conditions to 'hygiene factors' and 'lower needs' respectively, as secondary to personal and or social work satisfaction. Such a view is itself symptomatic of a dulling of aesthetic sensitivity to noxious forms. Research into motivation and learning that has revived interest in Herzberg and Maslow, such as that of Lewis Elton (1996), continues to read these writers through utilitarian, rather than aesthetic, frameworks, merely compounding their lack of sensitivity to environmental factors in learning.

CONDITIONS FOR LEARNING

So much for the *via negativa*, but is there a recommendation to follow the criticism? The Renaissance scholar Marsilio Ficino (1489, 1980) described an ideal curriculum grounded in Plato's concern with beauty. Following the number of the Muses, nine conditions offer a successful and enriching andragogy: three follow images derived from the Classical gods, three relate to the soul of the learner, and three refer to the learner's social and cultural context. We might refer to these conditions for learning as the mythological, psychological, and sociological, respectively.

In Ficino's account, first, certain gods (or images) give learning itself three distinct faces. Under Mercury, who is 'in charge of all inquiry', learning is instigated, or curiosity is aroused. Under Apollo is illumination – the competence generated by understanding. Under Venus is love of learning, especially shared enjoyment, as a reciprocity. Five hundred years ago, Ficino thus prefigured Jerome Bruner's account of the constitutive elements of intrinsic motivation (curiosity, competence, reciprocity), and had returned ideas about learning to a source in mythology or story, now echoed through Bruner's contemporary valuing of narrative.

Second, what we now call the psychology of learning, Ficino called learning in the soul. Its three components are will, acumen of mind or intellect, and tenacious memory. Each of these is intimately tied to imagination so that the primary motive power in learning is not located in the conceptual mind, but the autonomous imagination through which the world is read not literally, but metaphorically.

The third trio of contexts for successful learning, that we might call the sociological, Ficino relates entirely to guidance from significant others as guides: a prudent 'father', an excellent 'teacher', and a brilliant 'doctor'. While noting the gender bias, let us imagine the 'father' as 'management', the 'teacher' as 'lecturer', and the 'doctor' as 'counsellor'. Contemporary Higher Education appears to value management over the teacher, and the teacher over the counsellor. Yet the counsellor deals with the difficult symptomatic return of those charged emotional and aesthetic concerns of students who have been badly neglected, or indeed repressed, by management and lecturers.

We have not significantly improved upon Ficino's educational insights. Indeed, we have lost an essential factor through our current obsession with the technical-rational. Ficino, following his mentor Plato, placed beauty at the heart of learning, while we have systematically rationalized away aesthetic in motivation and learning, plucking the heart of beauty from the chest of education and forcing it into early retirement. Our rationale for this has been misplaced: we have stereotypically abstracted aesthetic, rather than formulating beauty as a practice.

REFERENCES

Ball, S J (1995) 'Intellectuals or technicians? The urgent role of theory in educational studies', *British Journal of Educational Studies*, 43, 3, 255–71.
Bataille, G (1993) *The Accursed Share*, 3 vols, Zone Books, New York.
Bronner, S E (1994) *Of Critical Theory and its Theorists*, Blackwell, Oxford.
Elton, L, (1996) 'Strategies to enhance student motivation: a conceptual analysis', *Studies in Higher Education*, 21, 1, 57–68.
Ficino, M (1980) *The Book of Life*, (trs. C, Boer) Spring Publications, Irving.
Foucault, M (1977) *Discipline and Punish*, Penguin Books, Harmondsworth.
Geertz, C (1997) 'Learning with Bruner', *The New York Review of Books*, 10 April, 1997, 44, 6, 22–4.
Hillman, J (1981) *The Thought of the Heart*, Spring Publications, Dallas.
Hillman, J (1986) 'Interior and design of the city: ceilings', in Sardello, R and Thomas, G (eds), *Stirrings of Culture*, The Dallas Institute, Dallas.
Hoyenga, K B and Hoyenga, K T (1984) *Motivational Explanations of Behavior: Evolutionary, Physiological, and Cognitive Ideas*, Brooks/Cole, Monterey.
Lyotard, J-F (1984) *The Postmodern Condition: A Report on Knowledge*, Manchester University Press, Manchester.
McKeachie, W J (1961) 'Motivation, teaching methods, and college learning', in Jones, M R (ed.), *Nebraska Symposium on Motivation*, (vol. 9), University of Nebraska Press, Lincoln.
Plato (1991) *Symposium* (trs. T, Griffith), The Folio Society, London.
Read, H and Armstrong, A H (1987). *On Beauty*, Spring Publications, Dallas.
Reber, A S (1993) *Implicit Learning and Tacit Knowledge: An Essay on the Cognitive Unconscious*, Oxford University Press, Oxford.
Schon, D A (1991) *Educating the Reflective Practitioner*, Jossey-Bass, Oxford.
Seabrook, J (1996) 'An English exile', *Granta*, 56, Winter 1996, pp.173–89.
Sinclair, I (1997) *Lights Out for the Territory*, Granta Books, London.

SECTION FOUR:
The Impact of Assessment on Motivation

18

Motivating Student Learning through Facilitating Independence: Self and Peer Assessment of Reflective Practice – An Action Research Project

Julie Mortimer

INTRODUCTION

Semi-structured group and one-to-one interviews with a sample of first-year undergraduate students, supplemented by analysis of original documents, provided the data for a focused study that centred upon two main issues:

- the design and use of portfolios as a reflective learning tool;
- the impact of the self and peer assessment strategies implemented, on the learning process.

The emergent themes of the study highlighted the students' personal reactions to reflective learning, their perceptions of self and peer assessment and their responses to portfolio compilation. Gaining reflective skills led to increased critical ability, and the adoption of a 'deep' approach to their learning as described by Gibbs (1992), and the analysis of the portfolios demonstrated an individual approach to learning. The importance of clarity of the criteria by which they made judgements about themselves and their colleagues has led to further development of the programme, particularly with regard to the owner-ship and sharing aspects of writing criteria. The emphasis on independence used in this approach, has led to increased levels of intrinsic motivation in the student's learning.

CONTEXTUAL BACKGROUND

The project arose through the opportunity afforded by the unitization of the institutional academic programme. Courses are designed with units of learning which collectively form a 'route' to an award. 'A "unit" represents a coherent learning experience and it has its own curriculum and assessment methodology, and mode of delivery.' (The Guide to UNN Curriculum Structures and Processes, 1995). An innovative unitized programme of learning leading to a BA Joint Honours award in which Professional Practice Studies (PPS), could be read as either a major or minor part of a route which also offered Childhood Studies and Subject Studies for Schooling, was the setting for two concurrent units in the first year entitled Self and Human Relationships.

The PPS programme is of an academic nature in that students develop analytical and reflective skills centred upon understanding of diverse occupa-tional and professional workplace cultures, but unlike a vocational programme, it does not seek to provide work-based experience culminating in accreditation within a specified occupation. The aims are designed to facilitate the development of the knowledge, conceptual and practical generic skills which the graduate needs for practice in the professional world of work. Such generic qualities that become known as 'graduateness' (HEQC Graduate Standards Programme interim report, 1995). An exploration of this notion is implicit in academic practice in many Higher Education institutions in the UK and Ireland (Walker, 1995) but it needs to be addressed explicitly, in order to gain a nationally shared understanding of what it is to be a graduate.

The PPS programme addresses this issue in an explicit way. In devising the units of learning 'Self and Human Relationships' I have attempted to meet some of the changing expectations of graduates which are being expressed by the various stakeholders, including the students themselves. In Self and Human Relationships this includes the acquisition of reflective and critical reasoning, grounded in the subject matter which encompasses: models of professional knowledge and practices concerned with human relationships in the workplace; a range of perspectives which focus upon self concept and a variety of social and cultural perspectives which centre upon the self in relation to the family and society. The acquisition of communication, presentation, interpersonal and self-motivated study skills which foster a 'deep' approach to learning, is facilitated through the linking of subject matter to the teaching learning and assessment strategies applied. 'Deep study implies a deep level of conceptual understanding as the intrinsic motivational goal. Information is examined to identify the underlying concepts and meanings,' (Gibbs, 1995). The philosophy underpinning the programme is founded upon Schon's (1983) model of professional artistry, which embraces the concept of reflection-in-action. Reflection in the context of the current enquiry is considered to be a process involving learning through analysis of experience to enhance understanding which leads to the ability to deal effectively with complex situations and decision-making in the professional context (Mortimer, 1995). The main outcome of this process is the reflective practitioner, that is, one who demonstrates artistry or excellence in their daily practice as a professional.

The operationalization of the programme gives the students the opportunities to draw on their own experience from life, from class membership while it is happening, and from other significant learning incidents. They are also encouraged to make connections between the theoretical concepts and issues of the subject matter and their own learning experiences, and to relate them to prescribed and incidental learning outcomes. The evidence for this learning is compiled into a portfolio, which is structured with the intention of emphasizing individuality, creativity and writing in a reflective genre. It was chosen because it offers an appropriate means by which continuous progression of learning can be documented. The assessment strategy is intended to inextricably link the progress each student makes from the inception of their learning on the first session and continues beyond the completion of the first year, (ipsative assessment) giving the students the basic skills needed for lifelong learning. Brown and Knight (1994) define ipsative assessment: 'It simply means that the scale of worth, the benchmark of which current performance is measured, is oneself; present performance is compared to past performance.'

The values of autonomy, empowerment and collaboration, which both graduateness and the professional artistry model of learning espouse, are mirrored in the assessment strategy. Self and Peer assessment is especially appropriate in the context of learning about self and others, about appraisal and its application to lifelong learning, to the employment situation, to career progress and continual professional development. The process of learning *how* to assess began with discussion of the nature and purpose of self and peer assessment. A progressive approach was implemented which encompassed reflection on learning as an integral part of each session, and facilitation of group tasks which raised awareness of the students individual performance levels, leading to in semester one:

- self and peer assessment of presentation skills;

- writing a reflective commentary upon the process which was tutor marked;

- completion of the portfolio dual assessed (students and tutor) (see Table 18.1).

In semester two there was self-assessment of portfolio with tutor moderation. Although all criteria were discussed with the students, they were tutor-set.

In my role as unit tutor I was accountable to both myself and the students in striving to deliver the best practice possible. I needed to evaluate the impact of this innovation on the students' learning. Another aspect of my interest lay in

Table 18.1   *Criteria for assessment portfolio: self and human relationships*

Learning outcome	Assessment criteria	Example of evidence submitted
1 Recognise and discuss issues concerning the role of human relationships in basic models of professional knowledge and practices	Demonstration of your: i. understanding of reflective practitioner and technical rational models of professional knowledge and practice ii. ability to relate your understanding of the above models to concepts of human relationships, in the workplace	Activity 8 and reflective commentary on group discussions, analysis of readings
2 Illustrate key theoretical issues underlying the concept of self	Critically reflect upon at least three key theoretical issues underlying the concept of self	Activities 3, 4, and 6, summary of group discussion, analysis of readings. Psycho analytical models of self Self-actualization Perspective transformation
3 Recognize and discuss further examples of social and cultural perspectives on the development of the self in relation to the family and society and relate them to your own experience.	Relate your own learning experiences to self development, in relation to family, culture and society	Activities 1, 4, 5 and 6, group discussion, analysis of readings Analysis of a critical incident
4 Begin to acquire skills in reflective practice	i. Demonstrate a reflective writing genre, illustrating reflective critical thinking ii. Adopt a deeper approach to your learning	Analytical reflective commentaries Diaries
Outcomes 1, 2 & 3	Connect the theory underpinning the three themes of the unit to professional practice	Activities 1, 2, 7 and 8, group discussion, analysis of readings

Table 18.1 *Criteria for assessment portfolio: self and human relationships (continued)*

Refer to evidence in portfolio on page	Self assessment/Rating	Tutor

My evidence demonstrates that
1. I understand the philosophies on which the reflective practitioner and technical rational models of professional practice are based and
2. that I am able to relate my understanding of the above to concepts of human relationships

	1.		2.	
outstanding level	9–10	☐	9-10	☐
high level	8–9	☐	8–9	☐
pass level	4–7	☐	4–7	☐
lower than pass level	0–3	☐	0–3	☐ *(please tick)*

My evidence:

shows an outstanding level of critical reflection	16–20	☐
shows a high level of critical reflection	11–15	☐
shows a pass level of critical reflection	6–10	☐
shows a lower than pass level of critical reflection	0–5	☐ *(please tick)*

My evidence shows that I have related my learning experiences to my self development, in relation to family, culture and society at an:

outstanding level	16–20	☐
high level	11–15	☐
pass level	6–10	☐
lower than pass level	0–5	☐ *(please tick)*

My evidence demonstrates:
1. a reflective writing genre, illustrating reflective critical thinking
2. Adoption of a deeper approach to my learning

	1.		2.	
outstanding level	9–10	☐	9-10	☐
high level	8–9	☐	8–9	☐
pass level	4–7	☐	4–7	☐
lower than pass level	0–3	☐	0–3	☐ *(please tick)*

My evidence shows that I have connected the theory underpinning the three themes of the unit to Professional Practice at an:

outstanding level	16–20	☐
high level	11–15	☐
pass level	6–10	☐
lower than pass level	0–5	☐ *(please tick)*

the debate surrounding assessment which encompasses quality in and equality of standards, fairness, validity and reliability in the context of a rapidly changing environment of increased technology and Higher Education for the masses (Smithers and Robinson, 1995). From this background the aims of the project arose.

AIMS OF THE PROJECT

The aims of the project were:

- to gain insight into the ways in which first-year undergraduates view self-assessment and reflection in relation to their learning of self and human relationships;

- to reflect upon, analyse and discuss the above views of self-assessment and reflection, and examine the implications of the analysis of the above data to assess the effectiveness of the teaching methodology, and the facilitation of critical and analytical thinking in the students.

One question arising from the aims centred upon the teaching and learning strategies applied, and the motivational factors, and their relationship to learning: Does using self-assessment and the compilation of a portfolio with reflective commentaries motivate a deep approach to learning?

The principles of a qualitative approach were adopted to guide the research methods used in the enquiry. The data collection commenced with a literature search. The research sample consisted of one-third of the total population of the group (six students), who were interviewed on a one-to-one basis. Two group interviews were also conducted with the same sample The documentary evidence contained within the portfolios was gathered from the whole student group (total population).

As this study involved students with whom I already shared a working affinity, and in the context of studying aspects of themselves, I gave careful consideration to ethical issues before establishing a research relationship. It became apparent to me that each person who was involved in the study needed to know what was expected of them and how it would be of benefit to them. Exchange theory (Hoyle, 1989) encapsulates this issue in terms of mutual benefits for those involved in a social situation. Discourse is necessary to build trust (Gibbs 1990) and to help create an atmosphere in which both the researcher and respondents can be as honest as possible with each other, regarding in this instance our perceptions and values in relation to the students' learning. This building of trust was particularly important , because I had access to students' reflective commentaries which were of a personal nature, and also because the interviews were recorded on tape, producing 'hard evidence'. The benefits to the students in this case included gaining experience of the research process as respondents, and individual and group reflection on the effectiveness of their learning.

Early in the research process an outline of the study and an ethical code was discussed and agreed with each participant. The rationale for this code was built upon the principles of : respect for the individuals' rights, the safeguarding of their interests, honesty in the purpose and nature of the research, trust in obtaining free and informed consent of subjects, and the maintenance of confidentiality, deriving from the work of Leininger (1984).

THE INTERVIEW PROCESS

The aim of an in-depth interview 'is to get informants to talk freely and openly about themselves, only initial stimuli being provided by the interviewer' (Powney and Watts, 1987). Open-ended questions were devised which were flexible, allowed for probing into deeper issues and to clarify meanings. The recorded interviews were transcribed, coded and indexed, and respondent validity was implemented, which ensured feedback of transcriptions to the respondents as a check of their recollections, and also as a method of deepening the perceptions of myself, the 'outsider interviewer' and the interviewees themselves. The outsider is defined as one who has no knowledge of the content or context of the study (Cohen and Manion, 1989).

FINDINGS

Three perceived major and inter-related themes emerged. Motivation was a prominent issue identified in all three themes. The themes are shown in Table 18.2.

Table 18.2 *Themes emerging from the study*

Theme	Issues involved
Personal reactions to reflective learning	Motivation Personal growth Confidence building Catharsis and emotional response Increased self-awareness Increased critical ability
Perceptions of self and peer assessment	Conducive environment Clarity of criteria Motivation Transferability Justification
Responses to portfolio compilation	Motivation A deep approach to learning Levels of difficulty Individuality Continuous progression

Theme one: personal reactions to reflective learning

The major issue to emerge within this theme was personal growth, to which the aspects of confidence building, catharsis and other emotional responses, increased self-awareness and increased critical ability were linked.

Students talked about the outcomes of using reflection to learn about value conflicts:

> I suppose I'm more conscious of what's going on around me. More conscious of looking at the other person's side of the argument and being able to think, how does it look from their perspective? It makes me think in greater detail about what's really going on around me.

> There was an incident I wrote [in a reflective commentary in my portfolio] about a girl that I was working with [on a group assignment]. I wasn't getting along with her and I can see by reading it now that I hampered the outcome of the assignment by the actions I took. And I would actually change how I went about dealing with that situation if I come up against it again, I wouldn't approach it the same way.

An explicit example of increased self-awareness can be seen in the following extract together with an increased critical ability and more implicitly, an increase in self-confidence, expressed in terms of maturity. There is also an implicit connection between, self-awareness and deep learning (Theme 2), in the analytical approach the respondent applied to learning situations in which she assessed her level of understanding and achievement.

> I'm definitely more self aware than when I first started, because I'm looking around, I'm more conscious of what's going on around me, analysing the situations I'm in, where I am with my learning. I feel like I have changed, I've become, I think it's made me more responsible which is a good thing and I'm more mature.

Several students described a greater understanding of their emotions in their reflective commentaries and evidence of catharsis emerged:

> I found them [the reflective commentaries really hard to do] because I chose to put really personal things in. One, for example was about my the day my Dad died and I'd never written anything in my life about that. So I found it really hard and it probably took me about three days to write it , but I felt better afterwards, I have come to terms with my anger.

The same respondent went on to display a deep approach to her learning: 'I am now able to relate what I have learned about bereavement theory to my own experience, and realise that I fully understand it.'

Design of marking criteria for dual assessment of portfolio

The following explanation of the design of the criteria for the portfolio assessment for unit two in the second semester, is included here to help clarify for the reader, the context in which the emergent issues in theme two (Perceptions of Self and Peer Assessment) arose.

The learning outcomes and the three major inter-relating themes of the unit were used as a basis for devising the criteria. The taxonomy is at level 1, that is, equivalent to the first year of a 3-year undergraduate programme. The students were therefore expected to demonstrate:

- understanding of theoretical concepts;

- critical reflection on experiential learning and theoretical concepts;

- connections between experiential learning and theoretical concepts.

The evidence for the achievement of learning outcomes was compiled by the student using evidence exemplars as a guide, and meaningful criteria referenced statements were linked to a 4-point banded rating scale. The scheme involved initial self assessment followed by tutor moderation.

The interviewees' perceptions moved from anticipated difficulty over its usage to a greater understanding of their own learning, and a positive attitude towards self-assessment, once they had actually experienced it.

The importance of sharing 'ownership 'of marking criteria with students is emphasized in the literature Stefani (1994), McDowell and Sambell (1996). In the first semester I had felt that the students would require a detailed structure for both the compilation of the portfolio and for the assessment criteria. Although I used several strategies with the aim of ensuring a shared understanding, I did not expect them to be able to write meaningful and clear criteria at that early stage in the programme. With the insight which this study has now afforded me together with triangulation with the literature, I uphold the view that production of their own criteria leads to more meaningful understanding and less anxiety for students.

The issue surrounding an environment which is conducive to self and peer assessment centred upon the students' understanding of the purpose of such assessment, a willingness to learn and an anxiety-free atmosphere. Students had been given the opportunity to learn the importance of linking critical self-appraisal in the classroom to the workplace, and in the wider sense to their personal development. Again, the questions on graduateness and core skills come to the fore. It is anticipated that the future graduate workforce should be self-appraisers, who are autonomous in their practice. The students expressed their understanding that appraisal from others was important but, in many working contexts decisions have to be made instantaneously, and the most effective and appropriate outcomes are achieved by practitioners working in isolation. Through this understanding they developed commitment to the self-assessment process.

Theme two: perceptions of self and peer assessment

The issue Clarity of Criteria highlighted the necessity of writing criteria which are clearly understood and interpretable by the students themselves. Referring to the Criteria for assessment of presentation (see Table 18.1), the view expressed by one student was shared by most of the interviewees.

> I don't think I could add to that, I don't think there would be anything I could put in. And when your doing a presentation these are the things [refers to criteria] that are important whilst doing it. If you fulfil all of these then you have done a good assessment.

However, in the group interviews it became apparent that some students had had some difficulty distinguishing the exact meaning of 'Logical flow of content' from 'Clarity of Articulation'. I had made the assumption that what I thought of as simple and clear criteria, would be thoroughly understood by them (see Table 18.1). The criteria for the self-assessment of the portfolio compilations were intended again to be clear in meaning, although they were more complex than the presentation criteria. There were several opportunities given for the students to share both their own and my understanding of what was expected of them in the interpretation of the criteria.

In response to questions about their perceived differences between engagement with tutor marked essays, which they experienced in other units on the programme studied concurrently with Self and Human Relationships, and self-assessment of the portfolio, the helpfulness of explicitly written criteria was highlighted. 'Now that I know what I am assessing and how to assess my learning and progress, I wish that I had done it a while ago, because my previous essay work was not critical enough, I didn't understand what was wanted.' Referring to essay criteria, she said: 'It's not as detailed as this [portfolio] criteria, It just says with reference to the literature, compare . . ., whereas this, this makes me think more critically about how to relate what I'm thinking to theory as well as to how that informs what I do' [in practice].'

Motivation and transferability

Griffin (1994) argues that the assumption that learning skills are transferable to new situations needs to be verified but in the context of this study, students gave evidence in their reflective commentaries and in discussion of designing and implementing coping strategies by making connections between how they were dealing with situations at home, in class, and in their every day life. Schon (1987) informs us that when people write about their experiences they become more interested in their work and positive changes occur in their actions. The powerful process of learning through reflective thinking and writing, together with self-assessment, has for these students led not only to increased self-awareness and critical ability, but to a change in the nature of their behaviour.

The students' levels of motivation and whether it was intrinsic or extrinsic was affected by their ability to:

- reflect upon their learning and progress;
- apply their newly gained skills in self and peer assessment to their learning as individuals and as members of a group;
- transfer those skills to new situations.

This was shown by their comments:

> I'm beginning to think that with what I have learned in Self and Human Relationships, and because I think I do quite well, I think, well, you know, I've got the capability to understand that, and to try and learn more and to do better, to look back upon what I've done and think, well, could I have done better or if I did well, why? And what way did I tackle it that made it successful?

> In terms of how I think about other parts of the course, this unit has helped a lot in the sense that I understand more that it is a process of learning that I am going through, as opposed to just turning up for the day, taking in some information, and then going home. I am very aware that I am actually learning when I am here.

> One thing that I do much better in all of my units now because of learning how to assess my achievements or identify a lack of them, through practical sessions in Self and Human Relationships where I used the opportunity to learn with and from my group members, I now am able to state my needs much more clearly to other tutors and I notice that I am getting more detailed feedback, which actually makes sense to me.

Extrinsic motivation and 'surface' learning

Some students, however, were more extrinsically motivated as demonstrated by their view that the compilation of the portfolio (theme three) was an 'easy option compared to exams'. 'I am always more worried about passing an exam, I try very hard to pass, to write down the theory, I don't worry about this portfolio writing, it's not as academic, and I don't need to try very hard to pass'. For those students for whom learning was seen as passing or failing, they used a surface approach to the portfolio compilation. Their ability to assess their own achievements was demonstrated less than those students who progressively reflected upon the process of learning. They were less able to relate their own experiences of learning to theoretical concepts.

However, most students were motivated by the way in which the portfolio structure and compilation gave them insight into their own progression and were constant in their deep approach to learning. These students demonstrated a higher level of critical ability in their reflective commentaries, increasingly drawing upon theoretical concepts. They felt that the portfolio compilation, as opposed to essay writing, which they encountered in other units of learning, helped them to differentiate between levels of difficulty through which they progressed.

I think they [assessors] want to see, they want to be able to identify that you know there are different stages, and are you going through them? and that's shown in a portfolio but not in an essay, because, I mean, you can write an essay in one night and that would just be it. With a portfolio you have to constantly work through it.

Justification

Anxiety was expressed in the allotting of highest criteria, to themselves, but they were not influenced by what others achieved, they felt it was important to justify allocation of highest scores by the amount and quality of evidence they submitted, but also felt the need for justification by tutor moderation. This process resulted in only two student self-assessment ratings being altered, one to a higher level the other to a lower. Overall, the students felt that it was a fair system.

I think I deserved the top score because I had thoroughly engaged with all of the readings, and class tasks which I related to my own experience and I know that I have achieved the learning outcomes, but it was good that the tutor agreed with me.

Some students, however, found the allotting of marks problematic and deliberated over what mark they thought they deserved in terms of how it would affect the achievement of either a first or second class award (the UK system of awarding degrees is divided by classification into first, second and third class degrees.) No problems arose over decisions on the level achieved which were denoted by the criterion references.

Conducive environment

The students described how they had built up trust in their group membership and in doing so felt that it was 'safe' to give each other constructive criticism.

When we first started to assess each other, I think we were all afraid to say anything which might have upset anyone of us, so we tended to praise and give high scores, but now I think we can be honest with each other about our contributions and our effectiveness.

Theme three: portfolio compilation and individuality

Although the students were using the same portfolio structure, there was no evidence of duplication in their completed form. Annotated bibliographies demonstrated a wide range of reading of subject matter. Students created relevant tasks for themselves based upon their personal experiences of learning, alone and in groups. They analysed themselves in their different life roles, as members of their own families, as workers (many were currently employed as well as being full-time students) as individual members of their student group, and in many additional roles which they identified individually.

Deep approach to learning and increased motivation

Further evidence of using a deep approach to learning which increases motivation can be seen in the following portfolio extract where a student is making connections between theoretical concepts (internal and external locus of control), her experiential learning and her reflection upon that learning.

> I realised as I read through what I had written that I was jealous of my sister. It is not a pleasant feeling, but now I think I understand the reasons why. I am not as good an athlete as she is, I have always thought she had better luck or (better) opportunities than me, but on reflection and because I have learned in this unit about an internal and external locus of control, I now know that's not the case. I need to concentrate on the things I am good at.

An increased self-awareness led in most cases to being more aware of others. There was evidence of this occurring in the students' reflective commentaries, where they wrote of being more tolerant of group members and of exercising patience and in some instances, compassion for peers whom they considered less able than themselves. Students described how relationships were improved because they had a greater understanding of not only how they themselves had treated particular group members, but also why group dynamics were not always positive.

CONCLUSIONS

Using a portfolio, which was structured to maximize inclusion of self and peer assessment strategies and reflective commentaries, has been effective in leading the way to fostering a deep approach to learning in most of the learners in this study. In summary there was evidence of increased critical ability, self-awareness and personal growth and the development of transferable skills. Learners demonstrated a progressive aptitude for relating theory to practice.

The perceived major issues concerning self and peer assessment derived from the students are:

- the importance of the creation of an environment which is conducive to the utilization of open and honest discussion;
- the fostering of a belief that self and peer assessment are beneficial to learning;
- the changing of extrinsic to intrinsic motivation through self-assessment;
- that clarity of criteria is essential to students' understanding of tutor expectations;
- that a precursor to effective peer assessment is the facilitation of collaborative group work;

- that self and peer assessment require integrity, critical awareness and its usage fosters the need to justify the outcome.

Assessment issues which need further development have been highlighted in the findings. Students' involvment with writing criteria leads to a greater understanding of the learning process (Stefani 1994) and this finding will be incorporated into the assessment strategy. Difficulties in marrying an essentially criterion referenced marking system to a banded percentage scheme need to be addressed. Some of the students were concerned that they achieved a high mark and they were less concerned about the level to which they had understood and achieved the learning outcomes expressed as criteria. The institutional unitization process attempts to standardize all assessed work into a rigid framework of numerical denominators within a marks recording system. Whilst this may meet the requirements of administration, it does not give consideration to the question raised in this study about the appropriateness of aligning marks to levels of achievment of learning outcomes, which are essentially of a subjective and qualitative nature, and may reduce the validity of the assessment.

The recognition of the importance of a direct relationship between the development and evaluation of assessment criteria, and the development of a programme of learning, has been a major outcome of this study.

The facilitation of independent learning leads to an increase in intrinsic motivation when:

- strategies are adopted which foster committment to self and peer assessment;

- learning by reflective writing is integral to the programme philosophy;

- emphasis is placed on both the process and progress of learning;

- committment to self and peer assessment is promoted when the learning and teaching methods centre upon the *student's* understanding of the purposes of such assessment;

- group tasks are followed by reflecting upon the group process, and recording reflective commentaries which demonstrate evidence of the learning which has taken place;

- opportunities are given for continuous feedback on progress being made (self, peer and tutor);

- situations are created which enable the student to link critical self-appraisal to the learning process, the workplace, and personal development.

Based upon the findings of this study, I have piloted a unit of learning for prospective teachers which incorporates the development and evaluation of assessment criteria by students themselves. The programme is structured to give direct and continuous feedback to both the students and myself, on the effectiveness of the strategies applied for facilitation of independent learning which fosters intrinsic motivation and a deep approach, and which focuses upon the provision of evidence of their progress. Themes emerging from this pilot study are reinforcing the importance of the direct relationship between the development and evaluation of assessment criteria and development of a more effective programme of learning.

REFERENCES

Brown, S and Knight, P (1994) *Assessing Learners in Higher Education*, Kogan Page, London.

Cohen, L and Manion, L (1989) *Research Methods in Education*, Routledge, London.

Gibbs, A (1990) 'Curriculum innovation and management of change', *Nurse Education Today*, 10, 98–103.

Gibbs, G (1992) 'Improving the quality of student learning through course design', in Barnett, R (ed.), *Learning to Effect*, SRHE and OU Press, Buckingham.

Gibbs, G (ed.) (1995) *Improving Student Learning through Assessment and Evaluation*, OCSD, Oxford.

Griffin, A (1994) 'Transferring learning in Higher Education: problems and possibilities', in Barnett, R (ed.), *Academic Community: Discourse or Discord?*, Jessica Kingsley, London.

Guide to UNN Curriculum Structure and Processes (1995), University of Northumbria at Newcastle, Newcastle-upon-Tyne.

HEQC Graduate Standards Programme interim report (1995), HEQC, London.

Hoyle, E (1989) 'Organisational pathos and the school: the micro politics of change', in *Approaches to Curriculum Management*, Open University Press, Milton Keynes.

Leininger, M M (1994) *Qualitative Research Methods in Nursing*, Graham & Stratton, London.

McDowell, L and Sambell, K (1996) 'Helping students to learn from assessment', paper presented at the Start Development conference, University of Ulster, May 1996.

Mortimer, J (1995) *Are you a Reflective Practitioner?: An Introduction to Reflective Practice for Nurses*, Educational Development Service UNN, Newcastle-upon-Tyne.

Powney, J and Watts, J (1987) *Interviewing in Education: Research*, Routledge & Kegan Paul, London.

Schon, D (1987) *Educating the Reflective Practitioner*, Jossey-Bass, London.

Schon, D A (1983) *The Reflective Practitioner: How Professionals Think in Action*, Penguin, Harmondsworth.

Smithers, A and Robinson, P (1995) *Post-18 Education: Growth Change: Project*, London Council to Industry and Higher Education, London.

Stefani, L (1994) 'Peer, self and tutor assessment: relative reliabilities', *Studies in Higher Education*, 19, 1, 69–75.

Walker, L (1995) (ed.) *Institutional Change towards an Ability-Based Curriculum in Higher Education*, Department of Employment, Sheffield.

19

Individual Differences in Student Motivation

Stephen Newstead

INTRODUCTION

There are many stereotypes about what motivates university students. In April 1997, as I was preparing this chapter, a newspaper report appeared describing research by a company calling itself High Fliers Research on what students did and what they expected out of a degree. It was called the Graduate Consumers Study.

The *Independent* newspaper (24 March 1997) carried the headline: 'Students abandon sex and drugs for mobile phones and laptops', and said the report 'uncovers a disturbing picture of sensible, organised young people equipped with mobile phones and personal computers'. It continued: 'Half plan to be earning £15000 or more after leaving university this summer'. The report concluded that: 'The Class of '97 are ambitious, materialistic individuals'.

All of these comments go against stereotypes, and suggest a very interesting picture of what it is that motivates students. I suspect the researchers are basically right in their claim that students' motives have changed in recent years. In this chapter, I want to argue that student motivation is central to Higher Education and is the crucial determinant of how students approach their studies and of how well they perform. I have been slow in coming to this conclusion. For a long time I held the view that the main thing that determined students' performance was their ability. Indeed, this may even have been true not too long ago. However, I have now become convinced that, in my own institution and elsewhere, student motivation is more important.

Much of the evidence that led me to this conclusion is circumstantial. I first came to suspect it might be the case in the context of PhD students. Most of these had good degrees, and all were, in my opinion, capable of getting a PhD. But not all of them did so, and it seemed to be their motivation – their willingness to overcome obstacles, their dogged determination to succeed, in some cases their sheer stubbornness – that determined whether they were successful.

But I have also been influenced in reaching this conclusion by the results of my own research on students in Higher Education. This has suggested to me that motivation is of crucial importance at all levels of Higher Education. I want to talk about three strands of research which have been factors in my reaching this conclusion: student cheating; students' motives for entering Higher Education; and the effects of modularization.

STUDENT CHEATING

A group of researchers at Plymouth has been interested in student cheating for nearly five years now. Our research is, we believe, the first research on the topic that has been conducted outside the USA. In order to put it into context, the general thrust of the American studies needs to be considered.

A short article by Davis *et al.* (1992) provides an excellent summary. The authors have administered a questionnaire on cheating to more than 6000 high school and college students. Their results are fairly typical of research in this area:

1. Cheating is commonplace; 76 per cent of respondents reported having cheated in either high school or college.

2. Cheating is less common at college than at high school.

3. Males report more cheating than females.

4. Stress and pressure for good grades are the main reasons for cheating.

5. Large, crowded classes in which multiple choice tests are used foster cheating.

6. Cheating is seldom detected and, even when it is, action is only rarely taken.

7. More able students are less likely to cheat.

Some of the techniques for cheating that the respondents in this study reported using are most ingenious. My favourite is one in which the four corners of the desk match the four possible responses to a multiple choice test and the students touch the appropriate corner to signal to each other the correct response. Others included tape recording the answers and playing back the tape through a Walkman during the exam, and writing the answers on a paper flower that was then worn on the person's blouse. One suspects that, with the advent of high technology devices, eg calculators with the facility to communicate with each other, the range of cheating behaviours is likely to increase. The Internet is also a rich source of opportunities for cheating.

Our own research has indicated that there is no case for complacency this side of the Atlantic. I wish to focus on one study in particular which investigated the occurrence of cheating in a single British university, and which enabled individual differences in the occurrence of cheating to be measured (Newstead *et al.*, 1996). This research used a list of behaviours which most people would regard as cheating. Respondents were asked to indicate whether they had indulged in that behaviour on one or more occasions during the previous academic year.

Our questionnaire also asked for personal details which are of potential interest from a psychological perspective since they may provide clues as to the reasons why students cheated. We looked at sex, age, and performance in the previous year's exams as predictors of reported cheating, and also students' reported reason for studying We also asked respondents to indicate their reasons for either cheating or not cheating.

The students were in intermediate years, ie they were not first years or finalists. The questionnaires were administered either by a research assistant who had herself recently graduated or by a student representative on the course; in this way we hoped to make the administration of the questionnaire as non-threatening as we could. Respondents were guaranteed confidentiality, and of course the questionnaires were filled in anonymously.

The results are presented in Table 19.1 in terms of the percentage of students who reported indulging in each type of behaviour. The behaviours are presented in descending order of frequency: the first behaviour, paraphrasing without acknowledgement, was admitted to by 54 per cent of our respondents, while impersonating someone else in an exam was reported by only 1 per cent. A rather crude generalization would be that plagiarism, ie copying without acknowledging the source, and data fiddling, are very common, being reported by 40 per cent or more of students. Exam-related cheating is less common, though note that copying from a neighbour and taking unauthorized material into an exam were reported by 13 per cent and 8 per cent of students, respectively.

In comparing the incidence of cheating between different groups we calculated a fairly crude 'cheating index'. This was simply the percentage of 'yes' responses given by each student to the 21 behaviours. Thus a score of 0 per cent would mean that the respondent had not reported cheating on any of the 21 behaviours, while a score of 100 per cent would mean that they had indulged in each and every one of the 21 behaviours. Group scores (eg for males) can be obtained by averaging over the individuals in the group. Not surprisingly, the actual scores do not reach 100 per cent, but they are nevertheless far from the 0 per cent that we might all, in our naïvety, have desired. A score of 28 per cent, for example, means that, on average, these students reported cheating on 28 per cent of the behaviours in our inventory, in other words on about six of them.

We found a number of group differences on this cheating index which are summarized in Table 19.2. Sex: there was a large difference between the sexes. Males engaged in rather more cheating (28 per cent) than females (18 per cent). Age: mature students engaged in least cheating, 18-year-olds most. Students aged 21–24 were in between, but closer to the younger age group. Academic performance: those who reported low academic performance in the previous year were far more likely to cheat. There is a clear decline in reported cheating across grades, with those students achieving First Class and Upper Second marks reporting significantly less cheating than those awarded Lower Seconds and Thirds.

Table 19.1   *Percentage of students reporting each of 21 cheating behaviours*

Behaviour (in rank order of frequency)	%
1 Paraphrasing material from another source without acknowledging the original author	54
2 Inventing data (ie entering non-existent results into the database)	48
3 Allowing own coursework to be copied by another student	46
4 Fabricating references or a bibliography	44
5 Copying material for coursework from a book or other publication without acknowledging the source	42
6 Altering data (eg adjusting data to obtain a significant result)	37
7 Copying another students' coursework with their knowledge	36
8 Ensuring the availability of books or journal articles in the library by deliberately mis-shelving them so that other students cannot find them, or by cutting out the relevant article or chapter	32
9 In a situation where students mark each other's work, coming to an agreement with another student or students to mark each other's work more generously than it merits	29
10 Submitting a piece of coursework as an individual piece of work when it has actually been written jointly with another student	18
11 Doing another student's coursework for them	16
12 Copying from a neighbour during an examination without them realizing	13
13 Lying about medical or other circumstances to get an extended deadline or exemption from a piece of work	11
14 Taking unauthorized material into an examination (eg cribs)	8
15 Illicitly gaining advance information about the contents of the examination paper	7
16 Copying another student's coursework without their knowledge	6
17 Submitting coursework from an outside source (eg a former student offers to sell pre-prepared essays, 'essay banks')	5
18 Premeditated collusion between two or more students to communicate answers to each other during an examination	5
19 Lying about medical or other circumstances to get special consideration by examiners (eg the Exam Board to take a more lenient view of results; extra time to complete the exam)	4
20 Attempting to obtain special consideration by offering or receiving favours through, for example, bribery, seduction, corruption	2
21 Taking an examination for someone else or having someone else take an examination for you	1

Source: adapted from Newstead *et al.,* 1996

Another variable we explored was reason for studying. These reasons were given in an open-ended question which asked respondents to indicate the single most important reason why they were studying for a degree. The responses were scored using a simple categorization system (see Table 19.3). It in essence divided students into those studying for a degree to avoid getting a job or for social reasons (stop gap); those studying as a means to an end, usually to get a better job or more money, but also just to get a qualification out of it (means to an end); and those studying out of interest in the subject or to develop themselves as individuals (personal development).

Table 19.2   *Scores of different groups on cheating index*

Group	Cheating index %
Sex	
Males	28
Females	18
Age	
18–20	27
21–24	25
25+	13
Academic performance	
First	21
Upper Second	21
Lower Second	25
Third/Fail	31

Source: adapted from Newstead *et al*, 1996

Table 19.3   *Reasons for studying and cheating index*

Reason	Cheating Index %
Stop gap (n = 83)	32
avoiding work	
laziness	
allowing time out to decide on career	
social life	
fun and enjoyment	
Means to an end (n = 561)	23
improving standard of living	
improving chance of getting a job	
developing career	
getting a good qualification	
getting worthwhile job	
Personal development (n = 200)	17
improving life skills	
reaching personal potential	
gaining knowledge for its own sake	
furthering academic interest	
gaining control of own life	

Source: adapted from Newstead *et al.*, 1996

The results are shown on the right-hand side of Table 19.3. Perhaps not surprisingly, those students studying for personal development reasons were less likely to cheat than other groups. Since they are studying out of interest in the subject or to prove to themselves that they can do it, they would probably only be cheating themselves anyway. Those studying as a means to an end were rather more likely to cheat, but the group who cheated substantially more than the others was the stop gap group.

We also asked respondents to indicate their reasons for cheating or not cheating on each individual behaviour. The reasons students give for cheating are principally to increase the mark, time pressure and that everybody does it. The main reasons for not cheating are that it is immoral, that the situation did not arise or that it was unnecessary.

These results are clearly of some practical importance. Students would appear to cheat rather frequently. I am sure that most lecturers will find these results surprising, and they clearly have practical implications. For the present purposes, I wish to gloss over these and to look into the explanations for our findings. Why should males cheat more than females? Why should older students cheat less than younger ones? There are a whole host of possible explanations, but the one which is best supported by the data is in terms of motivation, measured in our investigation by the reasons students gave for studying in Higher Education.

Females and mature students were much more likely to be studying for personal development reasons, and it is plausible to suggest that this is a major part of the differences obtained. A common distinction made in the literature is between performance goals and learning goals. Students with performance goals have as their main aim to obtain good grades in their studies. Those with learning goals wish to learn something from their studies (Dweck, 1986). This distinction has been shown to be related to school students' performance and to their ability to persevere with a demanding task. Performance goals are very similar to what we have called 'means to an end', and learning goals match up closely with what we have termed 'personal development'. We have come to believe that this distinction is an important one in explaining individual differences in cheating.

It would appear that students with performance goals are more likely to cheat, and that males and younger students are more likely to be motivated in this way. Those students with learning goals are more likely to be female and mature, and these students are less likely to cheat. We suspect that student motivation is one of the main factors underlying cheating.

STUDENTS' MOTIVES ON ENTERING HIGHER EDUCATION

Rhona Magee, Ann Baldwin, Hazel Fullerton and I are currently carrying out a longitudinal study – funded by SEDA and by the University of Plymouth – into student motivation (see Chapter 9, this volume). We are particularly interested in how motivation develops over the course of Higher Education. There is anecdotal evidence that Higher Education can sometimes serve to de-motivate previously highly motivated students, but few developmental studies of this have been conducted.

Our methodology is to look at motivation of students on entry and at various points during the first year. We are using a combination of questionnaires and interviews. We are also looking at the motivation of continuing students (ie second and third years) and how their motivation waxes and wanes throughout the academic year.

At the time of writing, only preliminary results are available. The ones I wish to present focus on the motivation of students right at the beginning of their career in Higher Education. We used questions developed by Entwistle and his colleagues within the ASSIST collection of tests which is based on the work of Beaty (1996). This enables one to determine whether students are studying out of:

- *intrinsic interest:* to develop knowledge and skills, or out of interest in the subject;

- *extrinsic interest:* to get a qualification, to get a job or to have an active social life;

- *no clear goals:* drifting into Higher Education and deferring taking a decision

The overlap between these categories and our own categorization used in the cheating studies is remarkably close.

There were differences in motivation as a function of age of student, as can be seen in Table 19.4. The picture is fairly clear. Older students tend to have an intrinsic interest in the subject rather than being interested in outside factors or having no clear goals.

Table 19.4   *Student motivation as a function of age on entry*

Age	Intrinsic interest	Extrinsic interest	No clear goals
18–20	11.5	13.3	8.4
21–24	12.3	12.3	6.4
25+	12.4	11.2	4.6

Gender differences in motivation are presented in Table 19.5. As can be seen in this table, not all effects are significant, but females tend to have an intrinsic interest in the subject while males are more likely to lack clear goals.

Differences in motivation across the various courses on which students had enrolled are given in Table 19.6. It is clear that there are large differences in the motives which students bring to these courses. For example, students in Graphic Design and Psychology are much more likely to have intrinsic interest in the subject on which they have enrolled, while Education and Business

Table 19.5   *Motivation as a function of gender*

Sex	Intrinsic interest	Extrinsic interest	No clear goals
Males	11.3	N.S.	8.2
Females	12.0		7.5

Table 19.6   *Student motivation as a function of course studied*

Course	Intrinsic interest	Extrinsic interest	No clear goals
Education	10.9	12.1	6.0
Business	10.9	13.4	8.5
Engineering	11.4	12.4	7.4
Geography	11.6	13.7	8.9
Rural Studies	11.8	12.8	6.9
Graphic Design	12.5	13.0	8.1
Psychology	12.6	12.6	7.0

students were more likely to report studying for extrinsic reasons. Education students, perhaps surprisingly, indicated a certain lack of clear goals as to why they were studying.

We also looked at motivation as a function of education prior to coming to university, and the results are presented in Table 19.7. Students straight out of A levels were less likely to be intrinsically motivated, and more likely to lack clear goals (this is no doubt related to the age differences reported earlier).

It must be borne in mind that these students are being investigated in the first week or two of their entry to Higher Education. We are looking at the motives that they bring to their university careers, rather than something that Higher Education has done to them. It will be interesting to see how their motives develop, but it is important to realize that different disciplines are dealing with different raw material. It is also clear that differences in motivation between different age groups, sexes and prior education exist before students enter Higher Education. It is not yet known how they will change during Higher Education, but clearly not every group is starting with the same level and type of motivation.

MODULES, MOTIVES AND MEMORY

In this final section, I wish to be a little more speculative and even controversial. I wish to argue that some of the things we are doing in Higher Education are

Table 19.7   *Student motivation and prior education*

Level of prior education	Intrinsic interest	Extrinsic interest	No clear goals
A levels	11.5	13.2	8.3
Othor	11.9	12.7	7.0

having significant effects on students' motivation, and that many of these effects are negative. I will have most to say about the current trend – or more accurately headlong rush – towards modularized and semesterized courses which are examined at the end of each semester. We have not yet analysed our data in the study just reported to see how motivation changes over the semester, but there is evidence from other sources that motivation is changed by the new structure.

First, there is evidence that students' approaches to studying change markedly over the course of a semester, and that this is largely attributable to the impending assessment. Entwistle and Entwiotle (1991) intervicwed graduate students in the year following their graduation and found that they all felt that the assessment system led to their adopting increasingly surface approaches to learning as the academic year advanced. We have empirical evidence to support this claim and to indicate that such changes happen during the course of a semester.

Newstead and Findlay (1997) used a shortened version of the Approaches to Studying Inventory to determine how students' approaches to studying varied over a 15-week semester. The questionnaire was administered in each of the first ten teaching weeks of the semester and then again during the examination period to a group of 20 final year psychology students. The results are presented in Figure 19.1.

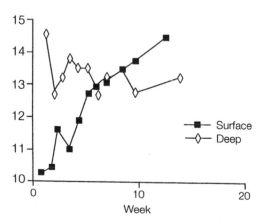

Figure 19.1   *Changes in students' approaches to studying over a semester*

It can be seen that there is a consistent increase in the adoption of surface approaches over the semester. The adoption of deep approaches decreases slightly – though not significantly – over this period. We are tempted to conclude that students start out with very good intentions of developing a deep, conceptual understanding of the material, but as the realities of student life impose themselves and as exams approach, there is a tendency to focus increasingly on rote learning of the material. I believe that modularization focuses students' attention much more clearly on examinations – which happen twice as often – and hence leads to more surface approaches than do yearly exams.

Also of interest in the Newstead and Findlay study was the finding that the teaching approach adopted by the lecturer seemed to have little effect. The lecturer on one of the option courses that the students were taking deliberately tried to foster a deep approach, for example, by using 'journal writing' (Hettich, 1991). There was no evidence that this had any effect: the changes over time were much the same over all the courses. It seems reasonable to conclude that students are influenced primarily by the assessment system, and that individual lecturers can have only limited effect.

Some recent evidence collected by Conway *et al.* (in press) provides corroborative evidence for this from a very different perspective. Conway *et al.* have looked at students' memory for information learned during courses taken as part of their psychology degrees. They looked at the different forms of memory students held when they were given multiple choice exam tests. When giving their answers (in a real test situation) students were asked to indicate whether they remembered the answer or whether they 'just knew' it. 'Just knowing' a response is taken to indicate that the information has been integrated into one's existing knowledge framework – it has become conceptual knowledge. Remembering, on the other hand, indicates a more surface form of learning.

When tested immediately after a course had finished, most students indicated that they remembered responses. What is more, those students who indicated that they just remembered responses tended to do well in these exams. However, when the information was tested again some six months later, the better students were now those who 'just knew' the answers – in other words, students who had developed a conceptual understanding of the material.

It is extrapolating from this evidence, but not much, to draw certain conclusions. First, exams taken just after a course has finished encourage rote learning. And second, it is only by letting the information be integrated, which takes time, that conceptual knowledge is developed. Modularization coupled with testing at the end of each semester will simply not allow the information to be conceptually integrated – it will not pass beyond the surface, 'just remember' stage.

I do not wish to say that modularization and semesterization should be abandoned – I suspect things have gone too far for this to happen. But we do need to be aware that we are now treating students differently and that this is having an effect on how they study. There may well be ways round the problem – but we need to acknowledge that there is a problem before any change can happen.

CONCLUSIONS

I have covered a number of different approaches to student motivation. My evidence is not conclusive, but I think I have demonstrated that motivation is important in Higher Education. I have also, I hope, indicated just how variable motivation is, with students being motivated in very different ways. Differences between males and females and between younger and more mature students seem particularly marked. It would appear that motives largely determine the extent to which a student cheats. The evidence that modularization has had an influence on motivation is largely speculative, but if it is true it has major implications for the way in which we organize the curriculum.

REFERENCES

Beaty, L (1996) 'Learning orientation: study contracts', in Marton, F, Hounsell, D and Entwistle, N (eds), *Experience of Learning*, 2nd edn, Scottish Academic Press, Edinburgh.

Conway, M, Gardiner, J M, Perfect, T J, Anderson, S J and Cohen, G M (in press), 'Changes in memory awareness during learning: the acquisition of knowledge by psychology undergraduates', *Journal of Experimental Psychology*.

Davis, S F, Grover, C A, Becker, A H and McGregor, L N (1992) 'Academic dishonesty: prevalence, determinants, techniques and punishments', *Teaching of Psychology*, 19, 16–20.

Dweck, C S (1986) 'Motivational approaches affecting learning', *American Psychologist*, 41, 1040–8.

Entwistle, N J and Entwistle, A (1991) 'Contrasting forms of understanding for degree examinations: the student experience and its implications', *Higher Education*, 22, 205–27.

Hettich, P (1991) 'Journal writing: old fare or nouvelle cuisine?', *Teaching of Psychology*, 17, 36–9.

Magee, R, Baldwin, A, Newstead, S and Fullerton, H (1998) 'Age, gender and course differences in approaches to studying in first year undergraduate students', Chapter 9 in this volume.

Newstead, S E and Findlay, K (1997) 'Some problems with using examination performance as a measure of teaching ability', *Psychology Teaching Review*, 6, 14–21.

Newstead, S E, Franklyn-Stokes, A and Armstead, P (1996) 'Individual differences in student cheating', *Journal of Educational Psychology*, 88, 229–41.

20

Motivation in Assessment

Linda Leach, Guyon Neutze and Nick Zepke

INTRODUCTION

> Assessment seems to be loitering expectantly in the corridors of higher education, thereby reinforcing the hope that it will soon enter the classroom to serve the learner'
>
> (Loacker et al., 1986, p 47)

We work with adult learners in a Bachelor of Education programme. This is an account of our discoveries about assessment of adult learners and how assessment affects their motivation. In this programme we base our approach on the ideas of humanist writers in adult education (Knowles, 1980; Freire, 1972; Mezirow, 1994; Brookfield, 1995). In particular we take up four key ideas in our practice. Adult learners tend to be more motivated where:

- assessment is an integral part of learning and is not separated from it;
- they have control of their learning and the assessment of it;
- there is a balance between maintenance and transformative learning and assessment;
- there is an opportunity for them to engage with subject matter intrinsically or extrinsically.

In this chapter we outline how we use these ideas in assessment to maximize learner motivation. We set the theoretical stage, describe our emerging assessment practice, then present some learners' views on whether it has indeed been motivating. Finally, we use these learner opinions to reflect on our own theory and practice.

ASSESSMENT

Assessment as learning

Assessment is an integral part of conscious daily life. We constantly are assessing feedback from ourselves, others and the environment. When we buy new clothes we assess first that we lack something. When we decide not to buy new clothes we assess that our wardrobe meets our standards or that we lack time, opportunity or money. Where we buy, depends on our assessment of price, quality or service. What we buy depends on factors such as our degree of fashion consciousness, taste, desire for comfort or feedback from others. When we don't wear what we have bought we make a judgement about the success of our shopping.

Assessment is also an integral part of learning (Heron, 1995). Successfully completed or not, it provides feedback. It is recognized by adult educators such as Boud (1995) and Brown and Knight (1994) as having a major impact on learning, both positive and negative. For example, an optimal level of challenge stimulates learning; success encourages learning and a sense of achievement; people may profit from a lack of immediate success as long as they have the opportunity to try again (Crooks, 1993). On the other hand, Crooks (1988) found that if challenges are too great, learners may be discouraged from further effort and that many limit their learning to meet assessment requirements.

Control of assessment

It is motivating for people to make decisions which affect their lives. When people exercise the right to choose their own clothes they feel in control. When unable to do so, for example having to wear a uniform, they may feel disempowered or resist. Given the right, people may even be happy to choose a uniform. However, denial of the right to choose clothes can also be motivating and spark resistance.

Adult learners' motivation is similarly enhanced by frameworks of rights and empowerment. Heron's (1995) moral argument for learners' rights in the assessment process asserts the right to take part in decisions which affect their welfare. Opportunity to exercise that right may motivate adult learners to use control of assessment to enhance their learning. Where students cannot access such control 'docile bodies and obedient souls' result (Foucault, in Marshall, 1989) although some individuals may find motivation in the removal of rights. To avoid the disease of docile pens and obedient voices, learners must be involved in the assessment of their learning.

Maintenance and transformation

Within society there are values and norms to which people are expected to conform. We shop for clothes to keep us warm, to maintain decency or to make us attractive to others. Occasionally we make a deliberate decision to defy social expectations and buy clothes to make a personal or social statement.

A high-profile male lawyer wore a kaftan in public places to protest against the taboo on men wearing comfortable clothes usually associated with women. A museum curator seeking sponsorship wore dirty running clothes to a meeting with company executives in order to transform the usual business culture. In their clothing statements, both were motivated to transform an existing custom or practice.

Assessment similarly can be maintaining or transforming. It can be used to maintain prevailing social, intellectual and economic perspectives as it does in competency-based assessment when professions or industries define what is to be learnt. Such an approach is motivating because it can give learners access to jobs and prestige. It is necessary for assessments to facilitate maintenance motivation. Adult learning theorists also argue that learners are motivated to transform their views of the world. Mezirow (1994) and Taylor (1987) identified a number of stages in the transformation process. Taylor focuses specifically on self-direction and identified four steps: disorientation, exploration, reorientation and equilibrium. Ideally assessment practices will enable students to transform existing perspectives, explore new ones and reorient themselves to achieve equilibrium

Motivations for learning

People do things for a variety of purposes. We may buy clothes for an extrinsic purpose, for example, to please an important person, we buy a garment of which we know they will approve; to meet the requirements of a particular situation, we may buy aprons or overalls. Extrinsic purposes are stimulated by external needs. People may also be motivated intrinsically, independently of external factors. We buy clothes to feel good and to lift our spirits; to co-ordinate with the rest of our wardrobe; to make a statement about our personality and our role in the world.

Similarly, learning has a variety of purposes. Some learning is done for extrinsic purposes, for example, because an important person expects it; because students need a particular qualification; to conform to the expectation of a social group, class or culture. Other learning is intrinsically motivated. People may learn for the pure joy of it; to achieve personal goals; to achieve transformations of their world view; and to give meaning to their experience. Assessment practices support both learning purposes. Adult learning theorists and assessment specialists (Knowles, 1980; Brookfield, 1995; Crooks, 1993; Boud, 1995) generally hold that the educator should aim to facilitate intrinsic learning. We distance ourselves from the should and hold that educators write assessments which enable learners to satisfy both intrinsic and extrinsic motives.

We try to incorporate these four key ideas in our assessment practice by designing assessments which:

- are part of the whole learning process through on-going discussion and feedback loops;

● respect the rights of learners to have a say in what evidence of their learning they will present; to help decide what assessment criteria are set; and to share in the marking;

● recognize learners' motivations and meet both maintenance and transformative purposes;

● facilitate both intrinsic and extrinsic motivation.

MOTIVATION IN RELATION TO ASSESSMENT PRACTICE

We now explore motivation in relation to our current assessment practice within a Bachelor of Education programme for teachers working with adults in formal and non-formal contexts. Our practice arises out of three years of continuous development. (Leach *et al.*, 1996). We use a version of criterion-referencing in which learners select the evidence they will present in portfolios, choose and negotiate criteria, and assess their own work. At third-year level, they contribute to the final grade in a negotiated process.

Assessment as learning

In our programme, assessment is not confined to one mega-event at the end of a course, or even a series of discrete minor events. Our assessment process is continuous and is part of the fabric of every teaching session. Assessment and learning are a whole. We agree with Boud (1995) that underpinning this whole are two key purposes: feedback to learners and accreditation of their learning. In our practice, assessment is informal, formative and summative. Our teaching sessions are full of assessment events in which formative and informal feedback are part of the learning dialogue.

We argue that this approach to assessment is motivational. Continuous feedback is an integral part of the learner's experience. When given as part of classroom dialogue, it clarifies what they know and opens doors on what they don't know, offers partnership and status in an on-going academic dialogue, and stimulates and challenges them to consider new perspectives. To achieve this, our feedback is specific, encouraging, constructive and challenging. We also give this quality of formative feedback on draft summative assignments. The comments we write on summative assessments are similarly designed to motivate by engaging with learners and their thinking. We try to make the accreditation purpose of assessment similarly motivating by involving learners in judging their work.

Control of assessment

Learners are involved in two ways in grading of summative assessment events. First, they have three options for determining criteria. They may use our set list, they may choose criteria from an extended list, or negotiate their own. Second, they may grade their own work or have it graded by a peer. We, the tutors, also have our say. Where the gradings disagree, we discuss the difference. If it cannot be resolved, a moderator's opinion is final. We do not give away full control of the assessment process.

In this process the learner has both tacit and explicit control. We argue that this is motivational. Tacitly it continues the engagement of the learner with the material throughout the assessment process, thus enabling them to retain control and ownership. Explicitly, through the self-assessment process, learners assume some power over the accreditation of their learning. This confirms the learner's status as partner in the assessment of learning.

Maintenance and transformation

We work within a world which expects educational institutions to certificate graduates to specified standards. Our assessment processes meet these maintenance requirements. All assessment focuses on pre-specified learning outcomes which reflect the expectations of the adult education discipline in conventional assessment events such as essays, reports, seminars and portfolios. Learners are graded on a traditional grading scale.

There are two transformational aspects to assessment. The first concerns content knowledge and learners' changing perspectives Challenging yet fitting feedback is designed to lead to new insights, actions and perspectives. The second concerns the assessment process itself. Learners transform their expectations from teacher-control to shared-control and their perception of their status from subordinate to learning partner.

It is our view that assessment is motivational in both its maintenance and transformation aspects. Learners are motivated when their expectations of content and process are met. Passing assessments is in itself motivating. Although not all learners are motivated by the transformational aspect of our assessment process, challenging feedback, participation in grading and the partnership relationship do motivate students to enter new learning territories.

Motivations for learning

Our assessment process tries to meet both extrinsic and intrinsic learner purposes. Learners who at any stage are pursuing extrinsic goals may complete set assignments, use set criteria and accept the grading of the lecturer. For example, learners juggling a range of priorities may want to complete an assessment in the quickest possible time without effort on optional extras like changing their world view. The same learners on other occasions may want to engage with us in partnership assessment by negotiating learning outcomes, assessment events and criteria, self-assessing and engaging with us in the complex dialogue of this process. In short, our assessment process recognizes both forms of learner-motivation.

LEARNERS' VIEWS ON SELF-ASSESSMENT

One of us is currently researching issues related to self-directed learning (Leach, 1997) and interviewing adult learners enrolled in our Bachelor of Education to find out what they think about self-direction. So far, fifteen people have been interviewed. They have been selected to represent all stages of the programme and achieve a balance between sexes, cultures and geographical location. A number of these learners have made some insightful statements about our assessment processes. We offer these here as learners' perspectives on our approach to assessment. We looked at the comments learners had made and noticed that they seemed to show a range of responses which reflected the transformation stages theorized by Taylor (1987).

Disorientation

To be honest – I don't like it . . . I still can't see any real benefit for me in this system. (A)

I've really struggled with this. Are others having problems designing their first three (criteria) or is it just me? (J3)

I think being told, 'This is how the assessment is going to happen', I think that's the easiest route . . . it also gives you some stability because you know what you're working to. Whereas if you set it yourself, sometimes you think 'Oh, am I doing this right?' . . . you're not always sure you're on the right track. (N1)

That was a bit scary for me because, coming from three years there . . . and you know what's to be expected. You know what to do. And then, coming here, it's just totally different, a big change. And I would admit that I sort of got lost . . . But it was a big change for me . . . I think the hardest thing was the assessments, getting used to the assessment. (J2)

Whereas if I was given a blank page and somebody said to me, 'Right, you are doing this course. Now these are the overall objectives. You decide on an assessment activity that is going to meet those criteria.' That would be harder than actually doing the assignment itself for me. That would be a nightmare. (S)

What would worry me about that would be, I doubt the possibility of sincerity in the whole thing because, I mean, assuming someone is the teacher and is going to be the one who signs off the results, there could only be a sort of semblance of the passing of control . . . So I feel it wouldn't be genuine self-control, genuine self-determination. (K)

Exploration

Yeah, at the moment just little by little because I can only cope with a little, a little bit at a time. And I can see that I've been given a little bit now and I am happy to play with it for a while. I'm not sure about the total, my total involvement in how I am going to be assessed but in talking to you . . . you say that can happen and I believe I'll be ready for it when it does. Tonight I'm not. (N2)

Of course, I fully appreciate that the last word belongs to the facilitator and the moderator but nevertheless I would appreciate the opportunity to say that I believe that I've met the learning outcomes and the requirements of assessment. (F)

I don't think I've ever gone along to any formal learning situation and thought that I would be able to have control over the learning. I guess you are conditioned to expect that. I don't think I've probably ever thought of an alternative in a formal learning situation – as yet. Maybe I am starting to think about it now. (B)

Reorientation

When I first came across it I thought 'Oh well, this is interesting' but it was unfamiliar. But I think after the first couple of times I used it I found it was quite comfortable . . . I was keen to try it . . . I think I'm getting better at this as I do it more . . . I actually enjoy this process whereby assessments are negotiated and you can actually look at the criteria by which you are going to be assessed . . . It gives me a better focus on how I should work on the material. (S)

Equilibrium

Umm, initially it [self-assessment] was the pits. I found it, just in the beginning, just so confronting, so in your face . . . Couldn't think of anything . . . The process does get easier. But learning from it is amazing. I think it's a really valuable exercise – an extremely valuable exercise. It helps me stay on track as to what it is that I was supposed to be talking about ... Because as you go back and look all the time and self-assessing, Now did I do that? Is that what I really want to present or is it this? So it allows for a clearer thinking process, for me anyway, and it does get easier with use, with practice. It does get easier. And yeah, I quite like it to the point now that I'm even getting that ... I read what the tutors say, but it's like, 'Yeah? So?' (J4)

It's [self-assessment] become so much part of the way I work here that I'd probably look for it and feel as if a bit was missing if it wasn't there . . . I think I would take it even if it wasn't there. (J4)

[If I wasn't offered the opportunity to take control of my learning] I would actively look for somewhere else to, where I would prefer to learn. (G)

CONCLUSIONS

As we looked at these comments this chapter hung by a thread. The range of views seemed to contradict our assumptions about assessment. An uncomfortable number of comments suggested that learners found the process unhelpful and a disappointingly small number were enthusiastic supporters. The Taylor progression from disorientation to equilibrium was evident but the weighting of comments seemed to be at the disorientation–exploration end of the continuum. However, further examination revealed a surprising and supportive theme. The time learners had spent in the programme almost exactly matched their stage in the transformation continuum. Learners at the disorientation stage were in their first year of study with us, while those at the equilibrium stage were in their third year with one person in their second year. Those at the exploration and reorientation stages were in their second year with one in their first.

The sequence of quotations above clearly signals the development of motivation through the process. Consider:

I don't like it . . . I've really struggled . . . you say that can happen and I believe I'll be ready for it when it does . . . I found it was getting quite comfortable . . . I think I'm getting better at doing this as I do it more . . . I was keen to try it . . . I quite like it to the point now that I'm even getting that . . . I read what the tutors say, but it's like 'Yeah? So?' . . . I think I would take it even if it wasn't there . . . I would actively look for somewhere else to, where I would prefer to learn [if control were not offered]'

The Taylor progression also fits two of the other key ideas about motivation in our assessment practice. For example, in relation to the learning and assessment connection, a learner at the reorientation stage said, '[negotiated assessment] gives me a better focus on how I should work on the material', and at the equilibrium end of the Taylor progression one said, 'But learning from it [assessment] is amazing.'

In relation to learner control, one person at the exploration stage said, 'I don't think I've ever gone along to any formal learning situation and thought that I would be able to have control over the learning. I guess you are conditioned to expect that. I don't think I've probably ever thought of an alternative in a formal learning situation – as yet. Maybe I am starting to think about it now.' Two learners at the equilibrium stage made really powerful statements: 'I think I would take it even if it wasn't there' . . . 'I would actively look for somewhere else to, where I would prefer to learn.'

On the evidence presented here we are unable to claim that motivation through assessment serves the needs of extrinsic learners. In the data we have it is difficult to distinguish extrinsic from intrinsic motivation. However, the motivational power of the assessment process is demonstrated by the following statement: 'And yeah, I quite like it to the point now that I'm even getting that . . . I read what the tutors say, but it's like, "Yeah? So"?

Although Taylor's progression does not absolve us from the difficulty of having learners who do not enjoy the process, nor is the model itself fully validated in the restricted range of data we have available, it has been a useful framework for reflection on the impact on motivation of our assessment philosophy and practice. We shall continue to consult learners and consider their perspectives in the future development of our assessment practice.

REFERENCES

Boud, D (1995) *Enhancing Learning Through Self Assessment*, Kogan Page, London.

Brookfield, S (1995) *Becoming a Critically Reflective Teacher*, Jossey-Bass, San Francisco.

Brown, S and Knight, P (1994) *Assessing Learners in Higher Education*, Kogan Page, London.

Crooks, T (1988) 'The impact of evaluation practices on students', *Review of Educational Research*, 58, 438–81.

Crooks, T (1993) 'Principles to guide assessment practice', paper presented at Assessment of Learning Conference, Palmerston North.

Freire, P (1972) *Pedagogy of the Oppressed*, Penguin, Harmondsworth.

Heron, J (1995) 'Self and peer assessment', paper presentation at Central Institute of Technology, Wellington,

Knowles, M (1980) *The Modern Practice of Adult Education*, Cambridge University Press, New York.

Leach, L (1997) 'Self-directed learning: a never-ending story?', paper presented at the Higher Education Research and Development Society of Australasia Conference, Adelaide.

Leach, L, Neutze, G, Zepke, N (1996) 'Walking the talk: a critical examination of an assessment partnership', paper presented at the Assessment of Student Achievement Conference, Auckland.

Loaker, G, Cromwell, L and O'Brien, K (1986) 'Assessment in Higher Education: to serve the learner', in Adelman, C (ed.). *Assessment in American Higher Education*, Office of Educational Research and Improvement, US Department of Education, Washington.

Marshall, J (1989) 'Foucault and education', *Australian Journal of Education*, 33, 2, 99–113.

Mezirow, J (1994) 'Understanding transformation theory', *Adult Education Quarterly*, 44, 4, 222–35.

Taylor, M (1987) 'Self-directed learning: more than meets the observer's eye', in Boud, D and Griffin, V (eds), *Appreciating Adults Learning: From the Learners' Perspective*, Kogan Page, London.

Index